THE LIFE AND TIMES OF A VERY BRITISH MAN

THE LIFE AND TIMES OF A VERY BRITISH MAN

KAMAL AHMED

BLOOMSBURY CIRCUS
LONDON · OXFORD · NEW YORK · NEW DELHI · SYDNEY

BLOOMSBURY CIRCUS
Bloomsbury Publishing Plc
50 Bedford Square, London, WC1B 3DP, UK

BLOOMSBURY, BLOOMSBURY CIRCUS and the Bloomsbury Circus logo are trademarks
of Bloomsbury Publishing Plc

First published in Great Britain 2018

A catalogue record for this book is available from the British Library

Library of Congress Cataloguing-in-Publication data has been applied for

ISBN: HB: 978-1-4088-8918-3; TPB: 978-1-4088-8915-2; eBook: 978-1-4088-8916-9

2 4 6 8 10 9 7 5 3 1

Typeset by Newgen KnowledgeWorks Pvt. Ltd., Chennai, India
Printed and bound in Great Britain by CPI Group (UK) Ltd, Croydon CR0 4YY

To find out more about our authors and books visit www.bloomsbury.com
and sign up for our newsletters

For Maud and Noah

And Mum and Dad

'It required years of labour and billions of dollars to gain the secret of the atom. It will take a still greater investment to gain the secrets of man's irrational nature.'

Gordon W. Allport, *The Nature of Prejudice*, 1954

'There is no reason for you to become like white people and there is no basis whatever for their impertinent assumption that *they* must accept *you*. The really terrible thing, old buddy, is that *you* must accept *them*.'

James Baldwin, 'Letter to My Nephew on the One Hundredth Anniversary of the Emancipation', *The Fire Next Time*, 1963

'Keep on movin'. Don't stop, like the hands of time. Click clock...'

Soul II Soul, 'Keep on Movin'', 1989

CONTENTS

Introduction: Dear Britain   1

1 Mum. And Dad   29

2 Preventable evil   61

3 Go home   103

4 Zoo time   129

5 Happy face   163

6 Dear Sudan   195

7 I can't tell you how I felt when my father died   223

8 Prejudiced, me?   231

9 Reconciliation   261

Conclusion: In-group   285

Afterword: Mr Powell and Mr Trump   291
Acknowledgements   301
Notes   305
Index   321

Introduction
Dear Britain

I have six photographs of my father.

Which is not many, really, is it? Given that he is responsible for one half of me.

They are old photographs from the 1960s when I am a little boy and he is a svelte young man in drainpipe trousers and a white wool, roll-neck jumper. His skin is dark, ebony.

Cool. So very, very cool.

Each photograph is black and white with a thick, white border.

One is of my father with a lawnmower, looking proud. There are not that many men from Omdurman, Sudan, who knew what a lawnmower was. Not then – not in the 1960s, before you could type 'lawnmower' into Google. He is leaning back with a 'ta-da!' look on his face, hips pushed forward with a flourish, shoulders flung back.

A matador with a Qualcast.

Another is with me, a baby in his arms. My father is laughing as I giggle out of control, being tickled. There is an older lady in the picture, almost cropped out, with horn-rimmed spectacles, a sensible 1950s dress and a grey cardigan. Her skin is soft, pale, white.

That's my grandmother.

Beloved, wise, kind – a woman who eschewed harsh words and argument, passions at odds with a certain type of quiet Englishness that imbued her very being. As different from my father as water is from fire.

A third picture sees my father and me sitting on a drystone wall: I am older, maybe three, which would place the photograph around 1970. I am wearing a striped top. In another we are both looking out from a castle window. A proper English castle with turrets. It's a place called Berry Pomeroy, near Torquay.

The fourth and fifth are similar, from a set all taken on the same day.

The final photograph is on a moor, Dartmoor, also in Devon. The sun is out. We are on holiday. I am sitting on my father's knee; he in the classically inappropriate dress of the immigrant recently arrived in England – and ready for a day out in the countryside he has read so much about at school, thousands of miles away. Leather slip-ons are not the ideal footwear for a walk across scrubby, steep grassland dotted with heather and sheep poo. Even if they are paired with Pringle socks.

My father is in his late twenties.

Forty years later he will be dead.

And these are all the photographs I have of him – six four-inch squares of history that I do not remember because at that age memory has no longevity. At the age of three, the narrative of our life is largely lost to the immaturity of our brains.

I keep the pictures in an envelope. On the front of the envelope is the name 'Elaine', written in fountain pen. Elaine is my mother. It's my Auntie Marjorie's writing. My Auntie Marjorie is from north Wales. She must have sent them to her sister-in-law many years ago.

Not many young men from Saharan Africa ended up holidaying in the south-west of England in the era of the Beatles and Harold Wilson with a pipe. Not many grammar school-educated women from a small village in the north of England married men from Sudan in an era when wearing a miniskirt was a flag of social rebellion. And even fewer had children. So, there weren't many people like me around in those days, looking out from castle windows, eyes expectant, smiling.

Not many at all.

The debate of our age is the debate about identity. Who are we? Why do we do what we do? Why do I like this thing? And not like that? Who are the in-group? The me group. And who are the out-group? The other.

For anyone not white in a country which most assuredly is, much of that identity is expressed via one obvious fact. The colour of the person's skin.

In my case, brown. Not a big definite colour like white or black, but a tertiary colour. A secondary colour. A mixed colour.

And hang onto that thought, because it throws up a whole host of competing trends and tides as we try to make sense of those big questions about who we are, where we live and what that says about us – the British. Because I most definitely am British. A Very British Man. Not a Very English Man, oddly, because English seems more exclusive, less me. British is that most malleable of words, attachable as easily to Britain First (Taking Our Country Back) as it is to British values and British Summer Time, which is more my kind of Britain, lazy days lying in sun-kissed meadows. Comfortable, soft Britain.

Now – and this is the odd thing given the importance of that outer signal – if a surgeon did not know the colour of our skin, she or he would find it impossible to deduce from rummaging around in our insides, looking at the texture of our blood in a test tube or counting how many teeth we have. Strip off that obvious layer and we are all the same – a pretty remarkable set of electronic impulses, muscle tissue and organs which come together to form a human being and member of the one 'in-group' that is strictly defined and impossible to dispute, the human race – *Homo sapiens*. Wherever we live, whatever our background, whatever our 'ethnicity', we laugh at jokes that are funny and feel sadness when someone we love dies.

And here is a second thing that is worth considering. All human beings are born prematurely in comparison with the rest of the mammal world, and as such are a relatively blank canvas, emotionally. That the vast majority of our brain development happens in the world around us (our brain doubles in size in the first year of life) rather than during pregnancy, means that 'inputs' from that outside world – via material culture (tools) and emotional culture (society) – are vital. If we wanted to arrive in the world with the cognitive ability – the cognitive smarts – of a chimpanzee newborn, pregnancy would need to last about twenty-one months. My guess is a rather limited number of mothers would gladly sign up to such an arduous metabolic and mental task.

This short gestation, relatively helpless childhood and long adulthood, gives us an ability unique in the animal kingdom. We learn about life and who we are in the outside world and we decide how to make sense of it. Our brains are not hardwired from birth. No one is born prejudiced, born with a desire to put some other group to the sword. Our beliefs and ideas become hardwired via the stories we tell ourselves and the cultures we build, and those stories and cultures are ultimately under our control and can change if we will it.

We are evolutionarily special in our ability to identify a problem and come up with a solution because we have given ourselves so much thinking time. Our race's attempts to do so have led to world religions, wars and scientific breakthroughs that take the breath away. And, as Yuval Noah Harari argues in *Sapiens*, if you can create myths, of differences, of superiority, of 'otherness', of the danger of the 'out-group', you can also unmake them, in surprisingly short order. 'In 1789 the French population switched almost overnight from believing in the myth of the divine right of kings to believing in the myth of the sovereignty of the people,' Harari writes. As we British say of the weather: if you don't like it, a different lot will be along in a minute.

And from these two facts – that underneath those thin layers of skin we are all the same and force of will can change any story we tell ourselves – flows a significant thing. Grounds for optimism.

Whatever the problems of now, they are not necessarily the problems of the future.

This book started in November 2008, the 4th to be precise, a Tuesday. And in that sense it is like a lot of books about race and identity because what happened on that day changed the whole meaning of what it was to be brown or black or white in the modern world. That was the day Barack Hussein Obama was elected 44th President of the United States. The *New York Times* credited the moment with 'sweeping away the last racial barrier in American politics'. The paper said the historic event had been achieved 'with ease'.

Every American presidential election is an event of international bearing. The demise of the world's only superpower – culturally, economically, militarily – is oft predicted but still the nation resolutely 'lifts its lamp beside the golden door', blazing that certain trail, showing us what we might become. Maybe warning us.

The election in 2008 had more resonances than most not because of what President Obama promised he would do but because of what President Obama symbolised. Not just to Americans, but to all of us obliged to tick the box 'other' when it comes to race and identity. All of us not a member of the majority 'in-group'. All of us who are members, to a lesser or greater extent, of the 'out-group' – the other in a society that we call home. Black, Asian, Jew, Irish, Romany, Muslim, Hindu, Buddhist – we could look at ourselves, look at our country, a little differently that one day later and ask ourselves some simple, profound questions. Could I achieve that? Could my country achieve that? A journey spanning just 143 years, from a nation that enslaved its black people to one that was led by a black person.

Who some people claimed wasn't black enough.

For the in-group, white people, this was also a moment. Had peace finally been declared? President Obama was the most powerful man in the world. Could we leave all that messy, ugly racial tension behind? Maybe all we were waiting for was the opportunity, the trigger. And here it was, made flesh.

For me, the most remarkable thing about President Obama among a long list of remarkable things was not so much that he was black, but that he was mixed-race, with a black Kenyan father and a white American mother. Among all the millions of words expended about the possibilities of a post-racial world, not many had been about this rather obvious fact and its significance to the mercurial, sometimes grotesque, sometimes uplifting, conversation about race this country – Britain – has been having since the thirteenth century and Edward I's decision to expel Jewish people, the other, from the sceptred isle. I had recently left the *Observer* newspaper where I worked as an editor and thought someone should write about it. I rang up some old friends there and made my point.

'You,' they said. 'Why don't you write about it?'

So I did, and this is what appeared the weekend after that historic day:

In the good old days, otherwise known as the 70s, I used to wear rainbow-coloured jumpers, cords with a wide leg that flapped over my Adidas Gazelle trainers (brown suede, three beige stripes – absolute classics) and rode a Raleigh Arena racing bike made in Nottingham with drop-handlebars and five whole gears. It was a happy life. The only black people you saw on television were playing for the West Indies cricket team or were being made fun of in *Mind Your Language* on ITV. 'Mixed-race' hadn't really been invented. Not yet.

The article tried to tell a story, or at least a bit of one, a sliver of an argument I thought worth making. It spoke of my mother who is white and British, so British she is actually *from Yorkshire* where being British is less important than being from Yorkshire. Which is very British. And my father, dead now and so no longer able to argue the finer details of why a science degree would have been so much better for me, his son who was far too interested in intellectually suspect 'arts subjects' for his own good. He was black – properly African, strong, definite black – and from Sudan. And that made me, their only child … well, no one was really sure in the good old days what that made me. Half-caste, some people said.

What President Obama did was raise a mirror in which I could see myself reflected. The *Spectator* said that the man in his forties from Chicago, Illinois, was someone who 'scrambles categories', made simple definitions difficult. James Baldwin wrote decades earlier – because he spotted things in front of us most only understand once they see the fact relayed in hindsight's pleasingly accurate rear-view mirror – of the 'web of ambiguity' that infiltrates our person. A web that should not be denied, evaded or overlooked if we do not want to risk diminishing our very selves. It is a web that we are all part of – black, brown, white – to a lesser or greater degree.

'It's very British of course, mixed-race,' I wrote in 2008. 'In America the segregation between races is still deep and largely unyielding. Here, we prefer integration over separate lives. The Policy Studies Institute pinpointed it first in a report 10 years ago and revealed that Britain's black and Asian populations were marrying across ethnic lines at a "staggering rate". Half of British-born Caribbean men, a third of Caribbean women and a fifth of Indian and African Asian men had a white partner. Not so much black Britain as brown Britain.'

My mother and father were two of those people, taking a leap of faith and love in the 1960s – remarkable as a decade for its opposition to whatever was then the norm and, more, was considered 'normal' in the way that everything else was considered 'abnormal'. Before my father, most members of my English family – and they were and are a wonderfully warm and generous-spirited English family – had never met a person who couldn't trace their Caucasian antecedents back generations.

We forget just how big a deal that was.

Brown Britain was my Britain. Just after President Obama was elected I was filling out a survey which asked my racial origin. There was, as usual, 'black, Afro-Caribbean' and 'black British' as well as 'mixed', meaning white and black. Now, a decade earlier I would have put black British, which I always thought of as a political definition, because not being white was more than just having different coloured skin, it changed the way you viewed the world and the world viewed you.

But this time I didn't. I clicked on 'mixed', some black and some white, a rare nod to my mother that arrived courtesy of the political and social change that had blown in across the Atlantic from Washington DC.

'The world has shifted,' I wrote:

Too late for my father and perhaps for many millions of others. But it has shifted. It has shifted for that little boy with the Raleigh bike. It has shifted for the first-generation immigrant who wants to join that sophisticated class where the colour of your skin is not more important than the content of your character. Politics here, too, must now shift.

Last Wednesday I listened to a recording of Obama's acceptance speech. He spoke of 'the brief union between a young man from Kenya and a young woman from Kansas who weren't well off or well known, but shared a belief that, in America, their son could achieve whatever he put his mind to'. I had to concentrate so that tears did not flow.

The response to my article told me something significant about race and identity in this country for the simple reason I thought I was saying something commonly understood. What I did not realise was that for many of the people who read it, it was revelatory. Not revelatory in its intellect or its insight – it wasn't overflowing with either – but revelatory in a rather more mundane sense. It was the start of a conversation *between* two groups of people – in-group and out-group – that had evaded us up until that point.

It revealed to one audience, white people not much versed in such issues, that race and identity are complicated; one can be both 'black' in sympathy and 'white' in sympathy, almost interchangeably. At one and the same time you can feel great anger, say, at the latest statistics that show an unlevel playing field for black, working-class children let down by the British schools system, and you can also empathise with those who sit, fearful, wondering why the world has changed so rapidly around them, those who do not feel that anyone is listening to their concerns.

To another audience, the more than one million people in Britain who look like me, it was an articulation, an expression of something rarely touched upon. We 'mixed-race' people didn't really have our 'thing', not quite fitting into anyone's neat circles of identity. Now here we were, on the front page of every newspaper in the world and leading every television bulletin. Identity was not always about neat circles. It could also be a Venn diagram, an intersection of white and black. President Obama, for goodness' sake, was one of us.

It was at that moment that the first inklings of an idea began to form. If the 'world had shifted', what had it shifted to? Something more optimistic, something replete with opportunities never before imagined, something that included all the sides in a debate, that, in what I knew was a faintly ridiculous metaphor, found its personification in me and people like me. I had spent the first forty years of my life trying to fit in with my country: shiny shoes, nice suits, nice accent, short hair, whatever you do, don't frighten the horses. Now the world, this new president, was demanding my country fitted in with me – this was the future, climb on board. And the thing was, everyone was welcome. The reason why so many white, liberal people who read my article took something from it was because it was a piece about race that did not paint them as the enemy. It was a time for a place called Hope, that stubborn little bugger that we keep trying to beat to death.

That was ten years ago. And ever since, I've been collecting little bits and pieces, talking to lots of people, reading, thinking and scribbling things in notebooks. The outcome of that rather chaotic process is this book. And it is not, actually, the book I originally intended to write. Which, of course, is exactly how President Obama started his book about his life, *Dreams from My Father*. Don't worry, I haven't got delusions of grandeur.

You see, my original book plan, from 2008, would have drawn a broad narrative arc and called it progression. It would have argued that events in America, that surveys of the young in Britain that showed declining racial prejudice, that the flowering of a new generation of people that looked past skin colour now meant we were living in a country, to remember the awkward phrase alighted upon by my employers at the time, the Equality and Human Rights Commission, 'at ease with our diversity'. I would have argued that the positive wheel of history was turning and we could increasingly look back on the brutalities of race and racism as the peculiarities of a bygone age. At a school rugby match where we were watching our sons pummel into one other with frightening regularity, a friend and fellow father turned to me and said that race, for these young and growing people chasing around the pitch, was no longer an issue.

But by the time of that rugby match, maybe 2014, my mind was already changing. And that changing mind made this book different. And by that I don't mean less optimistic, but I do mean more realistic. It is different because of a myriad of challenges that quickly became apparent. Britain isn't America; we have our own delicately refined instincts when it comes to identity and race that can only be discovered by looking at our history. I was in danger of confusing the optimism of a new president thousands of miles away with a change of substance in our own, parochial, story. That the uplifting note from the White House would sound clear across the ocean, rather than become lost in our own thick forests, subdued and shadowy. Where America is often scalpel-sharp in its technicolour, the murders, #blacklivesmatter, the raging demonstrations, the anger, the reaction, the Yes We Can!, the loud, public discourse; Britain is quieter, less expressly violent, less expressively hopeful, covert, whispered, uncomfortable, unsure. Swirling issues of identity swim just under the surface, a surface covered in calm, all British polite.

There are breakout moments. Rare, angry moments that reveal truths under that calm. One happened fifty years ago, and suddenly now was snagging at my memory. In 1968 a Conservative politician walked into a hotel function room in Birmingham and spoke of 'the River Tiber foaming with much blood'. Enoch Powell articulated a different narrative from the one I was initially trying to construct in the book I never wrote. He spoke of an unheard and unheeded mass of English people, white people, scared, as he described it, by what they saw happening to the streets they lived on. New Commonwealth immigration – the arrival of 'the coloureds' – was upending the country and tipping us towards Hades, he argued. In 2008, the fortieth anniversary of that speech, I would have considered it historically interesting but not resonant. Not resonant with many people in Britain, this new Britain that I believed – from my comfortable London eyrie – was being forged with a relentless and unstoppable energy. Now, on the fiftieth anniversary of that speech, I am not so sure. Powell's words, agree or disagree with them, think them true or revel in uncovering their grotesques, are not only historically interesting; they are, once again, resonant. Resonant in this country. Resonant around the world.

Fear of 'other' is back, and with it a challenge to optimism.

The echo of Enoch Powell defined the challenge from one side. Equal and opposite came the challenge from the other side. From the side still beaten back, still not getting the fair crack of the whip we were told would be in our hands by now. The challenge of the case of Bijan Ebrahimi, an Iranian refugee murdered in 2013 by a white neighbour who liked a can of super-strength lager while he went about his business in the Bristol suburb of Brislington. Ebrahimi was beaten to death and set alight, events that happened despite seven years of complaints to the police who either ignored him or saw him as the problem. Ebrahimi's case never received the coverage of the murder of Stephen Lawrence, the teenager from south-east London whose death revealed that official, institutional incompetence and prejudice can compound the effects of rank violence. But it was no less shocking. You do not have to dig down too far beneath this country's great strides on diversity (and they are great) before you hit rock with a dull ring, find that the truths of race and racism are still with us, hiding under that glittering soil of kumbaya togetherness so many of us were busily shovelling. In years past, I believed the aggregate narrative was travelling ever upwards, that the singular events, the shootings, the murders, the attitudes, the comments, would slowly decline towards oblivion.

I was wrong.

What is the new thesis, then? The new story of this country that I love, that has nurtured me, that has embraced me in the warm arms of opportunity, of security. This country that has also cold-shouldered me, so subtly at times I did not even notice. 'Just glad to be here', I would think. Because this is Britain which, we were told when we were young, used to rule the world and invented everything. A country that you were damn lucky to call home. We read the geography books about the poor, developing world, which is where dark people came from, and watched the films about the scary Zulu savages fighting our white gentlemen.

And that other one with the dog called Nigger.

And laughed along at school at all the Paki jokes.

Because, what if someone *did* send you home? The pictures of Africa I had seen didn't look anything like the comfortable suburbs of west London with their clipped privet hedges and cars that were washed on a Sunday. Africa was full of mud huts. And starvation. And war. And chaos. And trees that people sat under, doing nothing, lazy buggers. And I didn't want to live in a mud hut. Or sit under a tree.

This thesis is different. It is not one of unalloyed optimism. But it is not one of complete pessimism either. It is one shaped by a belief, by a belief born of being part of both this country and a country abroad. It is a belief born of that constant division in me, that constant internal chatter of one against the other, my own self-contained discussion. That internal debate – I am sure present in so many – needs to become an external one, a national conversation. In a country where so many want to transmit what is their truth, partial, filtered, aggressively put, it is time to find our receive button, switch it on and listen.

I use the word conversation. Contact theory proposes that talking to each other is better than not talking to each other. Or shouting at each other. And a conversation, if it is to go anywhere, needs to understand where the participants are coming from. All of them.

First, there are the people that are angry, and there are lots of them.

Those black people who have had enough of being told that solutions are just around the corner when all the studies show chronic failures, that Afro-Caribbean people are still more likely to be in prison than they are to be in the police. People who want to tear down statues to Britain's imperial past and wonder why the only non-white people on plinths in Parliament Square are Nelson Mandela and Mahatma Gandhi. No black Brits, you see. Or women of any colour, frankly, until they decided to cast a bronze of Dame Millicent Fawcett, the leading member of the suffragist movement.

Those of the Muslim faith being told to account for themselves in a country where searching 'Muslim' and 'terrorist' on Google brings up over 51.5 million matches. There are 2.8 million Muslims in Britain making their way, adding to the great richness of this great country. How do you think they feel? How would you describe the coverage of that group of people in the media?

Those white people who feel resentful that a country with a long and sometimes noble tradition of welcoming new groups of people to its shores is accused of 'racism', a blunt club of a word. People who feel wary about new communities separate from theirs. Communities that behind garden walls and closed front doors live a life of difference, a challenge to how Britain sees itself, what Britain is. People who wonder why 'white working-class' children are doing badly at school and who make the seemingly reasonable extension that therefore 'racism' is actually a problem they face as well. Clever people tell them that they have all the power. As white people. It just doesn't feel like that, scraping a living in social housing that is falling down around them.

And the vast majority, of whatever colour, who would just like to be left in peace to get on with their lives, taking what opportunities they can, the chance to live and love and laugh, unhindered by the arbitrary hurdles of prejudice and cant.

I make no special claims for myself as the author. I went to a 'bog standard' comprehensive school and a good university and performed without great spectacle at both. Not for me the double firsts or A* grades of the sedulous. I am not an academic. I am not a social historian. I am not a psychologist. Many smart people have written many smart books on the issue of identity. As one waspish newspaper commentator suggested when it was announced that I was writing this book – isn't fifty a bit young for a memoir? It's not as if I have discovered a cure for cancer.

There is also the problem of memory, upon which much of this book is based. Memory is partial, often wrong, miscast or foggy in detail. For that I apologise in advance. Alain de Botton, talking on American National Public Radio about Marcel Proust's *In Search of Lost Time*, said: 'I think the odd thing about memory is that not all memories are as clear as one another, just as not all moments of the present are that clear. So it's very possible to remember with incredible clarity a moment that occurred to us, you know, in early childhood, while the whole of last week seems lost in a kind of murkiness. And if someone says "Hey, what have you been up to?" we can't remember anything. So, our minds store information in very bizarre ways.' I am still not sure what my madeleine moment is – the tasting of a cake that set Proust on a route back to childhood.

All I have to sell is my very ordinariness. Anybody could be me. I grew up on an everyday suburban street of terraced houses in west London. I didn't go abroad much on holiday because Mum, who brought me up on her own, didn't have too much spare cash. Her parents, my grandparents, never travelled across a sea, even the Irish one, preferring Devon to Alicante. The only thing not so ordinary about me was something pretty extraordinary my mother did many years ago. And that was marrying my proud black dad in the 1960s when niggers and coloureds were still part of Britain's lexicon. This book is as much their story as mine, a story of a different type of Britishness, a narrative woven deep into our nation's tapestry but still so rarely visible.

That union meant the son of Elaine and Seddig was different. Meant I was pulled both in one direction – British, and touched by all that this nation has achieved, from Buckingham Palace to Soul II Soul – and another – not-white, carrying 'otherness' along every step of my fifty years, aware that when I walked into a room I was likely to be the only person who looked like me.

It has been a life of reconciliation, very British in its own way, compromising, just rubbing along, few rules and gloriously inconsistent. Reconciling my mother's history and my father's, reconciling my discomfort at even describing myself as 'black' – given that I did not suffer the privations of many black people failed by this country. No one ever posted excrement through my letter box. No one ever beat me up because of the colour of my skin.

It has been a life spent trying to understand, understand why so many brown people like me wondered, when young, if it was actually possible to become 'white' and change our name to something simple and normal, like Neil. People make a set of assumptions about who I am because of what I look like. Whereas the inner me is so full of different identities I often baffle myself. Michel Foucault wrote: 'Do not ask who I am and do not ask me to remain the same.' This is a complex and ambiguous world where many people are standing, daggers drawn, demanding clarity – whose side are you on? In a world with a hundred sides, splinters of glittering glass floating within us.

What has changed since 2008? The notion of a singular progression to a new, positive future has been disrupted, the world has moved to a state stamped 'unreconciled'. The poor are angry with the rich. The conservatives are angry with the liberals, and the liberals are angry right back. The young are angry with the old. The old wonder what hit them and count their money. The metropolitans are angry with the provincials, the provincials angry with the metropolitans. London – big, cynical, messy, artful, beautiful London, my home – is a capital separate from the country it heads, echoes of it only heard in the larger urban centres of Britain. Wealth has become divorced from effort, with returns on capital (riches) outstripping returns on labour (work). The average weekly income is still about the same as it was a decade ago. There have only been three elections since the Second World War when real incomes were falling: 1945 after the desperations of that war and two in the last decade, 2010 and 2017. That is how unusual these times are.

We cannot fix on a target – an understanding – in a world that keeps throwing us curve balls. And we sit, grumpy, in our own tents, marked out clear on the battleground, standards flying, like the prelude to some medieval conflict, fearful or rejecting of the people outside – the others, the people over the hill.

And all this leaves questions. What kind of country are we? What kind of country do we want to be? If this is where we are, what is the alternative? And whenever big questions are asked of who we are, we ultimately come down to one thing – identity. The science of life is called biology. The science of labour and consumption, economics. There is no science of identity because there are no laws. If I drop a ball it goes down. That's gravity. And for all the attempts by the historians and the psychologists and the politicians and the sociologists we are still unable to unlock the human emotions of prejudice and discrimination, hope and idealism, fear and pessimism. We can split the atom. We cannot look inside people's very souls.

And with that knowledge there is only one place to start this conversation. With a big, generous, open-hearted handshake. A big, communal 'I get where you are coming from.'

My name is Kamal Ahmed and I am fifty years old. I grew up in London, a city where taxis thirty years ago would not pick you up past midnight and certainly would not travel to south or east London, code for 'black places we do not go to'. Now, I get an Uber, invented by an American and often driven by an Iraqi PhD student or a Somali refugee who swears blind he supports Brexit to stop 'all those Poles hanging around on street corners who get all the jobs'.

My mother took me on bucket-and-spade holidays, where my face would be the only brown one on a beach crammed with windbreakers and straw hats, pale legs and seagulls, sand gritty in our crab sandwiches. My father left home when I was young and for much of my life was a distant figure who tiptoed in and out of contact over the years, the man from a restless, young country where he grew up comfortably off and was lauded as the first son.

England, cool, reserved, *planned*. Sudan, hot, in your face, loud, *chaotic*. These are the currents that are alive in me. The contradictions and joys of different influences, a feeling understood by many other members, I suspect, of the mixed-race, different face of Britain. Different identities alive in one person and alive in our country.

Britain has found it hard to have the conversation about what it has become, now it has arrived in the twenty-first century. Our very Britishness has stopped us talking about our very Britishness. I do not speak Arabic. Have visited Khartoum just once. And therefore I have never had the 'from home' narrative to fall back on, the stories at my father's knee to use as nourishment. The romantic red dust of the Sahara is not mine, the call to prayer is not mine, not in the way the River Thames is mine, the sands of a Devon summer holiday beach are mine, a pint down the pub is mine. I am as British as they come, like hot buttered toast and bacon sarnies. And still something of an alien in my own country.

Elaine

'If you want a coloured for a neighbour, vote Labour.'

    Please explain.

'No blacks, no Irish, no dogs.'

    Please explain.

'Keep Britain Tidy. Kick out Pakis.'

    Please explain.

1

Mum. And Dad

My mother once wanted to be a nun. This came as a surprise, decades later, when she told me. She was about fourteen and at the local grammar school in south Devon where she lived with her mother and father, Norah and Roland, and two younger brothers, Anthony and Philip. My grandparents and my uncles. A surprise because as far as I was concerned my mother was about as cool on God as one could imagine. She was a campaigner, a person suspicious of the Church and its structures, of organised worship used as a cover for a myriad of social ills, like power and who had it. And gender, and who won which battles. If the Church of England was the Conservative Party at prayer – as it was once described by the suffragist Maude Royden – then Mum was having none of it. That's what I thought.

My surprise at my mother's early religious leanings was based on a child's-eye view, that perspective that believes your parents came fully formed into existence on the day you are born and have no pre-existing hinterland. It's that same perspective that produces surprise when you stumble across a teacher in the real world, doing the shopping. I only knew Mum as 'a grown-up', and assumed she had always been one. She was the adult who warned me with ashen face after the election of 1979 that Margaret Thatcher would 'bring no good to Britain'. I was not quite clear why, given – from what I could glean from the news – the rubbish was piling up on the streets, the people who collected the bins and buried the dead were always on strike and the lights went off pretty regularly because there wasn't enough coal for the power stations, causing a scramble for the candles in the cupboard under the stairs.

At the age of eleven all I wanted to do was play football and ride my bike down to the canal where a few mates and I had built a den in the trees. Mum would often admit with a laugh that she was always shocked when the Conservatives won an election because 'I don't know any'. She thought Tony Blair was a bit, well, capitalist.

Finding out about that hinterland, her childhood, her younger years, not only painted a picture of the post-Second World War Britain my mother grew up in, but also explained why she once 'got God'. Mum is one of the smartest people I know, the person who taught me that the obvious position on any subject is not always the wisest, and that there is a difference between an initial reaction and a considered thought. I think she may even now know a few Tories, having mellowed a little in her old age.

Mum was born in an era of traditional England, a quiet England, the type of England held dear by many, a folk memory connected to blood and soil and history which is regularly dismissed by those of a metropolitan, sophisticated bent. It is held onto, hard, nevertheless, with a tight knot of pride by many in Britain who wonder why they are not allowed to say 'in the good old days' without someone pointing out a lot of bad things about the good old days like it was illegal to be gay, that many women had to give up work when they had a child, that debilitating poverty was widespread. And racism. 'Okay, but I still like the idea. The memory.'

It was an England that can make the heart swell a little. A celebration of a difficult-to-define peaceableness, a romantic notion coloured, I am sure, by misremembering and ignoring, for that moment of nostalgia at least, all that is wrong with how we are and were. It is a sepia-tinted history and it matters, even if much of it was a construct, a romantic dance with a past that only had a casual relationship with reality. Country lanes resplendent with hawthorn-infused hedgerows, so high you were only able to glimpse the view of the green and pleasant land when passing a five-bar farm gate. Wooden, not metal. High streets populated by independent grocers and shops called things like Dingles, where staff in bonnets weighed the sweets, while in the butcher's next door freshly carved hams were packed in greaseproof paper for each and every customer ('Hello Mrs Chase!' 'Hello Mrs Mills!', because they were all women, of course, doing the shopping). Cars *poop-pooping* their horns as young scamps scattered on the road in front of them, breaking up their game of bat and ball. Ruddy-faced milkmen delivering fresh pintas in the morning and in the afternoon the coal arriving in sacks to be lugged around the back and dumped in the coal hole behind the conservatory. The England of that certain type of rose-tinted Sunday evening television drama before they find the dead body in the barn.

It was a comforting story, told of a country searching for stability in a storm. Everywhere today the talk is of noise and rapid change and how we – in the twenty-first century of artificial intelligence, social media overload, the political dismemberment of populism, the literal dismemberment of terrorism – have never seen anything like this, ever. And we wonder why people need an anchor, something solid to hold onto, white knuckled, in these rough and turbulent seas. We could do with listening a little more to why people like remembering old, curling photographs of children playing in the woods, climbing the highest trees, before the killjoys arrived, the health and safety police, the endless lobbies with their new rule books on this and 'you can't say that', and we all became scared about paedophiles and street crime, hoodies and drugs, and no one going out anymore and just cowering behind their locked doors worrying about social armageddon. Let me have my little imagined community in all its monocultural glory, just for a bit. It's comforting.

Elaine Mary Sturman was born on 23 April 1943, Norah and Roland's first child. She arrived, a little early, in her Auntie Ivy's house, directly behind her grandmother's in a small village called Thorpe Hesley just outside Rotherham. Yorkshire was a county built on steel, a garlanded duke at the top table of the industrial revolution. In the 1740s the process of producing 'crucible steel' was honed in nearby Sheffield, a far harder and stronger metal product than previous efforts, allowing for an increase in production which made the city the centre of European steel-making. Sheffield plate followed soon after, a method of fusing silver onto copper, 'plating' the cheaper product with the precious metal and bringing a solid silver substitute to the growing middle classes. A century later, Yorkshire was manufacturing half of all the steel made on the continent.

Metal production encouraged metal production, a magnet acting to attract. Henry Bessemer moved his steel company to Sheffield in 1856, inventing the Bessemer Converter which allowed for the mass production of the alloy that was building the modern world. By 1911, 75,000 skilled steelmakers and engineers were employed around Sheffield, the giant, fireball furnaces fed by the coal pits of Barnsley and Doncaster. In 1913 came stainless steel and the cutlery industry; the First World War increased demand, as did the peace, the continent's largest economies battling for production supremacy, fear of another conflict never far from the thoughts of those that wielded power. Growth seemed a one-way bet and by the start of the Second World War, Sheffield was a thriving city of 500,000 people; employment was plentiful; immigrants came, not from strange, far-flung countries, but from the rural world, the fields and valleys of the Peak District and the Pennines, the dales of North Yorkshire. They lived in poor housing for poor people, built by the Victorians in serried ranks, back-to-back. Mum remembers the excitement of the time, the huge factories, the glorious light, sunbeams caught in the steam of industry, people with a purpose, marching to work every morning and home every night having *made* something via the sweat of their brow, the ingenuity of their hand, their understanding of science, knowing that this was the place to be, the heart of a brave new future.

A brave and dirty new future. Heat (equivalent to a fifth of that provided by the sun) and sulphur-stained smoke billowed from the factories into the air, caught in those sunbeams. Chemicals poured into the rivers, producing toxic foam which lay filthy on the water, often several feet thick. Britain's engine had a stinking exhaust, and that mattered for Anthony Sturman born four years after my mother. He was severely asthmatic, and home was a place surrounded by seven hills, a trap for pollution. After his first birthday, a doctor took Norah and Roland to one side to tell them some difficult news. Anthony would, possibly, not survive another year in Yorkshire, the soot-stained county. He needed to live somewhere where the air was clean, fresh. The Sturmans, traditional Yorkshire folk whose family used to farm the fields north of belching, steaming Sheffield, would have to move.

After depression, war, so much dislocation, this was another cost, the home that had to be sold at a loss because of restrictions against speculative gains on house sales. People like Roland and Norah didn't talk much about such things – this was not the age of expressing emotions, it was the age of keeping what was inside, inside. They didn't talk much about how it felt for Norah to leave her identical twin sister, Mary. Roland, his brothers. What it felt like to leave a settled community they knew, were anchored in, could take sustenance from in its very familiarity, when a distance of a few miles meant much more than it does today. Foreign lands were as much the next-door county as the next-door country.

South Devon, by the sea, more clement, was the decision. Roland could look for a job in the civil service and play the organ at the local church. They sold up, packed up, and left – left behind their families and their friends, a life they knew for a place strange and remote. It took a day to make the journey by car, setting off as dawn turned the sky from black to grey, with bacon sandwiches, I-Spy games and thermos flasks for sustenance. Arriving in time for sunset over the English Channel.

My family struggled for a while, making ends meet in a house provided by the church and then the council. Roland and Norah saved carefully and finally were able to buy a house on the top of a hill, 52 Highland Road, Torquay, with the glittering sea just visible from the bedroom in the roof.

Mum's father worked in the Food Office down the road in Newton Abbot – a rural market town where tourism mixed with farming and the wealthy mixed with the poor – at a time when the overhang of rationing meant that families still had to make do with dried egg and 'government cheese'. He played the organ at St Matthew's church in Chelston, Torquay, once every day for evensong and twice on Sundays. He was also the choirmaster, a significant post. Anthony and Philip were in the choir and attended regular choir practice. Mum wasn't allowed, and would turn the music pages sitting next to her father on the big stool at the organ, much wider than the piano stool at home where Roland would practise so early in the morning Norah had to tell him to stop for fear of offending the neighbours. My grandfather was a little suspicious of women in choirs, thinking their voices a tad thin and reedy and women being, well, women. Mum had a good alto voice, and would sometimes sing at the back, out of sight, helping to round out the male voices. Norah looked after the family, the home. She did not work, she did not drive – although I am not sure anyone asked her whether that was a decision she had made proactively. Women of her generation weren't really offered choices. The number of women in work fell after the Second World War. Academic and well-publicised papers with titles like 'The Purpose of the Family' made urgent pleas for a revitalisation of the 'art of motherhood'.

Norah and Roland fitted into their new Devon life, just like millions of families fitted in after the war, made do, got on with it via a set of unspoken rules of politeness and privacy, a generation which had earned its chance of a quiet life, had lived through two great conflicts, seen their loved ones taken away from them, been through a depression never equalled. And their oldest daughter decided that being a nun might be good because her quiet family who didn't fuss had enveloped her in a High Anglican cloak (there was incense at the church services) and all its attendant attractiveness, its rituals and routines. The teenage enthusiasm didn't last, Mum dropping God as she ticked off the years at Newton Abbot grammar school. But it gave a hint: inside, Mum wanted to be different, not follow the path of local job followed by family and domesticity. She just wasn't sure how.

Mum doesn't remember seeing a black person as she grew up. In 1940s Britain, 'others' were mostly Jewish people and the Irish, around one million, of a total population of 50 million. But in rural Devon, there weren't many Jews or Irish people either. If we're honest.

This was a Britain coming to terms with a changing world and still wary, in part – grumbling and uncomfortable with what it saw as threats to its system, a system defended with the lives of many millions of its people and, rather less conveniently, many millions of 'others' of different backgrounds and colours. 'Shockingly, British fascism revived quickly after the war,' David Kynaston wrote in his history of this post-war world, *Austerity Britain*. 'However the Jew was about to be replaced by the black immigrant as the prime "other".' So started the long difficult journey.

The numbers of black people living in Britain in the 1940s were small, about 20,000 to 30,000. During the war – when the need for labour was acute – there had been some small-scale projects to bring in Caribbean migrants. A few hundred black workers arrived in Liverpool under one scheme, to the consternation of local skilled workers who 'resented being associated in the minds of English people with the unskilled negro labourer'. With peace declared, it was now time to rebuild the country and for that the country needed hands to toil. The Ministry of Labour cast around for solutions to the shortage. We needed people to come here. Even if some people didn't want them. 'I do not think that any scheme for the importation of coloured colonials for permanent settlement here should be embarked upon without full understanding that this means that coloured elements will be brought in for permanent absorption into our own population,' was the opinion of one senior civil servant, Sir Harold Wiles. The Ministry of Labour itself fretted that 'many of the coloured men are unreliable and lazy, quarrels among them are not infrequent'. When the *Empire Windrush* arrived from Jamaica with fewer than 500 passengers on board in 1948, ministers scrambled for reassurances that 'no encouragement will be given to others to follow their example'. The colonial secretary, Arthur Creech Jones, described it as a 'mass movement'. Five hundred people would not quite fill a row of seats at Wembley Stadium.

There was another solution to the labour problem: thousands of white Europeans displaced by war. Many of them Poles, a far safer bet in the eyes of officials. Black immigration could be counted in the hundreds; European immigration in the tens of thousands, 51,000 alone in the agriculture sector. But it was the former that sparked that word 'mass', that sparked a letter to Clement Attlee from eleven Labour MPs arguing that 'an influx of coloured people domiciled here is likely to impair the harmony, strength and cohesion of our public and social life and to cause discord and unhappiness among all concerned'.

And here was Britain's problem – a problem that was to stalk its attitude to immigration, race and identity from then to now.

It came in two parts, which pushed against one another.

As head of the empire, there was a widespread belief that 'citizens' of those countries which Britain ruled should be given the right to settle in Britain, seemingly in the belief that people, to quote Baron Hailsham, Quintin Hogg, 'would come and go'. That revolving door would keep numbers stable and communities intact. It was also a useful way of filling jobs.

In opposition to that, Britain – an island – is also a country that has struggled with a historic fear of 'other' which, in the last seventy years, has been most easily defined by one descriptor: colour. We've had different ones of course, and spent a good few centuries pulling ourselves apart over religion, chopping traitors' heads off, burning monasteries and using the rack against people who looked exactly the same as those in power. Colour has been easier, frankly – no need for trials and inquisitions, colour is obvious, it is identifiable and after the war it was becoming more prevalent. The Labour MPs with their working-class constituencies who wrote to Clement Attlee, spoke of a country in the 1940s that enjoyed a 'profound unity without uniformity', a country 'blest by the absence of a racial colour problem'. It was rather more dormant than absent, a seed in the desert soil ready to germinate at the first sign of nourishment.

Britain has long had a problem with 'other', whether you were a French Huguenot speaking your own language, building your own churches and silk-weaving your way to wealth in the eighteenth century ('offal of the earth' according to one London priest, Dr Welton), an Irish labourer in the nineteenth century ('The most improvident and the most filthy in their habits,' according to Dr Duncan, the first Medical Officer of Health for Liverpool) or a Jewish émigré from Hungary in the twentieth century (who faced the fascism of Oswald Mosley, and the more prosaic discrimination of London County Council about which houses Jewish people could live in). We are just not very good at admitting it.

In the immediate aftermath of the war, the open-door, economic-need attitude prevailed, inching Britain towards a more liberal approach to immigration. There was little discussion, as the historian Randall Hansen points out, 'in parliamentary debate, the press or private papers' that there 'was the possibility that substantial numbers could exercise their right to reside permanently in the UK'. The public were not part of any conversation. They were not consulted. Their opinions not sought.

In flirting with this 'liberal' approach, the establishment in Westminster made a number of miscalculations. Mass, cheap, international transport was coming, fundamentally reducing the barriers to movement. Life in 'the mother country' appeared more attractive than people in Britain understood when you were taught at school in Jamaica or Sudan that this country was the guiding star, the home, to good fortune. Once you advertised that labour and jobs were to be had here, it should have been little surprise that people came, the young looking for adventure when the alternative was a tough social and economic life in countries often beset by conflict, maybe, and poverty, certainly. Britain offered a rich mix, which led to many hands reaching for the lever marked 'search for a better life' and pulling on it with enthusiasm.

When Norman Tebbit spoke in reverential tones about his father growing up in the depression of the 1930s and 'getting on his bike and looking for work', he was attempting to contrast a pre-war generation with those who took to the streets in the early 1980s to protest about the grotesque conditions they lived in (called riots in the media, uprisings by others more sympathetic). He received warm applause at the 1981 Conservative Party conference. Inadvertently, he was also making the most powerful argument for immigration imaginable – people getting on their bike, on a plane, on a train, and looking for work, a better economic future. Very British, in fact. Some might even go so far as to describe it as a 'British value'.

Two ideas, then, in conflict. On the one side the attitude to empire and Commonwealth – these are 'our people' – on the other the attitude to the more visceral issue of colour, and by definition, race – these aren't 'our people'. It was a contradiction that was to sit, glowering, dangerous, at the heart of the debate about the British and our attitude to others, from *Windrush*, via Enoch Powell, riots, mass immigration, all the way, in different form, to the Brexit vote.

And, it was a contradiction I could understand. One side of me was British to its very core. The other, immigrant stock. The stranger.

Czeslaw Knott was the only 'other' my mother was aware of at school. It is likely Czeslaw was the son of Polish immigrants who were given the right to stay in Britain after the war. In what has been described as the first mass immigration legislation signed by the government, the Polish Resettlement Act of 1947 – also known as Churchill's Promise – granted more than 250,000 Poles, many of whom fought alongside British forces, the right to live in Britain. With Poland partly annexed by the Soviet Union – and the rest operating as a satellite communist state – many Poles decided to stay in the UK. They often lived in old military bases, introducing 'Little Polands' across the country, Nissen huts resplendent with flowers to mark saints' days, allotments with rabbits and chickens and fruit and vegetables, just like at home, orthodox Catholic church services in rudimentary chapels. One of the largest was at Stover, four miles north of Newton Abbot. Czeslaw could well have been the son of some daring Polish fighter ace. But Mum admitted she didn't know. She never spoke to him.

Now, let's pause for a minute and think a little about what Britain did seventy years ago. Two hundred and fifty thousand Polish people. Welcomed to Britain with very little debate, to a country with a justified reputation for being a safe harbour. Full of good people who take the stranger as they find them, as long as the stranger takes to them and respects who they are. Just imagine for a moment if 250,000 people from the Indian subcontinent had arrived in Britain in 1947, whether Hindu or Muslim, and, having fought alongside British forces as they did, then built communities dotted across the English countryside, recognisable in Mumbai or Chennai, 'Little Indias'. Or from the Caribbean – 'Little Jamaicas'. What would have been the reaction then? Of course it is different, distance is not just a geographical concept, it is also a cultural one. But our attitude to Poland after the Second World War is instructive. It shows what can be done, that accepting large groups of foreign-born people is not beyond the wit of a country if the initial story we tell ourselves about that 'great arrival' is positive.

Mum lived in blissful ignorance that her life was 'blest by the absence of a racial colour problem'. No one in Devon spoke about a 'colour problem' or of faraway lands. She remembers having fish and chips from the shop at the bottom of the steep hill, Sherwell Rise, in Torquay. She remembers falling in love with French literature, which set her on a path, she believed to adulthood, of study and translation. A favourite was Armand Salacrou, the French existentialist dramatist, who wrote 'the existence of a world without God seems to me less absurd than the presence of God, existing in all his perfection, creating imperfect man in order to make him run the risk of Hell'. My mother had moved quite a way from wanting to be a nun.

So, she studied French at university and travelled to Paris and Marseille and met Salacrou and talked about the complexities of existence and how drama could make sense of how we live. She stayed with a friend, Régine, in a hotel in Marseille. It had to be cheap because Elaine Mary Sturman didn't have much money. And it was, and, as is usual with things that are cheap in big cities with immigrants, that was where the big city let its immigrants live, an economic zoning policy. Régine was horrified at where they found themselves: 'Nous sommes tombées en plein quartier arabe,' she whispered urgently over supper. Mum thought it was all quite exciting, falling into the middle of the Arab quarter. For the first time, she saw lots of black people going about daily lives not so far removed from hers and started to think a little about difference and whether a purely English approach to the world was for her. The 1960s was the decade of change, the buzz of the new, a decade for sloughing off that old, woolly coat and trying on a miniskirt for a change or a Biba mac with skinny sleeves. Mum was beguiled, was stirred by the beat of new possibilities.

At her university, Birmingham, she befriended the students from north Africa, 'all beautiful' as she described them and certainly a long way from the Davids and Johns and Williams of Devon life, ordinary life. They talked with passion about the Middle East, about United Nations resolutions – which they could quote by number – about Israel and Palestine, about how they would be going back to their countries to battle for change, rather than sit about chewing on their pencil ends wondering about the meaning of life. In French.

How different was that from British life? As different as shepherd's pie was from couscous and fiery chilli lamb, with extra red pepper and lemon juice on the side. It was the time to try everything, anything marked 'new' and 'exciting'. Mum, eyes wide, joined the Africa Society which held intense discussions about the self-styled 'Marxist socialist' dictator, Kwame Nkrumah, and independence for Ghana, made up of the former UK colonies of the Gold Coast and British Togoland; about the assassination of the first leader of Congo, which gained independence from Belgium in 1960. Patrice Lumumba was killed by secessionist forces in January 1961 and dark rumours swirled about the involvement of the CIA (Lumumba had turned to the Soviet Union for support) and MI6, which maybe shouldn't come as a surprise – Anthony Eden had wanted the Egyptian president Gamal Abdel Nasser 'destroyed' and David Owen, when foreign secretary, had asked officials whether it was possible to have Idi Amin killed.

Major world events were happening and suddenly my mother, called Pudding at school because she was from Yorkshire, plugged in. She dated Amin from Sudan and didn't tell her parents. Mum was young, charged up. The old life of 52 Highland Road appeared more distant, a life where good people didn't talk about politics and the only thing that would necessitate a conversation about the *Telegraph* newspaper delivered every day was whether anyone could help out with the crossword. Yes, the Suez Crisis was on the wireless – and that is exactly where it stayed.

After graduating, Mum doubled down on her city life and moved to the largest and flashiest of all, London. She joined the government's Crown Agents, the arm of Whitehall which dealt with supplying what were now largely former colonies with everything from finance to pens, weapons to printing presses for postage stamps. She kept her links with that exciting North African diaspora, those sent to Britain, often by wealthy families, to complete their studies; who ate ox tongue on great rugs sitting on the floor, laughing and talking 'current affairs'; who dipped strange flatbreads in concoctions made from beans – *foul* and hummus – and smoked from shisha pipes, the fragrant tobacco filling the air. These exciting new people who also joined in and ate watery burgers and pale chips at the local Wimpy with a knife and fork, ketchup in the tomato-shaped dispenser, which you squirted out of the plastic stem on the top; went to the milk bars for shakes under fluorescent lights, had a dance at the sparkling clubs in a city which was emerging from a claustrophobic post-war world.

Amin introduced Mum to Hameed, a friend from Sudan, and his wife, Erica, from Germany. Erica and Mum shared a flat above a parade of shops on Highbury Park Road in north London. The Beatles' film *Help!* was on at the cinema, the Rolling Stones released '(I Can't Get No) Satisfaction', tailored red coats were in fashion, launched by Mary Quant with the funny haircut, and Elizabeth Lane became the first woman to sit as a high court judge. The Race Relations Act was the first piece of legislation to outlaw discrimination 'in public places'. The BBC launched a new children's programme called *The Magic Roundabout* and the groovier adults sniggered at what they supposed were the drug references. Mum knew the future belonged to her.

Hameed had a proposition. Would Mum mind going to Heathrow to meet his friend and cousin who was arriving from Khartoum, a young research scientist who had received a scholarship from the capital's university and was coming to Britain to study bilharzia, a debilitating disease also known as snail fever, spread by parasites burrowing into people and cattle? Yes, my mother said, of course. And that's how Elaine Mary Sturman became the first white person Abubaker Ismail Ahmed ever met.

What must it have been like arriving on that plane, stepping into air 20°C colder than you are used to? The light greyer, the sun weaker, the people reserved, when all your life you had been surrounded by heat, sun-split azure skies, by the smells of spiced food, and dust and sand, people in your face, urgent, excited, the atmosphere of the market still pricking your memory.

Not this damp rain.

My father was in his early twenties and a successful science student. He didn't see himself as part of the mass immigration movements from the Caribbean, India and Pakistan – those that had come to Britain to answer the call for bus drivers and hospital workers, manual labourers and mid-skilled engineers. My father was different.

Abubaker Ismail Ahmed had received a scholarship to study in Britain from Khartoum University, one of the finest in the country in the 1960s, if not in the whole of northern Africa. The state was going to pay for him to study abroad – the obvious and natural route for anyone looking to succeed. Go away, learn, and come home – ready to share your knowledge and help build a new nation, stumbling, unsure, on its route away from colonialism.

Abubaker Ismail Ahmed was the oldest of four children – and in Sudan that meant a lot. Being the oldest child and being a boy gave you family rights. You were treated with respect by your younger siblings, at school you held your head a little higher, your position in the world was a little more significant, you were expected to achieve. In many countries across North Africa and the Middle East, welcome to the concept of the 'little prince', the first son doted on by the family. Dad was the Little Prince.

His great-grandfather was Ismael Sajer El Keiry, who, his sister Asma told me proudly years later, could trace the family's roots back to Mahdi royalty. And beyond that, the Pharaohs, she insisted, before going on to explain, inter alia, that Sudan also had the best grapefruit juice in the world ('Much sweeter than Egyptian') and 'our pyramids are older'. This isn't quite true but certainly you can visit the Kushite pyramids north of Khartoum by rolling up in your 4x4 with air conditioning and walking the last couple of hundred metres, with just a few passing farm hands and a clutch of goats for company.

Dad's family were senior figures in Omdurman society, Sudan's second city on the other side of the Nile from Khartoum. They helped found one of the city's best-known schools, Ahlia, in response to increasing Sudanese demand for education for the masses and the lack of government provision. The school was built despite concerns from the authorities that a better-educated society would 'increase the clamour for office chairs'. My great-grandfather was one of the first Sudanese *mamour*, or district officials, for the city. Before that they had all been Egyptians appointed by the British. Under him, the whipping of Sudanese locals by colonial officers was banned.

My father was expected to respect his place in a family of some standing. A family of somebodies. He was going to be somebody.

'Being the first son and grandson, much pressure was put on Seddig [my father's everyday name] to become an important man,' Asma said of her older brother, love obvious in every word. 'He was the darling.' My family were governors of cities, we didn't sit around under trees doing nothing, and Dad, the family straightforwardly believed, would carry on the tradition.

He grew up in a large house, a compound 2,000 square metres in size. It was one of the few brick houses in the city. In the large courtyards shaded by trees, thinly sliced meats and onions were left to dry on large trays, ready for the cooks who worked in the kitchen, preparing dinner. The children were called to meals by their nanny. They had one each. Over the dining table hung a rope which was pulled by my grandfather to signal that the next course should be brought. Servants scurried.

The walls were dotted with photographs of a proud father and mother, him resplendent in army uniform with a rifle and tall hat, feathers and shiny boots. Her, head covered with beautifully embroidered, white cotton, neck heavy with jewellery, surrounded by shy children – apart from one, my father, staring defiantly into the lens, chin raised. An imposing wooden desk stood in one room, behind which my grandfather worked on government business.

This was my other family. We weren't bunnies from the jungle, you see.

It was a grand world. It was a stifling world, bureaucratic and traditional. In Britain it would have been called Victorian. In Omdurman, it was just Sudanese. The rules were strict and enforced; respect for elders – mothers, fathers, grandmothers, grandfathers – absolute. No talking back, no cinema, no playing outside the compound walls; the order was to study, to be an engineer, a doctor, follow a path as set and immutable as, say, the laws of physics.

And my father chafed at the strictures and argued – often wildly – with his parents. His was a country in turmoil, the air thick with experiments in democracy and revolution. The streets were full of urgent talk of the type of place Sudan wanted to be, the Communist Party on the one side, the Muslim Brotherhood on the other, secular versus Islam. Gunfire was threateningly common, weapons taking the place of discussion; different forces fighting, sometimes road by road, for supremacy; governments rising and falling, accompanied by the soundtrack of crackling bullets.

It wasn't a time for staying at home. Seddig was out there, fist raised, chanting for democracy. Like so many late teenagers, people in their early twenties – whatever country they are from – he had all the solutions. If only people would listen.

He was shot at during one demonstration and the man on his shoulders was hit, killed. My father lay under the bodies, still, playing dead, as crowds streaked for cover, screams ringing out. My family speak of it quietly now, believing that my father's stillness, the holding of breath, saved his life. They nearly lost Seddig that day, the family hero, the boy who always took the lead as the sheriff when the children from outside the walls came over to play, who showed – in his great move to Britain – that he didn't really need his family as much as they needed him, didn't really need anything tying him down, went away to make a different life without his own strict mother; closer in the end to the Mother of Democracy than the woman who bore him.

'He wanted to rush off, change everything,' Asma said. 'He was so fun, outgoing. I am introvert.'

She pauses. Readjusts her headscarf.

'I think the family liked him more than me.'

This was the 1960s in Sudan for Seddig, just like it was the 1960s in Britain for Elaine. They grew up thousands of miles apart but were fellow travellers, excited by what appeared the endless possibilities of change. They had glimpsed a new world, through snatches of television, through scouring the papers for news, through academia. And they determined to have a part of it.

Where to go, to drink at the bar of the future? The pick was easy. Sitting at the centre of the new world for my father, just as for my mother, was London; and, just as for my mother, for my father a city both vibrant and dirty, forging a life somewhere between the American mix of modernity and fearful, segregated authority and the stultified, more foreign, European continent. London wasn't just the capital of England, it was the capital of the English-speaking world and of the crumbling British colonies. It was lusciously historic, its twisting, narrow streets, its churches and cathedrals, and so modern with its Underground and expressways and cinemas and nights out at the London Palladium, flashing neon lights bright at Piccadilly Circus. Pick a place, any place, that would be the destination of choice, the destination to put yourself at the beating heart of all that was going to be ripped up by its roots, this fresh, fair world so many wanted to see, then London was it.

'If you want a coloured for a neighbour, vote Labour.'

What kind of country was this, that my father arrived in? Nineteen sixty-four was the year Harold Wilson came to power in Britain promising to unleash the 'white heat of technology' and the year my father stepped off that plane at Heathrow. In the general election of that year, one constituency in Birmingham – Smethwick – bucked the national swing towards Labour. It was won by the Conservatives after a campaign which included: 'If you want a coloured for a neighbour, vote Labour' posters. And variants of the same. Including wanting a 'nigger for a neighbour'. Which might be considered even worse than 'a coloured', one supposes. Although it was unclear who had put the posters up, Peter Griffiths, the victorious Conservative candidate, said: 'I would not condemn any man who said that. I regard it as a manifestation of popular feeling.'

Popular feeling. Two words that have often been used as a powerful ram against all that is viewed as modern and liberal. 'Popular feeling' as a code for conservative feeling, traditional feeling, could-we-just-have-the-good-old-days-back feeling. Popular feeling from the 1960s to today, sometimes more prominent in the national conversation, sometimes quieter. An admission that many people do not like too many 'others' – who are portrayed as a challenge, a risk – and should be allowed to say so. And are not. I am not sure my father could sense 'popular feeling' when he arrived in London, because London is a place never much bothered by 'popular feeling', seeing it as something peculiarly provincial.

But it is a stubborn strand in Britain's political and cultural history, often strong in its sentiment and ugly in its execution. It comes back again and again to tap us on the shoulder and say: 'Remember me?'

A candidate for UKIP in the general election of 2017 re-tweeted a cartoon saying: 'If you want a Jihadi for a neighbour, vote Labour', across an illustration of a lorry being driven by Jeremy Corbyn with lots of, ahem, non-white people piled up in the back, hanging off the doors. John Bickley, UKIP's immigration spokesman and the re-tweeter in question, said he was unaware of its historical resonance and apologised 'for any offence caused'. Which one might describe as a 'third-party' apology – being sorry for the reaction of the audience rather than the substance of the content. Content that many voters might think, in the warm privacy of a pint in the pub with their friends, is right. Aren't you worried about having a jihadi for a neighbour? Even if the chances of having a jihadi for a neighbour are about as high as having a white, racist fanatic for a neighbour who wants to drive a truck into a mosque and kill people. And what if we just transposed the word Muslim in place of jihadi and had done with it? And how would it feel if the word Muslim was then swapped for Jew? Who would re-tweet it then?

Peter Griffiths beat Patrick Walker, the Labour shadow home secretary – a man mocked for standing in a seat blighted by factory closures and a waiting list for council houses 4,000-strong while living a hundred miles south in the rather more genteel surroundings of Hampstead Garden Suburb.

'How easy to support uncontrolled immigration when one lives in a garden suburb,' Mr Griffiths said.

'No blacks, no Irish, no dogs.'

When he first came to London, my father lived in a small flat in the centre of the city, then a soot-covered, glowering part of the metropolis not long out of the clutches of the pea-souper fogs caused by the burning coal of millions of stoves and fireplaces. And from his new home, a few square feet, not thousands, he contemplated where he had arrived.

This country that he had learnt about at school, learnt its language so well he would take a postgraduate scientific degree in a script not born of his mother tongue. This country which everyone he knew, had grown up with, understood, but whose understanding of Sudan was limited to colonial rule – Britain's – and how 'ownership' or otherwise affected relations with France. He maybe felt it in his bones, that realisation that acceptance would only come slowly, grudgingly, if at all. That realisation that must creep into the hearts of so many first-generation immigrants who arrive with such hope and often die unsure and unfulfilled, never completely a member of the jealously guarded in-group. This country, with people so generous. This country still raddled with a confused crossness that someone, a different someone, is somehow Taking. The. Piss.

My mother's initial exciting breakout to feed this fresh decade's wanderlust was to France – an intense adventure for someone who had grown up in south Devon. For my father, the horizons were wider, as they are so often for those millions of sons and daughters of countries that have a link to a colonial ruler – a past that put one nation above all others. The political scientist Tayib Zein al Abdin described Britain as 'the best country in the world'. My father agreed, heard about it at school. When al Abdin arrived in the UK to study in 1969 there was a rude awakening. 'All the white women refused to sit beside me on the bus,' he wrote, finding a country 'anti-Muslim, anti-Arab and anti-Africa.'

'It was, gentlemen, after a long absence, seven years to be exact, during which time I was studying in Europe – that I returned to my people. I learned much and much passed me by… The important thing was that I returned with a great yearning for my people in that small village in that bend in the Nile.'

The Sudanese author, Tayeb Salih, wrote in *Season of Migration to the North* of a journey back to Sudan by an unnamed narrator who has been studying in London for seven years. During those seven years he sleeps with a myriad of women drawn by his 'exotic roots' – largely invented, it turns out, the storyteller a-wooing on tales of living in the rainforests and charming snakes. It is the traditional story of the Sudanese émigré, that he or she eventually returns, pulled back by the scent of the Nile. My father always said that he could 'smell rivers'.

But no great yearning developed for Dad. Many of my Sudanese family studied abroad – it was part of what the wealthier classes did. They are nearly all back home now, aunties and uncles, cousins. But for Dad, Britain was freedom. Freedom from Sudanese life marked on one side by the control of a family and on the other by the chaos of a country still searching for its place in the world.

London was full of culture and pace, the global meeting place where you could discuss politics late into the night with your new-found friends from the North African diaspora as well as intense young English people who believed, like you, that the world was there to be changed. People like my mum. Ask my father why he stayed in Britain and he would answer 'energy'. Racism? Those people who wouldn't sit next to you on the bus? My father, the 'little prince' who was more grown up now, would have been hard-pressed to notice. And if he did, he wouldn't have cared very much.

My father committed wholeheartedly to his new home, his new life, his new girlfriend, the new him, the break from the past so many immigrants are driven by. My father wanted to live far, far away from his home, geographically as well as culturally. He had no time for the romance of 'nation' and 'soil'. His was a global community of individuals, internationalism not nationalism. He never taught me Arabic, never took me to Sudan, never gave me a present with an Islamic flavour, never told me stories as he stirred a pot full of bubbling goat stew. His idea of 'tea' was two slices of supermarket brown bread with compressed garlic sausage in the middle. I didn't like garlic sausage. That was followed by a tin of rice pudding to which he added sugar. I did like rice pudding with added sugar, although I had to be careful not to spill it as my father got cross about things like that.

Dad owned a *taqiyah*, but he never wore it. The Muslim cap sat, orange, on a shelf for all the years he was alive in Britain, a reminder of what my father wasn't. For me there was no rose-tinted 'going home' narrative beloved of film-makers. I am very proud that my father came from Sudan, and it is due to him that my experience has been so different from the majority of people who live here. But I am more proud about what he achieved in Britain and the hurdles he clambered over. I am proud of Sudan as an intellectual exercise. But, my father never gave me a homespun story about Sudan, because he wanted to spin a different one.

He went on holidays with my mother to Devon with a bucket and spade. He went to the cinema. He drank wine seriously – much to his cousin, Hameed's, distaste – and invested in a couple of wine businesses. Understanding a sommelier's 'nose' and investing in alcohol – a neat riposte to alcohol-free Sudan. He became a research scientist at the Institute of Ophthalmology, tucked away on Judd Street, central London, moving on from bilharzia to the study of the pathology of the eyes. He became an expert in the use of the electron microscope. He worked at Moorfields Eye Hospital, renowned throughout the world. I once remember seeing his name on a scientific paper on the cell structure of rabbits' eyes and felt like taking it to school to show all my friends, despite not understanding a word.

Admittedly, Dad never really understood that very English quality – being polite – often leaving Mum exasperated as her parents drew deep on their Christianity and welcomed to the family what to them must have appeared something tantamount to a Man from Mars. 'A few pleases and thank-yous would make things so much easier,' Mum would say wearily in the evening, after another uncomfortable encounter. 'Why?' my father answered. You didn't thank family, it would be rude. Many years later, Mum admitted that she didn't really understand it from Dad's point of view. How bizarre must it have seemed for Abubaker Ismail Ahmed, sitting around in Torquay cafés eating ice cream, while the people at the next-door table stared.

Mum went to work on the morning of her wedding, taking the Number 4 bus from her home in north London just as she did every day. In the afternoon she met Dad at the registry office in Finsbury Park. The guest list was short. Her mother Norah came from Torquay and her Auntie Mary from Rotherham. Anne, her closest friend from university, stood alongside Elaine Mary Sturman as she made her pledges.

A little earlier, the registrar had taken Mum aside, wondering if this young, white woman really understood the risks apparent to all about marrying Abubaker Ismail Ahmed. 'You know we won't be able to help you if you go to Sudan, get stuck?' he said in a low, conspiratorial voice. Mum thanked him for his concern. 'Can we get on with it?' When it came to signing the grand book with their names, my father so confused officials with his signature (Elsony, the family name, Abubaker Ismail Ahmed, his given name derived from his parents and grandparents, and Seddig, his 'everyday name'), they had to make up a new certificate and write 'formerly known as' by my father's entry, which settled, if nothing else, the needs of local authority bureaucracy. The small wedding party had cake afterwards back at the flat on Highbury Park Road. 'I don't think Mum and Auntie Mary were very impressed,' my mother said.

It is always difficult to explain why marriages break up, and that is not a subject to detail here. Suffice to say that reconciling Elaine from Torquay with Seddig from Omdurman proved too difficult and maybe, in the end, two such independent people were better cutting their own path. My mother and father stayed together for a few years before divorcing – Dad leaving our family home with the small back garden and the front gate with the wobbly post – to focus on work; Mum staying to focus on work and me, struggling to retain a civil service career that didn't have much room for 'single mothers' with a small child who needed picking up at 5 p.m. from the childminder – a large, white woman known to all as Auntie Jessie. Auntie Jessie, who had her own understanding of otherness, being married to a Pole.

My mother may have lost her marriage, but she did not lose that urgency of difference. When the Duke of Edinburgh visited the Crown Agents' offices, my mother stayed steadfastly at her desk. 'All the executives were white, all the clerical staff black,' she said. Mum could smell hypocrisy like Dad could smell rivers. She found it difficult to understand why my father wanted to go to the Black and White Minstrel Show at the Victoria Palace, complete with 'mammy' gags and wide-eyed, blacked-up dancers, complicated dance routines and Gilbert and Sullivan songs. He thought it was fun. 'I don't think he ever believed that the "no blacks" signs in the windows referred to him,' Mum said. 'He was different, he was from Sudan, maybe he really did think he was descended from the Pharaohs.'

Mum gave up, in the end, on the civil service – becoming a teacher after it was explained to her that a posting abroad was impossible as a single mother with a child. Fathers, of course, were paid to take their families. Teaching hours were more flexible, the holidays better and I was able to go to the school in south-west London Mum taught at – so less need for Auntie Jessie. 'What, are you, like, Mrs Ahmed's son?' friends at school would ask sceptically given that teachers didn't actually exist in the real world – particularly as mothers – and also that we were 'different colours and everything'. I insisted that I was, and on the long walk home with Mum up the Fulham Palace Road to catch the train back to Ealing, concentrated on playing being a rattly Underground service, complete with station stops and a *rrrrrrrr* sound of the silver and black doors opening to let the passengers on and off.

Last year I applied to be the Director of News at the BBC. I got through to the final four, a result I was pleased with, given I was the only candidate who had not spent many decades in broadcasting. The shortlist of two white men, one white woman and me created some social media comment. I was the only one with a name that would have been out of place in an English novel from the 1950s.

'I bet the Muslim gets it.'

'The BBC – they'll want a brown. Stitch up.'

I didn't get it.

I am brown.

I am not a Muslim.

2

Preventable evil

Asked to name a speech, any speech, about race and many people, probably, could pick out two. One by Dr Martin Luther King Jr, 'I Have a Dream'. And one by Enoch Powell, which became known by the shorthand title 'Rivers of Blood', but which Powell, the Conservative MP for Wolverhampton South West, preferred to call 'the Birmingham Speech'. Powell delivered his on 20 April 1968, sixteen days after Dr King was murdered by James Earl Ray's sniper's bullet. The shot shattered Dr King's jaw and severed his spinal cord. It's 4,112 miles from Atlanta, Georgia, to Birmingham, West Midlands. The speeches are a universe apart.

For my mother and father the events of April 1968 defined an era. In America, the fighter for racial emancipation gunned down, creating shock around the world. In Britain, the articulation of a calculated political argument against substantial, non-white immigration. An articulation of an apparent anger that has waxed and waned but has never found peace, never wholly disappeared. Not even now. Powell made the case against my mother and father, and by extension, me.

His was the case for the prosecution. The intellectual ballast for the 'send them home' brigade.

I have been to the Midland Hotel in Birmingham where Powell delivered the speech that he knew would go up 'like a rocket and stay up'. It is now called the Burlington Hotel. The occasion was the fortieth anniversary. In a different room at the same hotel on the same day in 2008 someone was there for the same reason, and his name was Nick Griffin.

Griffin was then the head of the British National Party, one of the many incarnations of the UK's fractious far right. He was once a member of the National Front, founded in 1967 – the year I was born, the year of *In the Heat of the Night,* the film that I watched over and over when I was younger because it was cool and American with Sidney Poitier and Rod Steiger; a film set in Sparta, Tennessee, the proper Deep South. A film about a black police officer and a white police chief and an uneasy coming together in a time of segregation. '*Virgil?*' the white chief, Gillespie, asks. 'That's a funny name for a nigger boy to come from Philadelphia. What do they call you up there?' Virgil, cool … so … cool … like an iced flannel on the back of the neck when the temperature is nudging 35°C: 'They call me Mister Tibbs!' No one made films like that in Britain.

No, here the National Front used to march up and down the streets of west London, with Union flags and barking dogs, the streets where Mum and I used to go shopping on the bus. The National Front believes Britain 'should remain a white country', that all non-white immigration should be halted, and that millions of non-white people living in the country they – I – call home should be deported in a 'phased and humane way'. 'Where?' I always wondered, reminded of Lenny Henry's joke that £1,000 would more than cover his bus fare back to Dudley. Griffin was a man who said he was not what lots of people thought he was – a racist. He was also a man who argued 'we must secure the existence of our race and a future for white children', a man who spoke of 'organised Jewry' running the media and, when arrested by the police in Wales under the Public Order Act after publishing a magazine 'likely to stir up racial hatred', commented to a friend on the phone that the police were 'very civilised … no Jews or Pakis'.

We walked right past each other – me, brown and working for the Equality and Human Rights Commission (EHRC); him, white and leading the far right in Britain – in one of the plainest, slightly too narrow, most English of hotel corridors with swirly patterned carpets. That is my country all over.

Nick Griffin – who has been invited to garden parties at Buckingham Palace with the Queen – doesn't know Kamal Ahmed – who has also been invited to garden parties at Buckingham Palace with the Queen. And why should he? I recognised him. He was almost around the corner, heading towards the lifts, as my brain ground through its mental gears. The puffy pale face, the slightly drooping mouth, the unruly eyes which look in slightly differing directions. A year later, the BNP would enjoy its greatest ever electoral success, polling just over 6 per cent in the European parliamentary elections and securing just under one million votes. Griffin became a Member of the European Parliament. There was talk of the BNP becoming the next Front National, the French party which had taken the extreme position on race – the identification of 'other' as the problem of substance – and made it mainstream, bundled together in a messy coalition with anti-establishment sentiment and economic resentment.

It didn't happen for the BNP. And why it didn't happen is interesting. Britain is uncomfortable with outright rejection, of people, of groups, of races. It generally makes us feel awkward. We may cloak prejudice (which is different from racism, not involving at its core the function of power and who holds it) with all sorts of words, and we may believe that nothing in life is, in the end, equal. Not in outcome, anyway. But the British way is marked by the phlegmatic, the non-emotional response, the rational. Not the whipped up, the frenzied, because, if we're honest, that is all a bit excitable and a bit 'foreign'. It is also something to do with fairness, a slippery concept, eel-like in quality and almost impossible to define. But we believe in it, nevertheless. Ideologues make us uneasy, those that are too definite in their solutions for any ills make us shuffle in our seats; we flirt, coquettish, but in the end do not consummate. The Nazis and the fascists and the real racists in Britain may be thugs but there is, today if not in the past, a toytown edge to their bluster, their flags and their boots. Britain is a country which looks at a man shouting through a megaphone and wonders what time *Countdown* is starting.

This position raises its own challenges. We do not reach for overarching solutions, but that can keep us blind to the problem running, in this case, just under our different-coloured skin. France and Germany vote for extremist parties and then pull back from the brink – enough people, at least up until now, knowing the route is just too awful to contemplate. But those elections that throw up such testing results are a vent, an outlet for pent-up emotions for those who feel unloved and disregarded.

And it demands that there is a very public conversation about what is in plain sight. In Britain such outlets are less obvious. And that can lead to eruptions of anger, that pent-up steam finally finding somewhere to go, to leak out. That we are not fascists marching around with our arms raised in flat-handed salute shouldn't be taken as permission from the political classes to ignore the factors that allow extremism to flourish.

By 2014 Nick Griffin had lost his seat and been kicked out of the BNP after some internal battles too laborious to bother ourselves with here. In 2017 he announced his intention to emigrate to Hungary which he said had become a refuge for 'westerners' who shared his view that the world west of the Danube had become too brown and too overrun, leaving 'aboriginal Whites' with nowhere to go but east and the sanctuary of a country that Griffin assumed was sympathetic to his views – one town mayor had said, after all, that he was engaged in a 'war against Muslims' and gay people.

'I hope that Hungary, the Hungarian government, the Hungarian people, will welcome people who are genuine refugees from western Europe but keep out the liberals who have brought western Europe to this state in the first place', he told the Hungarian website *444*. The Hungarian ministry for the interior responded that Griffin was a 'persona non grata', leading the former BNP member to tweet that he was now 'banned from New Zealand, Australia, Canada, Hungary and Ukraine'. The anti-immigrant's attempt to become an immigrant had failed. That man I had almost bumped into six years earlier.

On that day in April 2008, Trevor Phillips was the chair of the EHRC and had just given a speech I had a hand in writing. It was deliberately provocative to go to the place Powell had spoken at, and we at the EHRC knew it. The very fact of that geography made sure there was coverage. The speech had a simple message: that large parts of what Enoch Powell had said were wrong. Integration between different communities was possible, the speech said. Britain needed immigrants to be economically successful (a huge missing piece in the 'immigration debate' through the ages), the speech said. Immigration was not a numbers game as Powell had insisted: one immigrant is not one too many. Multiple loyalties are possible, where one identity – I'm British – doesn't necessarily clash with another – part of me is Sudanese. Like love, it is not a zero-sum game. When I was young I supported the England football team and the West Indies cricket team.

There were about 200 people in the audience. 'Whatever we feel about immigrants, immigration is part of our future,' Phillips said under the gimlet gaze of those 200, many from Britain's bashed-about equalities sector, whose attention to every word and its meaning or possible meaning, or possible offence, is as acute as those delicate machines calibrated to sense approaching earthquakes half a world away. 'The real question will be whether we can, as a modern economy, seize the restless tide of talent that is currently sweeping across the globe.'

An economic argument abutted tight against this huge, cultural, sometimes ugly, debate about otherness. 'There is creeping resentment in all directions which can only be halted by a policy of manifest fairness. I believe that the more we talk about immigration the better. Many think that this is not the time or the place for this debate. I understand their anxieties. If we cannot talk about it now, then when?'

They asked questions, those 200 people, motivated by a belief that progress can come from law and effort, from tackling prejudice and calling out racism. Those people who mean so much to people like me because, whatever ills the equalities lobby can have thrown at its door, without them we would only have Powell and others like him, and there are many, who didn't seem very friendly towards me. At all.

What about terrorism and immigration, Phillips was asked. Terrorists here are mostly not immigrants, but are British-born, he answered.

What about uncontrolled immigration? Yes, migration should be managed. And the only actual uncontrolled immigration is from the European Union and they are not really brown in the slightest. So, immigration is not an issue of race any more. Some conflate it – still – for a reason.

Karamat Iqbal asked about poor white boys and girls. Yes, there are lots of groups left floating, undernourished, at the back of Britain's economic queue and equality is about all of that stuff as well. 'Their problems are compounded because no one is speaking up for them,' Iqbal said. Which is true.

In an upstairs, smaller room, about thirty people had witnessed a rather different event. The *Birmingham Post* reported that BNP member, Peter Mullins – who had stood for the party in Powell's own constituency in 2005 – 'recited Powell's speech in full, breaking down in tears at the climax'. Mullins gained 983 votes for the BNP in 2005, forty-six behind Doug Hope of the UK Independence Party.

Griffin is not a man to agree with Phillips, but he did say that Phillips had every right to speak as Britain is 'a free country'. But, be warned, Powell will be proved correct; 'There's going to be a cross of fire, of burning cities right across the middle of the British Isles.' Northern Ireland-style peace walls would need to be erected within three years to keep warring communities at bay. Ten years after those words and the only peace walls in Great Britain and Northern Ireland are still in Northern Ireland. Keeping apart two groups of white people.

Let's start with a different speech by Enoch Powell. Why? Because it is easy to paint everything in black and white, see every argument as binary, bad and good. But without understanding, first, this different speech it is impossible to understand 'Rivers of Blood'. Because 'Rivers of Blood' was the second chapter of a Powellite thesis. It was a thesis tightly bound with two historic and intertwined themes that Britain was struggling to comprehend and deal with through the 1950s and 1960s – the end of colonialism and the rise of mass immigration. My mother and father were living through dramatic and rapid political change – indeed, they were the personification of that change, a change that would question Britain's very place in the world and cause men like Enoch Powell to lie awake at night in their pyjamas, beneath stiff, starched sheets and worry about the mother country as the clock ticked on the mantelpiece.

This different speech was made nine years before 'Rivers of Blood'. It was 1959, and followed the death of eleven Mau Mau detainees at the Hola prison camp in Kenya. Britain was engaged in a bloody war, a colonial power slowly losing its grip on a nation. The Hola detention camp near Garissa in eastern Kenya was used to imprison Mau Mau fighters and execute a project of 'rehabilitation', shorthand for beatings and enforced labour. When the prisoners, who had not been found guilty of any crime, refused to dig part of a new canal, they were struck with batons, blood soaking into the scrubland, jaws fractured, skulls split. One dead for each mile the canal was supposed to cover. The government at first claimed that contaminated water drunk from a cart was to blame for the deaths. They put out a press release. But, evidence is evidence, reality is reality. An inquest revealed the truth, under lazy fans whirring in a Kenyan courthouse.

In the early hours of 28 July 1959, Enoch Powell rose to speak in the House of Commons on the matter of the Hola massacre and the government's approach to its colonial territories. In his seminal biography of Powell, *Like the Roman*, Simon Heffer says that even at 1.15 a.m. the chamber was 'relatively full'. At the end of his speech the *Daily Telegraph* reported that Powell 'put his hands across his eyes', apparently to wipe away tears. Denis Healey, who was to become Labour defence secretary and Chancellor, described it as 'the greatest parliamentary speech I ever heard, it had all the moral passion and rhetorical force of Demosthenes', the Athenian politician and orator: the man who said 'you cannot have a proud and chivalrous spirit if your conduct is mean and paltry; for whatever a man's actions are, such must be his spirit'.

Reading Heffer's book, I put great scribble marks in the margin. A moment of note, I was telling myself. Much of the official narrative of the time about the Mau Mau had relied on a steady, destructive demonisation of who they were, making them the 'other' – sub-adult, child-like, not deserving of the rights of fellow men and women. It is a common technique, used through the ages to reduce the need for engagement. If your enemy is mad, hateful, your position is more easily described as just, munificent. Mau Mau oaths, which they made in secret as verbal contracts of loyalty, were portrayed as close to witchcraft, utterances made by simple folk who needed to be educated on the correct, the British, way forward. In 1954 the *Birmingham Post* wrote that 'these oaths involved such depravity and obscenity that little or nothing of their details has been, or ever will be, broadcast to the general public'.

Growing up, Powell was a bogeyman to me, nothing but a negative buzz, a man who made it personal, who allied immigration with race, who fretted over my effect on the country's very core, a figure gaunt (at school, friends called him 'crocodile face'), creeping up at me in nightmares. This was my feeling about John Enoch Powell. He was mad, hateful. He was my 'other'. And then, well, this, written of the detainees who had been described as the 'lowest of the low': 'I would say it is a fearful doctrine, which must recoil upon the heads of those who pronounce it, to stand in judgement on a fellow human being and say: "Because he was such-and-such, therefore the consequences that would otherwise flow from his death shall not flow."'

No one was prosecuted following the Hola massacre.

'It is argued that this is Africa, that things are different there. Of course they are. The question is whether the difference between things there and here is such that the taking of responsibility there and here should be on different principles. Nor can we ourselves pick and choose where and in what parts of the world we shall use this or that kind of standard.'

For people like Heffer, Enoch Powell's intervention 'sits ill with the accusations of racialism made against him a decade later'. I may not agree with much of what Heffer says – and in this case he does not touch on the underlying and uncomfortable us (British) and them (African) logic of Powell's position – but I want to listen to him. Because that is the point, isn't it? Listening to the people you do not agree with, not putting them beyond the pale, making them the other.

Heffer is well read, a man who carries an intellectual air. We meet over lunch in central London. He is a little late and apologises profusely. He refuses offers of a 'proper drink' – he has a funeral to go to later that day – and chooses a simple fish dish. He talks about Powell as you would a friend, which Powell was to Heffer (they first met at Cambridge in 1981, where Heffer was an undergraduate). Heffer tells stories as he sips his water. Once, when approached at a station and asked if he was Enoch Powell by an excited fan, Powell, in his distinct West Midlands drawl, replied: 'I am told I bear a striking resemblance to him.' Heffer does a remarkably good impression of the former MP for Wolverhampton South West.

On weekends together, the Heffers and the Powells would tour the churches of Essex, near where Heffer lives and grew up, and Powell would point out intricate architectural details, setting them in historical and religious context, the classics scholar's approach to knowledge on show, often to the bemused and impressed bafflement of his hosts. My uncle, Anthony, not a classics scholar but a man lifted by the beauty of architecture, was similarly in love with English churches and not averse to similar explanations. I would kick around after him, on endless summer holidays, scuffing my shoes in the dust and wondering when we could go for cake and lemonade.

Heffer's point is that Powell's 'Rivers of Blood' speech can only be seen as one part of a man's life. Even if you think him a demon. His life serving in India during the Second World War, where he learnt Urdu and read into Indian history; his reaction to the events at Hola; his apparent, maybe confected, shock that his speech of 1968 was used by those motivated by race to make a case *against* black and Asian people being afforded the same rights as white people, being welcomed, being offered that 'proud and chivalrous spirit'.

I push him a little more. Shouldn't he have done? Shouldn't Powell have realised that language matters and that the public, the audience, rarely have the time or the inclination to 'put things in context', and just hear the headlines from the speech. And those sounded like – were – 'panic, the black man is coming'.

Heffer pauses. Yes. Maybe his friend, who was voted Number 55 in the BBC's poll of 100 Greatest Britons, one above Sir Cliff Richard, should have thought about the reaction when he spoke about black people gaining the 'whip hand' and quoted people's supposed fears about 'the negro'. Thought about me. And my father. And maybe he did. And said it anyway. Heffer may not think Powell a 'racialist'. The speech, though, can still be racist.

Here we go.

'The supreme function of statesmanship is to provide against preventable evils.'

Enoch Powell is wearing a three-piece suit, dark grey, white pocket square, tightly knotted, dark tie. It is mid-afternoon, the best time to deliver a speech, time enough to cut together a broadcast package for the 6 p.m. news bulletins. He is standing in the small upstairs room of the Midland Hotel, a sheaf of papers in his hands, which he refers to intermittently. Typed on the paper by his wife, Pam, the 3,000-word speech in Courier type. 'I agreed with every word,' Pam said later. 'I never thought it would cause so much controversy.'

In front of Powell is a table upon which are set water-glasses and a jug. The glasses are empty. The jug full. On Powell's left, a man, slicked-back hair, strict parting, similar three-piece suit, pocket square, tightly knotted, dark tie. He is a member of the Conservative Political Centre of which Powell is chair. It is the group's meeting. Behind them, a mirrored wall, reflecting the faces of the audience, all white, mostly men.

On that Saturday in April, the week after Easter, my mother, recently graduated from Birmingham University, is probably in Devon with her parents, and maybe even my father. I'm not sure my father owned a three-piece suit. Three days later, two days after Ted Heath sacked Enoch Powell from the Shadow Cabinet, is my mother's birthday. I am six months old.

'In seeking to do so, it encounters obstacles which are deeply rooted in human nature.'

Powell's delivery is nasal, the accent distinct. He speaks in short sentences, most of the speech delivered looking directly at those in front of him. It is clear he has rehearsed, prepared carefully.

'One is that by the very order of things such evils are not demonstrable until they have occurred: at each stage in their onset there is room for doubt and for dispute whether they be real or imaginary. By the same token, they attract little attention

in comparison with current troubles, which are both indisputable and pressing: whence the besetting temptation of all politics to concern itself with the immediate present at the expense of the future.'

The opening of the speech, laying out the core offer to the audience in that Midland Hotel room and, vitally for the speaker, his local voters and a wider, political, national audience.

Powell wants this speech to have impact. Actually, he needs it to, having seen a similar effort in Walsall two months earlier – in which he spoke, probably erroneously, of a white child stranded in a classroom full of black immigrant families (and revealed that some of his white voters saw him as the 'MP for Central Africa') – pass by with little note. Two years earlier, Powell had experienced a political shock, a premonition of his own political mortality. His parliamentary majority was cut to 6,585 as Labour swept to power in the general election, led by Harold Wilson. The member for Wolverhampton South West had to blow the whistle a little louder this time. Maybe he even had an eye on the leadership, this speech another tactic to unsettle Heath, a launch pad for a third force in British politics: 'Powellism'.

Extracts of 'Rivers of Blood' had been sent to the broadcasters that morning, and a camera crew is there from one of the local TV stations, at the back, jostling for space. No one is going to miss Powell this time.

That first sentence bites hard – 'preventable evil' immediately raising the idea, the theme, that there is a threat in our midst, here in Britain. That first sentence also has another role, associating Powell directly with 'the supreme function of statesmanship' – as he defines it, the man who has spotted what others have not. It could, of course, be defined differently. The supreme function of statesmanship could be to explain matters to the public that they may not like to hear but are nevertheless worth hearing and considering for the good for the country's prosperity. The supreme function of statesmanship could be to explain why immigration is good for the economy, our wealth, and why it has happened, the link back to our colonial past. Powell stakes out a different territory for his self-evident truth.

'Above all, people are disposed to mistake predicting troubles for causing troubles and even for desiring troubles: "If only," they love to think, "if only people wouldn't talk about it, it probably wouldn't happen." Perhaps this habit goes back to the primitive belief that the word and the thing, the name and the object, are identical.'

Powell insists he is not trying to cause trouble – a forward defensive play against what he knew would be one of the main criticisms of him. The use of the word 'primitive' is another defensive gambit: only those of simple intellect believe that talking about a problem exacerbates it, putting Powell above, he maybe hopes, those who will claim, loudly and persistently, that his comments are 'incendiary'. It has long been the position of those who believe in limits to immigration that when they try to speak they are struck down by a liberal, pusillanimous and damaging omertà. Powell spoke of it in the 1960s.

This is what Trevor Phillips, my old boss, had to say about it in a speech in 2008: 'The right's public justification for reticence is usually that political correctness has unfairly silenced them. Somewhat comically, this point of view has been widely and consistently peddled by writers and publications which hardly ever stop yelling about immigration, only pausing from time to time to complain that they are being gagged, before resuming a deafening roar of outrage.'

I had a hand in writing it.

'At all events, the discussion of future grave but, with effort now, avoidable evils is the most unpopular and at the same time the most necessary occupation for the politician. Those who knowingly shirk it deserve, and not infrequently receive, the curses of those who come after.'

Powell is acting to save the future.

'A week or two ago I fell into conversation with a constituent, a middle-aged, quite ordinary working man employed in one of our nationalised industries. After a sentence or two about the weather, he suddenly said: "If I had the money to go, I wouldn't stay in this country." I made some deprecatory reply to the effect that even this government wouldn't last forever; but he took no notice, and continued: "I have three children, all of them been through grammar school and two of them married now, with family. I shan't be satisfied till I have seen them all settled overseas. In this country in 15 or 20 years' time the black man will have the whip hand over the white man."'

Politicians want to show their connection to ordinary people. It makes their arguments less easy to attack and distances controversial opinion from the speaker. Powell deployed this storytelling technique again and again, the repetition of examples of 'real people' speaking, taking individual experience and making it the norm, making common what may well have been unusual or apocryphal, with no hunt, no need, for a countervailing narrative – the blessings of immigration remaining silent, those stories untold.

Heffer admits that Powell was constantly in danger of repeating 'street truths' – urban tales twisted in the telling. 'There were many myths about the immigrant population doing the rounds in Wolverhampton, according to Jones [Clement Jones, the editor of the city's paper, the *Express & Star*, which spent much time fruitlessly trying to find evidence for the stories in Powell's speeches], some of which ended up in Powell's constituency correspondence and which he will treat with his usual sincerity.' Or as convenient bolsters for his arguments, his own prejudices and confusions, the patriot, the romantic defender of 'real Britain'?

The use of the phrase 'the whip hand' is telling, toxic, the turning of the whip of the slave master against him. Immigrants are not just coming here, they are coming to take over, what the black writer Reni Eddo-Lodge calls 'fear of a black planet' in her book *Why I'm No Longer Talking to White People About Race*. Twenty-two years after 'Rivers of Blood', almost to the day, Public Enemy released one of the world's most famous and important rap albums, *Fear of a Black Planet*. I played it a lot in my student flat in Leeds, on vinyl in those days, the revolutionary of Headingley ready to fight 'the powers that be'. Unless I had a politics essay to finish on the repeal of the Corn Laws.

'I can already hear the chorus of execration. How dare I say such a horrible thing? How dare I stir up trouble and inflame feelings by repeating such a conversation? The answer is that I do not have the right not to do so. Here is a decent, ordinary fellow Englishman, who in broad daylight in my own town says to me, his Member of Parliament, that his country will not be worth living in for his children. I simply do not have the right to shrug

my shoulders and think about something else. What he is saying,
thousands and hundreds of thousands are saying and thinking –
not throughout Great Britain, perhaps, but in the areas that are
already undergoing the total transformation to which there is no
parallel in a thousand years of English history.'

In 1964 the British Election Study asked respondents if there
were 'too many immigrants'. The figure agreeing with that
statement was 85 per cent. By 1966 it had risen by 1 per cent,
and by 1969 it was up again to 89 per cent. The BES did not ask
'coloured people' the question – people like my father; or me,
for that matter, if I had been old enough. For I was, indeed,
'coloured'.

In his speech forty years later, Trevor Phillips said: 'It would
be wrong not to acknowledge that Powell's public rhetoric
reflected the private thoughts of many white Britons.' Heffer
said that Powell's critics 'had to accept that he spoke for the
majority of the country, however unsophisticated that majority
might be'. Jones's *Express & Star* received tens of thousands
of letters, at some points threatening to overwhelm the local
postal service. Nearly all came to praise Powell, not bury him.

And then, Heffer raises the point that will come back, again
and again, as the years tick by and the debate ticks on. He
writes of the clash between the 'provincialism' of 'Rivers of
Blood' – where it was delivered, out of London, the quoting of
the views of ordinary people, however objectionable to some,
the have-nots; versus the 'metropolitan' – the haves, *The Times*
newspaper (which described it as an 'evil speech'), the liberals
(Jeremy Thorpe, leader of the Liberal Party, suggested that
Powell could have breached incitement law), Ted Heath (who
sacked him) – the comfortable, padded against the realities

of white flight and economic hardship by the soft, exclusive cushions of wealth.

This is the reason Powell's speech has resonated over the last fifty years. Here was a man who could claim to be speaking up for people who felt that very few of those in power – the people who could actually do things to change the world or at least the street they lived on – articulated a narrative about their concerns. The immigrants, the blacks and the browns, had a growing equalities lobby, always agitating about how these incomers felt or were being treated. They – the people who were here already – had nothing very much. The very fact that that sense is still with us today should make us pause and wonder why.

'In 15 or 20 years, on present trends, there will be in this country three and a half million Commonwealth immigrants and their descendants. That is not my figure. That is the official figure given to parliament by the spokesman of the Registrar General's Office.

There is no comparable official figure for the year 2000, but it must be in the region of five to seven million, approximately one-tenth of the whole population, and approaching that of Greater London. Of course, it will not be evenly distributed from Margate to Aberystwyth and from Penzance to Aberdeen. Whole areas, towns and parts of towns across England will be occupied by sections of the immigrant and immigrant-descended population.'

The numbers game, a vital point in Powell's argument, and actually here probably a slight underestimate of the numbers of foreign-born immigrants there would be in the UK by the 1990s. 'The size of London', the 'size of Leeds', the size of any suitably large city – as if immigrants were flying in on some large, alien spaceship to land on the heads of the unsuspecting. The sheer mass of immigration sketched out to sound as preposterous, as rejectable, as frightening as possible. 'By the toll of a billion deaths man has bought his birthright of the earth, and it is his against all comers; it would still be his were the Martians ten times as mighty as they are. For neither do men live nor die in vain,' H. G. Wells wrote in *The War of the Worlds* in 1897. We have long been obsessed with the fear of invasion, collected ourselves in readiness for the fightback.

And then, what of Commonwealth? That word at once romanticised if abroad – our old colonies, good people helped by Britain, who helped us, with trade, slaves (if we're honest), who salute the Queen and read British history – and a danger if here, demanding their rights, threatening the culture, not of this blood and soil.

And that second, double meaning. The Commonwealth includes Canada, Australia, New Zealand, Malta and Cyprus – the White Commonwealth. But is this what Powell is speaking of here, when he has just quoted his eloquent constituent saying 'the black man will have the whip hand'? Or was he talking of the 'other' Commonwealth? Jamaica, maybe, or Nigeria; Sierra Leone, Ghana and Botswana; Swaziland, Uganda and Zambia; the exotic, the different, the brown and black immigrants coming to Britain; Malawi, Malaysia, Pakistan; India, Zambia, Trinidad and Tobago; places on the map that once said 'here be dragons', the dark heart; Kenya, that country whose people Powell had spoken of so passionately a few years before, having to wipe his hand across his eyes as the tears welled. This was the 'New Commonwealth' that pricked Powell's concern.

Powell knew his history and knew the context in which he spoke. You always need to paint in the background – what was being debated at the time – to understand the foreground – the speech itself. The fractious battle in Parliament in 1968 was over a question which has rumbled like so much thunder through the squally storms of Britain's post-colonial history, and one that has affected every debate about race and immigration in this country. It has created headaches and sleights of hand, the withdrawal of rights when no one was concentrating, classic misdirection. And it came down to one central question. What responsibility does the 'mother country' have to those it once ruled and granted rights and passports, those very British blue passports, as subjects of the Queen?

As Powell spoke in that Midland Hotel room, the Labour government was planning its latest effort to push the controversial Commonwealth Immigrants bill through a restless Parliament. The legislation, agreed later that year, effectively withdrew British passport rights from, particularly, Asian people who lived in the colonies. It built on the 1962 Act of the same name, a first attempt at restrictions described by Hugh Gaitskell, then leader of the Labour Opposition, as 'cruel and brutal anti-colour legislation'. The 1968 Act was more restrictive. Immigrants from the New Commonwealth would be obliged to show a 'close connection' to Britain through a blood relative, a grandparent or parent who was born in the UK. The Commonwealth secretary, George Thomson, said the legislation was 'wrong in principle, clearly discrimination on the grounds of colour, and contrary to everything we stand for'. *The Times* called it 'probably the most shameful measure that Labour members have ever been asked by their whips to support'. Speaking to the *New Statesman* in 1999, the patrician Tory peer, Lord Gilmour, said: 'That was why the bill was brought in, to keep the blacks out.'

To understand the roots of the issue you needed to travel to a city like Mombasa, a bulging capital looking out over the Indian Ocean. Up to 200,000 Asian residents – and former British subjects – were slowly being squeezed out of Kenya (jobs were harder to come by, restrictions on the ownership of businesses blocked) as Jomo Kenyatta, the anti-colonial campaigner who had risen to become president in 1964, sought to anchor his newly independent country in the soil of east Africa. 'Africanise' was the word used. Kenyan jobs for Kenyan workers. The Asian population could either take Kenyan citizenship, complicated and not always attractive, or leave. To go, where?

Britain – that country they had helped, heeding the call, the order, of the mother country.

When a British colony, immigration to Kenya from India had been encouraged, and at points enforced. In the late nineteenth century Indian workers had died in their thousands building the Uganda Railway, also known as the Lunatic Line, from the coast to Lake Victoria. Six hundred and sixty miles through scrubland and malarial swamps. Railways were colonial weapons, glinting iron tracks a sword of trade at the heart of the battle for the lucrative Great Lakes region. Speed was of the essence as Germany also scrambled – with its own line – to open up the interior of eastern Africa. The building of the Lunatic Line was to be organised as if it were a military campaign, collateral damage was inevitable, a price possibly worth paying. Workers died in the heat, the piercing sun, lions marauded and killed. There was the Kedong massacre, a clash between workers – who had attacked two Maasai women and stolen cattle – and Maasai tribespeople, amongst whom anger flourished with each piece of land lost. It left 600 dead, skulls cracked again, blood seeping into the earth.

With independence, mistrust crystallised. Many Indian immigrants had been granted enhanced-status jobs in administration and finance, the famous British 'buffer' between the officer class and the 'lesser' local African populations. It was similar in Uganda, where in the 1970s that grotesque, Idi Amin, played the loud chorus of 'otherness', calling 55,000 Asian residents 'bloodsuckers' as he demanded their expulsion from the country some had called home for over a century. Leave, or face the military prison camps.

Many came to Britain and I remember watching their arrivals on the news, coming down the steps of endless BOAC flights with their light blue, cardboard suitcases. My mother and I, and millions of others, saw these new strangers on our teak-encased colour television sets which we rented for a few pounds a month. (You had to stand up and walk over to the glowing brown box to change channels, all three of them, pushing the large silver buttons.) In 1967 it had been the same for Kenyan Asians. On £60 one-way tickets, they started arriving on charter flights, clutching their British passports, the blue ones. Many had never seen Britain before. And, at a thousand arriving every month, many in Britain had never seen anything like it either. A thousand being the size of a small village.

Powell always insisted that he was not a 'racialist'. And that talking about immigration was not the same as talking about race. But there is that persistent context. The Registrar General's numbers he refers to came in a response to a parliamentary question from Sir Cyril Osborne, a strong campaigner against immigration (and a man who didn't like 'repulsive homos' very much either). Sir Cyril asked specifically about the rising 'coloured population' and 'how many years it will take before there are more coloured than white people in Great Britain?' To which he received a tart response from the Labour minister, David Ennals, who suggested Sir Cyril look up the answer he had been given to the same question the year before by James Callaghan, then the home secretary: 'There is no prospect of the situation envisaged by the honourable member arising.'

This wasn't about the White Commonwealth. It was about the Black and Brown Commonwealth. In 1967 and 1968 it was the Kenyan Asians on their one-way tickets. Earlier, the *Windrush* generation from the Caribbean, asked to come to drive the buses, care for the sick and clean the hospitals, after fighting alongside Britain in the Second World War. After that, Asian immigration from India and Pakistan, asked to come to drive the trains, look after our teeth and clean our schools, after fighting alongside Britain in the Second World War.

And my father, who came here to fix people's eyes.

The context of otherness was colour. Race.

'As time goes on, the proportion of this total [the 3.5 million Commonwealth immigrants] *who are immigrant descendants, those born in England, who arrived here by exactly the same route as the rest of us, will rapidly increase. Already by 1985 the native-born would constitute the majority. It is this fact which creates the extreme urgency of action now, of just that kind of action which is hardest for politicians to take, action where the difficulties lie in the present but the evils to be prevented or minimised lie several parliaments ahead.'*

I like National Trust houses, Richmond Park on a summer's evening, the Specials, running, Bedruthan Steps (the home of giants on the north Cornish coast), the NHS, James Baldwin, Jonathan Coe, Britain winning gold medals at the Olympic Games, Liverpool Football Club, a good Victoria sponge cake, Mo Farah, village pubs, city pubs, Glencoe, *Broadchurch*, *The Office*, *Fleabag*, Soul II Soul, Radio 4, French wine, British lamb, Parliament, couscous, politeness, irony, *Very British Problems* on Twitter, olives, double-cooked chips, Miles Davis. At school I read Jane Austen, William Golding, F. Scott Fitzgerald, Shakespeare. At university Karl Marx, John Stuart Mill, Jean-Jacques Rousseau and Adam Smith. I am an immigrant descendant and I am British. And there's the problem, Mr Powell, right there. You can't see how anyone can really be both.

'The natural and rational first question with a nation confronted by such a prospect is to ask: "How can its dimensions be reduced?" Granted it be not wholly preventable, can it be limited, bearing in mind that numbers are of the essence: the significance and consequences of an alien element introduced into a country or population are profoundly different according to whether that element is 1 per cent or 10 per cent.

The answers to the simple and rational question are equally simple and rational: by stopping, or virtually stopping, further inflow, and by promoting the maximum outflow. Both answers are part of the official policy of the Conservative Party.'

Nikesh Patel arrived in the UK from Uganda in 1972 aged seven. 'So there was I, a seven-year-old, forced to leave my country of birth to go to another country I had barely heard of.' I wonder what I would have felt like, arriving in Sudan, under Powell's 'maximum outflow' plan (appreciative murmurs of hear-hear from the audience), a country as a child I had barely heard of.

'It almost passes belief that at this moment 20 or 30 additional immigrant children are arriving from overseas in Wolverhampton alone every week – and that means 15 or 20 additional families a decade or two hence. Those whom the gods wish to destroy, they first make mad. We must be mad, literally mad, as a nation to be permitting the annual inflow of some 50,000 dependants, who are for the most part the material of the future growth of the immigrant-descended population. It is like watching a nation busily engaged in heaping up its own funeral pyre. So insane are we that we actually permit unmarried persons to immigrate for the purpose of founding a family with spouses and fiancés whom they have never seen.'

Here is the punch. The funeral pyre, the destruction of a nation. Literal madness, a country planning for its own end. One, immigration of coloured peoples, will destroy the other, England.

'Let no one suppose that the flow of dependants will automatically tail off. On the contrary, even at the present admission rate of only 5,000 a year by voucher, there is sufficient for a further 25,000 dependants per annum ad infinitum, without taking into account the huge reservoir of existing relations in this country – and I am making no allowance at all for fraudulent entry. In these circumstances nothing will suffice but that the total inflow for settlement should be reduced at once to negligible proportions, and that the necessary legislative and administrative measures be taken without delay.'

We need to stop this.

'I stress the words "for settlement". This has nothing to do with the entry of Commonwealth citizens, any more than of aliens, into this country, for the purposes of study or of improving their *qualifications, like (for instance) the Commonwealth doctors who, to the advantage of their own countries, have enabled our hospital service to be expanded faster than would otherwise have been possible. They are not, and never have been, immigrants.'*

My father came here to study. And then stayed here to work, for the rest of his life. And pay taxes. And serve patients.

'I turn to re-emigration. If all immigration ended tomorrow, the rate of growth of the immigrant and immigrant-descended population would be substantially reduced, but the prospective size of this element in the population would still leave the basic character of the national danger unaffected. This can only be tackled while a considerable proportion of the total still comprises persons who entered this country during the last ten years or so.

Hence the urgency of implementing now the second element of the Conservative Party's policy: the encouragement of re-emigration.

Nobody can make an estimate of the numbers which, with generous assistance, would choose either to return to their countries of origin or to go to other countries anxious to receive the manpower and the skills they represent.

Nobody knows, because no such policy has yet been attempted. I can only say that, even at present, immigrants in my own constituency from time to time come to me, asking if I can find them assistance to return home. If such a policy were adopted and pursued with the determination which the gravity of the alternative justifies, the resultant outflow could appreciably alter the prospects.'

Go home. Long the vision, warmly coloured with romance, of those who fear a social implosion, a 'national danger', not just from the first generation of immigrants, my father, but from 'immigrant-descended' people, me.

'*The third element of the Conservative Party's policy is that all who are in this country as citizens should be equal before the law and that there shall be no discrimination or difference made between them by public authority. As Mr Heath has put it we will have no "first-class citizens" and "second-class citizens". This does not mean that the immigrant and his descendant should be elevated into a privileged or special class or that the citizen should be denied his right to discriminate in the management of his own affairs between one fellow-citizen and another or that he should be subjected to imposition as to his reasons and motive for behaving in one lawful manner rather than another.*

There could be no grosser misconception of the realities than is entertained by those who vociferously demand legislation as they call it "against discrimination", whether they be leader-writers of the same kidney and sometimes on the same newspapers which year after year in the 1930s tried to blind this country to the rising peril which confronted it, or archbishops who live in palaces, faring delicately with the bedclothes pulled right up over their heads. They have got it exactly and diametrically wrong.

The discrimination and the deprivation, the sense of alarm and of resentment, lies not with the immigrant population but with those among whom they have come and are still coming.

This is why to enact legislation of the kind before parliament at this moment is to risk throwing a match on to gunpowder. The kindest thing that can be said about those who propose and support it is that they know not what they do.'

It is usually children who know not what they do. And the allusion to the 1930s touches all sorts of bright little buttons.

Gunpowder again, an explosion ahead. The cowering bishops in their palaces so far from the ordinary voices, the people who fear the whip hand.

'Nothing is more misleading than comparison between the Commonwealth immigrant in Britain and the American Negro. The Negro population of the United States, which was already in existence before the United States became a nation, started literally as slaves and were later given the franchise and other rights of citizenship, to the exercise of which they have only gradually and still incompletely come. The Commonwealth immigrant came to Britain as a full citizen, to a country which knew no discrimination between one citizen and another, and he entered instantly into the possession of the rights of every citizen, from the vote to free treatment under the National Health Service.

Whatever drawbacks attended the immigrants arose not from the law or from public policy or from administration, but from those personal circumstances and accidents which cause, and always will cause, the fortunes and experience of one man to be different from another's.'

Powell looks steadfastly at his audience, the reference to the 1968 Race Relations Act – which banned the refusal of employment, housing or public services on the grounds of race – clear. These people do not need special treatment. Britain is not America, black people here have not had to fight, he argues, not battle their way back from slavery. There is no line in this speech that many Afro-Caribbean immigrants in Britain are well able to find slavery undesirable and recent in the boughs of their family tree. That the majority of Afro-Caribbeans are, in a sense, fighting back from slavery.

Powell looms steadfastly at his audience. If there is discrimination, then look to your own soul, to what causes that discrimination – the 'personal circumstances and accidents'. Victims can be perpetrators of their own misfortune. They are to blame.

Jenny Bourne, company secretary of the Institute of Race Relations, later wrote that 'after the April 1968 speech, a gang of white youths armed with bars attacked Asian youths outside a Southall school and attacks were reported in London's East End'. There is some evidence that attacks on immigrants increased more widely. 'Paki-bashing' became the subject of playground songs ('Ohhhh, down where the lights are flashing, we're going...'). London dockers and meat porters marched demanding the end of favours for 'the coloureds'. Powell 'gave a fillip to popular racism that made the lives of black people hell', said Ambalavaner Sivanandan, head of the Institute of Race Relations. 'He brought scholarship and reason to white working-class fears and prejudices.'

'But while, to the immigrant, entry to this country was admission to privileges and opportunities eagerly sought, the impact upon the existing population was very different. For reasons which they could not comprehend, and in pursuance of a decision by default, on which they were never consulted, they found themselves made strangers in their own country.

They found their wives unable to obtain hospital beds in childbirth, their children unable to obtain school places, their homes and neighbourhoods changed beyond recognition, their plans and prospects for the future defeated; at work they found that employers hesitated to apply to the immigrant worker the standards of discipline and competence required of the native-born worker; they began to hear, as time went by, more and more voices which told them that they were now the unwanted. They now learn that a one-way privilege is to be established by act of parliament; a law which cannot, and is not intended to, operate to protect them or redress their grievances is to be enacted to give the stranger, the disgruntled and the agent-provocateur the power to pillory them for their private actions.'

Two years before Powell's speech, James Mossman, a BBC reporter with an acerbic style, walked the streets of nearby Smethwick – where there were lots of 'coloureds for a neighbour' – and did something innovative for the time, a time before constant social media recording and documenting of our lives. He fitted an Indian immigrant, newly arrived, with a hidden microphone. The man then travelled around the local area, documenting his experiences. He wasn't allowed into a barbers' and the local church told him to come back later for fear of offending white church-goers. Everyday slights in a country now called home. Mossman interviewed local people about the new communities of immigrants that had just arrived.

'They should live in a district by themselves. They're not clean.'

'They're a nuisance when you've got to walk past them in the street, they won't move. They're a nuisance at work.'

'They're content with Kitekat [cat food] and dog food, instead of ordinary meat.'

'So far in Britain, few things could have been so ill-prepared as immigration,' Mossman said. Few politicians sought to explain why these strange new people were arriving, that the shadow of empire – and all that had brought Britain – created reciprocal duties. That a country grown rich on the control of other nations, would face its time, the time when many – who laboured in earlier generations, who bought the promise that British rule came with British rights – would seek to 'cash the cheque', to use the scalpel-sharp phrase of Martin Luther King Jr, three weeks dead on the day Powell addressed his audience in the West Midlands.

The panic over immigration, the anger, the shock among many white people was, in part, understandable and certainly had never been tackled at a level that gripped a nation, like Powell did. There he stood, with white pocket square, trying to speak to a certain community's soul. Britain had few policies to mitigate the effects of immigration on settled communities. They were left to fend for themselves.

That community had no narrative from the other side either. No Dr King to grip the nation in a different way, speak to a different soul. It had no public speaker, no poet allowed a platform, to paint a different mood, reflect back to Britain a different story of welcome, of that very British ideal, so sweetly put, of 'rubbing along together', getting on, playing by the rules. Who told the lovely, uplifting tales of immigration, the immigrants who came here to work, to contribute, to make a difference? Who romanticised, waxed lyrical about the story of this mixed island race, said that there was no funeral pyre, only candles of fortune? About what a great moment this was for the UK, a country unique in its diversity, and the way it deals with it? Boosted by it. Wealth, culture, bursting new life.

Only later came the social historians with their calmly collected oral histories of the black nurse and the Indian doctor. Who has ever said the supreme function of statesmanship is to ease what ails a nation, all of its citizens, to ease via explanation, via words and policies to help those shocked and affected, not with the metaphors of war but with the balm of good hope?

Jaswinder Chagger came to Britain in 1966 from India. The BBC asked him to watch Mossman's documentary fifty years later.

'The working-class person had no idea what was about to hit them,' he said. 'It does raise the question why, with cinema, TV and radio, why was this information not put forward? [They could have said:] "We're inviting the nig-nogs over because we need them, the factories are empty."'

Mr Chagger sounds like my father.

'In the hundreds upon hundreds of letters I received when I last spoke on this subject two or three months ago, there was one striking feature which was largely new and which I find ominous. All Members of Parliament are used to the typical anonymous correspondent; but what surprised and alarmed me was the high proportion of ordinary, decent, sensible people, writing a rational and often well-educated letter, who believed that they had to omit their address because it was dangerous to have committed themselves to paper to a Member of Parliament agreeing with the views I had expressed, and that they would risk penalties or reprisals if they were known to have done so. The sense of being a persecuted minority which is growing among ordinary English people in the areas of the country which are affected is something that those without direct experience can hardly imagine.'

A short pause. The anticipation. Now. Now, *the* story of the speech.

'I am going to allow just one of those hundreds of people to speak for me. Eight years ago in a respectable street in Wolverhampton a house was sold to a Negro. Now only one white (a woman old-age

pensioner) lives there. This is her story. She lost her husband and both her sons in the war. So she turned her seven-roomed house, her only asset, into a boarding house. She worked hard and did well, paid off her mortgage and began to put something by for her old age. Then the immigrants moved in. With growing fear, she saw one house after another taken over. The quiet street became a place of noise and confusion. Regretfully, her white tenants moved out.

'The day after the last one left, she was awakened at 7 a.m. by two Negroes who wanted to use her' phone to contact their employer. When she refused, as she would have refused any stranger at such an hour, she was abused and feared she would have been attacked but for the chain on her door. Immigrant families have tried to rent rooms in her house, but she always refused. Her little store of money went, and after paying rates, she has less than £2 per week. She went to apply for a rate reduction and was seen by a young girl, who on hearing she had a seven-roomed house, suggested she should let part of it. When she said the only people she could get were Negroes, the girl said: "Racial prejudice won't get you anywhere in this country." So she went home.

'The telephone is her lifeline. Her family pay the bill, and help her out as best they can. Immigrants have offered to buy her house – at a price which the prospective landlord would be able to recover from his tenants in weeks, or at most a few months. She is becoming afraid to go out. Windows are broken. She finds excreta pushed through her letter box. When she goes to the shops, she is followed by children, charming, wide-grinning piccaninnies. They cannot speak English, but one word they know. "Racialist," they chant. When the new Race Relations Bill is passed, this woman

is convinced she will go to prison. And is she so wrong? I begin to wonder.'

This is the narrative of fear. The elderly, helpless lady, swamped by the incomer, the brutal other, the aggressor. It has drama, elan, tension, written like a chapter from a novel. There were suggestions that Powell had never received such a letter, that the woman did not exist and that her story was an exaggerated amalgam of rumours put together to make a point. Journalists hunted the streets in the days following the speech and could not discover who it was. Powell would never say, arguing the letter outlining the woman's story had been sent to him in confidence.

Years later, investigations revealed the name Druscilla Cotterill, a woman who lived alone on a street in Wolverhampton, had lost her husband in the war and had, once, rented out rooms. Local people denied that Mrs Cotterill had ever had excrement pushed through her letter box. A dead dog was thrown through the window of another white family living on Brighton Place, but that was to do with a family feud. Children did bang on Mrs Cotterill's door and run away, just like they did on the London streets I grew up on, kids' stuff, noising up the locals. 'It wasn't meant nastily,' one of the residents said. Mrs Cotterill was invited into neighbours' homes for dinner, sitting and chatting with the new immigrant families. She appears to have been affected by a drink problem and who knew what grief she faced and needed to numb. She lived in two rooms in her house and locked up the rest. When she died, a bouquet was sent by those Caribbean immigrant neighbours who had apparently made her life such a misery.

Those immigrants who were carpenters and factory workers, here to make a difference. Not bogeyman aliens.

And not 'wide-grinning piccaninnies' – a phrase, which Powell would know, straight from the playbook of the American South and slavery – the idiot coon, astonished by the wonders, as was Topsy in the anti-slavery novel *Uncle Tom's Cabin*, of the 'Ma'srs House', always under threat of being eaten by alligators, with bright teeth and big, red lips, dark and stupid, funny, comedic, wilful and insolent; the tricky, slippery Negro, the golliwog companion from across the Atlantic. It has been claimed that Powell did not use the word 'piccaninnies' himself, he was merely quoting from the letter he received. At the beginning of the passage he says: *'I am going to allow one of those hundreds of people to speak for me'.*

'The other dangerous delusion from which those who are wilfully or otherwise blind to realities suffer, is summed up in the word "integration". To be integrated into a population means to become for all practical purposes indistinguishable from its other members.

'Now, at all times, where there are marked physical differences, especially of colour, integration is difficult though, over a period, not impossible. There are among the Commonwealth immigrants who have come to live here in the last fifteen years or so, many thousands whose wish and purpose is to be integrated and whose every thought and endeavour is bent in that direction.

'But to imagine that such a thing enters the heads of a great and growing majority of immigrants and their descendants is a ludicrous misconception, and a dangerous one.

'We are on the verge here of a change. Hitherto it has been force of circumstance and of background which has rendered

the very idea of integration inaccessible to the greater part of the immigrant population – that they never conceived or intended such a thing, and that their numbers and physical concentration meant the pressures towards integration which normally bear upon any small minority did not operate.

'Now we are seeing the growth of positive forces acting against integration, of vested interests in the preservation and sharpening of racial and religious differences, with a view to the exercise of actual domination, first over fellow-immigrants and then over the rest of the population. The cloud no bigger than a man's hand, that can so rapidly overcast the sky, has been visible recently in Wolverhampton and has shown signs of spreading quickly. The words I am about to use, verbatim as they appeared in the local press on 17 February, are not mine, but those of a Labour Member of Parliament who is a minister in the present government:

"The Sikh communities' campaign to maintain customs inappropriate in Britain is much to be regretted. Working in Britain, particularly in the public services, they should be prepared to accept the terms and conditions of their employment. To claim special communal rights (or should one say rites?) leads to a dangerous fragmentation within society. This communalism is a canker; whether practised by one colour or another it is to be strongly condemned."

'All credit to John Stonehouse for having had the insight to perceive that, and the courage to say it.'

Integration, the assimilation of strangers, how possible is that? It plays to historic conservative fears, traceable back to Edmund Burke, of rushed, crashing change, clashing with an organic, gradualist approach. There is no 'end state' that politicians can plan their way to; change should be slow, considered. Anything rapid, sudden – whether the French Revolution or mass immigration – is to be fought shy of. Powell often quoted Burke approvingly and spoke of 'the authority of acceptance', that things are as they are because they are as they are. Not always logical, but still correct, he argued, the romantic Powell, the England of warm beer and cricket pitches, nuns riding to evening service as the sun sets over hills and dales, settled by the song of the nightingale. A land to be defended. Burke himself was suspicious of the 'swinish multitude' undermining a nation's very being. He was talking about the French Revolution. Powell believed he had his own multitude to contend with, right here in Britain.

And what were the dislocating outrages John Stonehouse (a man who – as the last Postmaster General of the UK – oversaw the introduction of the second-class stamp and faked his own death) had so bravely argued against? That Sikh bus drivers be allowed to grow a beard and wear a turban, despite it contravening union bus-driving rules and being the source of complaints to the local paper after one driver, Tarsem Singh Sandhu, was sacked for the offence of returning so attired after a period of sick leave. 'It is time,' one comment in the local paper said, 'they realised this is England, not India.'

'For these dangerous and divisive elements the legislation proposed in the Race Relations Bill is the very pabulum they need to flourish. Here is the means of showing that the immigrant communities can organise to consolidate their members, to agitate and campaign against their fellow citizens, and to overawe and dominate the rest with the legal weapons which the ignorant and the ill-informed have provided. As I look ahead, I am filled

with foreboding; like the Roman, I seem to see "the River Tiber foaming with much blood".

'*That tragic and intractable phenomenon which we watch with horror on the other side of the Atlantic but which there is interwoven with the history and existence of the States itself, is coming upon us here by our own volition and our own neglect. Indeed, it has all but come. In numerical terms, it will be of American proportions long before the end of the century.*

'*Only resolute and urgent action will avert it even now. Whether there will be the public will to demand and obtain that action, I do not know. All I know is that to see, and not to speak, would be the great betrayal.*'

That famous quote, 'rivers of blood', that has haunted the debate across the decades, and is the only line I knew as I grew up in a country where every clash of a black person and a white person led to demands that everyone now agree that 'Enoch was right', was not quite the quote at all. It refers to Virgil's *Aeneid*, the mythical epic on the founding of Rome. Powell originally considered leaving it in the original Latin but one assumes he realised that may not have come across with the same impact on the early evening news bulletins. It is a quote from the high priestess, the Sybil, and is a response to a question from Aeneas, the Trojan warrior, who seeks knowledge on how attempts to build an empire will turn out. A painful process, with the River Tiber foaming with much blood, he is told. But ultimately, of course, successful, a greater end forged from the fires – Rome, in its own mind, was the greatest of multicultural civilisations.

Could Powell have understood that, and just not taken his argument to its own Latinate conclusion? Is that where we have arrived at now, not rivers of blood but a distinctly British settlement on the kind of country we want to be – cricket and grime music, Shakespeare and Benjamin Zephaniah, the Cotswolds and London, still just a hundred miles apart. 'If it was any old person, you might think they'd just picked a line they liked the sound of and used it, but Powell was one of the best classicists of the twentieth century,' Mary Beard, Professor of Classics at the University of Cambridge, answered when asked that question in 2008. 'He'd have been well aware of the meaning of the line.'

If he had followed through the analogy, it would have been a different speech, a speech about how Britain was forged from different strands, was indeed an immigrant nation, and through that had found strength. Of course, there were individual problems which must be dealt with, but no existential threat. Just like the arrival of the Jews and the Huguenots, there is nothing to fear. Only advantage to be had.

But that wasn't the right message for Powell, nursing a small majority in his seat in the West Midlands. He wanted fire, not salve.

Two years after the 'Rivers of Blood' speech, his majority rose to nearly 15,000.

Less than a third of pupils in the London Borough of Ealing are classified as white.

3

Go home

I grew up in Ealing, west London, a place where the sun always shone. A place for which the word 'suburb', with that whiff of condescension, could have been invented. Only two boroughs in London are larger, Croydon and Barnet, and they sound about as exciting. Names which to us who lived there all those decades ago carried a ring of solidity and calmness. The good old days.

To me and the millions who grew up in suburban Britain, these places were and are the foundations of an essential Englishness, the Englishness of John Betjeman, poetry sunk in those schools named after English heroes like Henry Fielding, magistrate, reformer and writer, and Ellen Wilkinson, the first woman to become Minister for Education. Poetry sunk in those carefully tended parks and gardens, a manageable, ersatz representation of the countryside that had been covered up by so much city. Poetry sunk in the roads of terraced houses with a tree carefully planted every tenth paving stone; neat signposted names, Cranmer Avenue, after the Reformation archbishop, and Blondin Avenue, from further afield, after the tightrope walker Charles Blondin, the nineteenth-century 'daredevil of

Niagara Falls'. And each suburb, the size of a small city, stuffed full of immigrants, chasing dreams far from home.

Return, return to Ealing,
Worn poet of the farm!
Regain your boyhood feeling
Of uninvaded calm!
For there the leafy avenues
Of lime and chestnut mix'd
Do widely wind, by art designed,
The costly houses 'twixt.

The Queen of the Suburbs was Ealing's title, coined by Charles Jones, the borough surveyor in 1902 and used by the estate agents and shopkeepers to encourage the new middle classes and merchant classes to arrive in their thousands. To live in the terraced houses with pocket-handkerchief gardens, houses built with Victorian sweat and dust, the same sweat and dust that constructed all of outer London, swallowing up the villages of the old counties with serried ranks of red-brick homes, a million jostling offspring of the railways that spread from the capital.

I have Isambard Kingdom Brunel to thank for my childhood home, slap bang in the middle of Ridley Avenue. Number 26. His Great Western Railway to the south-west of England – including Torquay, incidentally, where my mum grew up – had a stop at Ealing Broadway, opened in 1838. Ealing Town was born, with newfangled 'horse-buses' to take people to the station.

Our next-door neighbours were from the Caribbean, mother and father and three children, a son and daughter a little older than me and therefore impossibly cool, and a younger daughter, Deloris, a friend for games of 'had' up and down the street outside. At Number 10 were the Greek family. They also had a daughter and she would come out as well, in funny frilly clothes. I think she wore those funny frilly clothes to church.

Deloris had a test which would reveal how brilliant you were. Her older sister had told her about it. Were your gums dark, like morello cherries, or pale and pink, like uncooked bacon? Cherries was good, bacon not so much. 'Let me see yours.' I dutifully showed her my gums. They were sort of in-between. 'Hmm,' Deloris said. Clearly the testing matrix outlined by her sister hadn't considered this eventuality. 'So, you're half-brilliant,' she suggested helpfully.

That would probably do, I thought. Better than having rubbish pink gums. This was the problem of being mixed-race. In the 1970s and 1980s no one really knew where to put you. The term 'mixed' wasn't even a category on the national population census until 2001. 'Ethnic origin' had only arrived a decade earlier after more than ten years of protests, led by African and Caribbean communities, worried about what the data would, could, be used for. At a time when persecution by the police was commonplace, such concerns were understandable. 'Arab' didn't arrive until 2011. My father was an Arab.

Ridley Avenue was the type of street estate agents now euphemistically describe as being populated with 'charming urban cottages'. That means small – two bedrooms upstairs, three rooms downstairs. One was the kitchen that you ate in because you didn't have any other space rather than because it was trendy not to always use the dining room. Every supper was a 'kitchen supper'. The other was the 'front room' (i.e. the only room at the front of the house) and a bathroom at the back. There were two of us, my mum and me, and I always knew when it was bathtime because the music for *PM* on Radio 4 would come on. When my uncles arrived with their new cars I would hang around outside, leaning on them, in the hope that someone would ask me whose they were. Mum didn't drive then, she learnt later. Dad did, but his car was a pale beige Morris Marina, built by British Leyland, and therefore was only to be approached as rapidly as possible, head down, hoping no one would notice not only that my dad came to pick me up at the weekends because he didn't live with us – for reasons no one had ever explained to me – but also that he drove a nonsense car. I pretended to friends that Dad owned a Ford Granada with two-tone paint because that was the grandest car I could imagine. In reality, I still remember the smell of the brown plastic seats of that Morris Marina, burning the backs of my legs when you wore shorts in the summer sun. The steering wheel waggled alarmingly when Dad went over 60mph.

My road was already changing in the 1970s. There was an obsession with 'Georgification', turning the Victorian working people's cottages into miniature facsimiles of Bath townhouses. Sash windows were taken out and replaced with panelled glazing, bullseye glass used for effect. This was middle-class glass, middle-class change. When we first moved in – I was aged about three – not only was the road that mixture of families from different ethnic backgrounds. It was also slightly mad. The woman a few doors up parked her car not on the street but *in her front room*. The only room at the front. She had a garage door put in and driveway gates where the garden wall should have been. The council had helpfully lowered the pavement kerb so that she didn't bump her dark green Mini's wheels on arrival home. If you walked past when the garage door was in the raised position, you could still see the flowery wallpaper and the fireplace. Opposite her was a man whose house was almost fully obscured by an out-of-control privet hedge, twenty feet high. He ran everywhere. Up and down the street on what crazy errands I never knew.

By the time we left, a decade later – around the corner to a house with a dining room and a garden with a lawn – that mixture had changed. White families with young, flaxen-haired children had moved in. Houses were painted grey with eau-de-Nil detailing. It was a reversal of white flight. As London property prices started to catch fire the wealthier came back to re-colonise the places they had gladly left to the blacks and the Irish, the Indians and the Greeks and the people of no fixed ethnic abode, like me.

Of course, at that age, maybe six, maybe eight, you didn't care about colour very much, gums aside. You cared that your Adidas Gazelles were the right shade of brown suede, you cared about the Roadmaker world in your bedroom, carefully slotting together complicated towns where your Matchbox cars – invented in a Tottenham pub – lived alongside Lego houses – invented in Billund, Denmark. The towns were populated with Lego people, although not brown ones, not in those days. All Lego faces in the 1970s were yellow, which I assume someone in Denmark equated with white. Some people my mum knew did give me a brown doll once, as a present, but it was a little *de trop* as it had no clear role in that essential childhood boy obsession – creating magnificent traffic jams. The people, I am sure, were doing their best. They had stripped pine furniture. Like we did.

Mum was a single parent, battling to keep a full-time job alongside the washing (in the sink, by hand, up and down, up and down; the day we took delivery of an automatic washing machine I thought the Space Shuttle had arrived), the cooking, the cleaning, the shopping (on the streets where the National Front liked to march), and looking after a small boy who would creep downstairs and sit under the dining table for hours, hoping not to be found. Mum had a friend with a mixed-race child and father who wasn't around. We spent a lot of time with them. The friend's new husband worked in the petroleum industry, so they had a big house.

This was my London. My London where ethnic groups lived together, house next to house. What if we had been elsewhere, maybe Thorpe Hesley in Yorkshire where my mum was born. Or down in Devon, Torquay, where Mum grew up and never saw a brown face. And nor did I. On those endless, wonderful sea-infused holidays with my grandparents, by the beach, where we walked by the calming, never-ending waves and, when on long coastal expeditions, stayed in hotels where I wondered if the staff realised that I did know how to use a knife and fork.

With grandparents who loved me so much, my grandfather offering endless cricket matches in the park up the impossibly steep hill from their house until the sun set and the stomach rumbled ready for tea of honeyed ham on plates fired in Stoke-on-Trent and bread so thinly cut by my grandmother you could almost see the light through each slice. Traditional, English tea. But. My grandfather still said 'play the white man' when we sat, intent on our card game and I had maybe tried some tricksy little move to win at rummy. And I remember that comment to this day. And lying on my bed that night in the 'little spare room' upstairs (as opposed to the big spare room at the front where my mother slept or the attic where I had to sleep sometimes if the house was full for Christmas) and wondering if white people really did play fairer. And why my mother hadn't said anything to her father.

Fighting for ten-year-old boys. Some rules.

When preparing for a fight, the goal is straightforward: to optimise the pain felt by the other party whilst at the same time minimising the risk to yourself. Achieving this goal needs a modicum of speed (few fights between young boys last more than three minutes) and an ability to keep your head down and your eyes closed whilst at the same time flinging flailing fists to the fore. This needs coordination. There is also much panting and snorting – and a key focus on turning a fight with fists as quickly as possible into an ungainly wrestle because an ungainly wrestle is less dangerous. The result is often similar: a red-faced headlock, blazers awry, with one of you submitting with just the right level of nonchalance to suggest to the 'friends' crowding around chanting 'Fight! Fight! Fight!' that you always planned to lose that way.

Much later I wondered if anyone ever fulfilled the greatest ever pre-fight line in cinema (*The Breakfast Club*, Andrew to Bender: 'Two hits. Me hitting you. You hitting the floor'). I assumed not.

Much older than ten and fighting can cause actual bodily harm. Which is why most people, including me, retire at that early stage, mostly unhurt.

I had lots of fights when I was young, banging people's heads on the tarmacked floor, being punched so hard by a friend called Dylan (whom I had decided to tease for being, well, Welsh) that I remember it to this day. He had swung around, blond mop of hair, eyes blazing, and caught me cold on the cheek with his right fist, just outside the boys' toilets (complete with the average ceiling decoration for school loos in those days – clumps of dried-up 'bog-roll', set so hard they were to all intents and purposes fossilised). I never mentioned that he was Welsh again.

Actually, I should be more precise about my fighting past which, on reading the above, may sound a little wild. I remember having lots of fights, which is not quite the same thing as having them. Fights, by their nature, are memorable. Maths lessons, which I certainly had many more of, not so much.

But there is one fight I do remember.

And here it is.

It happened on a day I was wearing my new brogues. Which could cause pain, I knew, if applied in the right way. Kicking for example.

'Jungle bunny.'

Now, of course, I had been called that name before. And most often, I would ignore it, outwardly at least, despite the churn inside. Head down, flush spreading across my face, walking on. A bit weary, sometimes. Though it passed.

But, every now and again, and dependent on a confluence of incidents, would come a different reaction. Like this time. A mixture of those new brogues, a long, irritating day, heat. The result was not a forced shrug, not an 'I'll get over it'. This time came anger, the fight response, rather than the other two options – flee or freeze. This time the amygdala – that part of the brain which prepares the body to respond to threats with aggression rather more quickly than the other bit of the brain, the cortex, works out whether it is reasonable to do so – lucked out. When you are ten, this can tend to happen. Reason, and the avoidance of being hurt, the need for self-protection, comes later.

This is what I remember of the next two minutes and thirty seconds.

Once anger takes hold, the world narrows. Wide horizons become focused. My brogues, black, leather – the working-class shoe of the Irish labourer that clambered its way to respectability – became weapons. My vision was wholly dominated by those shoes, my eyes trapped on them, that effect when you spin around, dizzy, then try and stand straight and the ground lurches up towards you, on a different plane – my brogues, coming up towards me, and for some reason I was enormously strengthened by this. My shoes gave me the edge. I was armed. 'Aha, you have said something bad but you have not realised that I am wearing new shoes. Big mistake, fellas.'

Two boys. My age, maybe a little older, school uniforms (navy, black, I can't quite remember), satchels over shoulders, walking away from me, down the road, towards the houses with the higher numbers on the doors, away from the church and its attached hall where I used to throw away the sandwiches my mother had lovingly made me for packed lunch – over the fence of black iron poles, into the bushes. Because the bread was too brown and was that new healthy stuff called wholemeal which, in those days, knitted the roof of your mouth to your tongue and wasn't nice like white bread which had crusty edges and tasted of doughy joy. And Marmite as a filling, with butter, which on a hot day (and this was a hot day) would have gone a bit slimy by lunchtime and maybe even started turning a little rancid. I never told my mother that I used to throw away my sandwiches (and pour away the Bovril drink she put in a thermos because I just hated Bovril) even though I think she saw them sometimes, discarded along the street, quiet little monuments of dietary rebellion. And that probably hurt her a bit. And I'm sorry, even though it was forty years ago.

Really sorry.

Two boys. I was at my front door, just fishing out my key which I stored in a little grey, furry pouch to keep it safe and stop me losing it and making my mum angry.

'Jungle bunny. Go home.' And a snigger. *Hahahahahahahaha.*

I turned and moved as quickly as possible (first rule of boy-fighting, surprise), discarding my school bag, black with Adidas in white letters on the side (school joke: what does Adidas stand for? All Day I Dream About Sex – despite it being about the last thing ten-year-old boys dream about, football and Asterix being more our thing). Out of my front gate with the wobbly post, turning towards them, past the russet-coloured tree where I used to watch the ants walking up the trunk, across the cracked pavement still chalked for hopscotch, covering that ten metres which has stuck with me all my life, a blur of those Blessed Brogues and a hot sunny day, everything crushing in on me, pumping air in my lungs. Aim for those boys. I chose one to attack with all my pre-teenage might. Hit, hit, hit and kick, bloody well kick, cause pain, cause pain to these people whoever they are. These people who didn't have any idea when they snarked at that boy, who didn't know. What it was like to walk home from school to the street you grew up on, a few miles from the hospital you were born in and around the corner from the school you went to just like all the other local children. Who didn't know what it was like when someone says 'Go home' and you are just about to walk into your home so you are doing exactly what is being asked of you but of course their request means something completely different. And is therefore something you can't achieve. Even if you wanted to.

And I think he fell, the one I hit and kicked. And I hit and kicked him some more and I wanted to optimise pain and I ran back to my house and opened the door and slammed it, crash, behind me and stood in the hall with a ringing in my ears and my head feeling like it was overloaded with blood.

To silence. My mum was always home later than me.

Rat-a-tat-tat.

The door knocker.

RAT-A-TAT-TAT. Louder.

I crept to the door and looked through the spyhole. A woman, face looming, distorted by the fisheye lens I was peering through. A grown-up. You open doors to grown-ups. So I did.

'What the hell do you think you're doing?' the woman said. Probably shouted.

And that's all I remember, but I am sure she continued that I had launched an attack on what I assumed was her son and she had turned from a little further up the street I grew up on to see a child come out of a garden, a blur of fists and attack the person she had brought up from a baby and probably also made sandwiches for.

Without provocation.

So, give her a reason. But I couldn't. I was crying so hard. With rage, and fear, and just damn bloody upset. And she was a grown-up and you steered clear of arguing with grown-ups. I tried to push the words out but they would not come, would not form in my dammed and constricted throat. When you cry you are loud and at the same time mute. Eyes damp, throat dry like the crumbs at the bottom of my school bag. Words fail you at the moment you most need them.

And she turned around and walked back down our short garden path and closed the gate with the wobbly post behind her. And I shut the door and slumped to the floor, and there were my brogues and me and the returning quiet of an empty house. And I never told anyone. Until I wrote it down for this book.

In the 1970s racism wasn't a 'thing' that you wanted to identify and argue about. It was something you wanted to ignore, and just wished would go away. Like acne. But there it was, every bloody day, a difference that was picked on. Like being fat. Or wearing glasses. We were each our own police officer, trying our best to fight our own battles. Carrying a whole load of little secrets, little hurts in a pile which we didn't share because – and this didn't make us angry, it just was – that was the way of the world.

Muhammad Ali learnt to box because someone stole his favourite red bike when he was twelve. I know how he felt.

We all live in tribes. That was the lesson for that ten-year-old boy. We are different, groups of us are different, and you are shouted at for being different, insulted. There is an 'other'. And either it beats you or you beat it.

And here's why I lived in a different tribe. Not just from the vast majority who were white. But from the minority who were black.

Properly black. A friend once asked me if I would like 'some of his arse'. He was black and had married a black woman from Chicago, jumping over a wooden stick during the ceremony in America for good luck and to remember a black past of poverty. He had a big behind and was worried that I didn't have enough of one. My arse was skinny, you see. Like a white person's.

When I was young, I was the only 'half-caste' kid that looked like me in my school year, and in fact any year, apart from someone in a more senior part of the school with the unlikely name of Geek. Which caused children to whisper behind their hands: 'Hey, is that the brother of Geek?' when they saw me walking to lessons with my school bag slung over one shoulder – and laugh about my likely connection to 'Geek' who also had lighter brown skin and a shock of curly, not-quite-Afro hair which maybe his dad cut badly as well. Geek? I mean, that's unfortunate. As a name.

For him. As well as for me. Off to play basketball one night after school, Geek was in the back of the minibus and kicked me. He was understandably angry that this new kid had brought so much fresh mickey-taking upon his head, opened a new flank of attack when, if you were 'different' and a teenager and a boy, all you want to do was bloody well fit in. It was quite a sharp kick, a lashing out from his seat. But I didn't have my new brogues on. So I didn't fight back.

And I never asked him his real name either. Even though I'm pretty sure now it wasn't Geek. Improbable, really, that many people actually have that name.

That was the backdrop to life. In the good old days. When you were young. A constant thrum caught from everyday life, from snippets of television, brief encounters with the world of news that Mum listened to on the radio, watched on TV before sending you up to bed; or maybe you caught sight of a message stuck up in a newsagent's window looking for tenants. Or a glimpse of graffiti.

There was a substantive, defining difference and you had to understand it. Some people had a question mark hovering over them. And you were part of the 'some people'.

Why? Well, you never asked, not then. Why don't you like me? Why do millions of people decide to dislike other millions of people they have never met and would never hope to shake their hand? Even if they had the time.

Is it fear? A biological necessity, traced back to our ancestral selves when the tribe from over the hill really could steal your wheat and your goats? Am I helpless in the face of it, a guiding, necessary and deep part of the very make-up of all of us as human beings? Mapped in our DNA and as unarguable as the existence of legs and arms and hair.

Is it a cultural norm, honed over many centuries, repeated in a million stories that 'other' is less good than 'self' and all the joined selves that make up our imagined communities? Is it why we are irritated when there are too many Latvian plumbers on our morning commute? Or all the corner stores are run by brown people? Or not enough people speak English on the train?

Is it a reflection of economic disparity? If a market is a zero-sum game, then my up must mean your down. And that down might be easier to endure if I don't like you in the first place. Cuts out the blocking mechanism of empathy. Which can be convenient.

Is it to do with colour, one of the easiest markers of difference and the most definite attribute we cling to at times of stress? My colour may not be the most interesting thing about me, but it is the most obvious.

Is there something in nation, blood and soil, in place of birth? That I feel settled when I see a red bus, the Union flag, pomp and ceremony, signs for London, capital of the world. Does it matter that some Scots might not like the English very much in the same way that it matters that Hendrik Verwoerd believed in the segregation of races in South Africa? Is prejudice the same as racism? Does it matter who has power?

Or is it just an irrationality, as inexplicable as Meursault's decision to kill an Algerian Arab in Albert Camus' *L'Etranger* – our attempt to construct an explanation for the 'tender indifference of the world' as futile as the court's attempts to understand why Meursault shows no remorse, before sending him to his death, this 'Monsieur Antichrist'.

Why don't I like you?

Identity, the discomfort of strangers, who feels at home, and who doesn't.

There is some human urge swirling within us to defeat it, or at least mitigate it. The social, fair-minded animal who wants to put salve on conflict. That prefers talk of Us, rather than Them. There has been a long and noble effort amongst a group of well-meaning – and I mean that in a literal way, not the faintly suspicious way it is now used to suggest someone weak in the face of reality, iron logic – public-spirited individuals who have done as much to help this world ease pain as doctors trying to cure cancer.

And I would include my mother in that group. To this day.

As a child my mother gave me improving books like *Discovering Africa's Past*, which told me that 'African history was hidden for a long time because those in Europe who explained it had not put their prejudice behind them, but had gone along with closed minds, convinced of their natural superiority.' I was young and more interested in kissing Yvonne Gibbons who sat at the desk behind me at school on the Fulham Palace Road in south-west London. But I still have that book, jacket cover bleached by the sun from red to pink after a life lying on a table by the window.

I am officially 'different' in this country, 'mixed' for the purposes of the statistics-gatherers. A category apart, an additional data cell, a separate column on the spreadsheet of society, away from 'the majority'. 'Mixed' is a weird word, isn't it? Almost pejorative, mixed as in not pure, mixed up, mixed picture, mixed results. I once said – when a teenager and starting to become interested in such things – that I wanted to be called 'shared race'. I looked around hopefully at my friends. They looked back at me as if I had suggested I wanted to be the first brown person to land on the moon.

'Like we're guests, sometimes,' as one close Asian friend described it to me. 'Just happy to be here and always wondering if someone is going to tap us on the shoulder and politely ask us to leave.'

And he was born in Wigan.

'Keep Britain Tidy. Kick Out Pakis.'

A piece of graffiti scribbled on the cover of a bright orange exercise book at school.

By me.

By a boy grappling in a world where half-white and half-black didn't have an anchor. By a boy who – lacking bravery – didn't always kick up at the bullies and sometimes kicked down, targeting the people who were targets. By a boy who thought that if only people from the Asian subcontinent learnt to speak with an English accent then 'racism' would cease, failing to realise that 'voice' wasn't really the issue. By a boy who wondered if 'Pakis' were the problem because they were – like – different, I kept being told. Not like me, who was trying to be the same as everybody else and could show that by writing bits of graffiti on my exercise book, just like the white boys did. (Pointless, of course.) By a boy who did not understand that people with backgrounds from Pakistan or India or Bangladesh or anywhere weren't the problem, any more than I was, and that prejudice had to be solved by the perpetrator, the in-group not the out-group. By a boy who remembers vividly the video of a young black girl – maybe seven, the daughter of a family friend – rubbing at her arm and neck visible above a pretty summer dress and saying she 'didn't like all this brown stuff'. A boy who asked his mum why the girl said that because the dress was not brown but yellow. And heard the reply: 'It's her skin. That's what she doesn't like.' By a boy so shocked by that, it is an image that has stayed with him as he has grown into a man and had his own family, including a daughter who sometimes, not often, wears a summer dress, even though she prefers trousers and black T-shirts dedicated to Twenty One Pilots. By a boy who thought it was the victims of racism who were the ones who had to change because that was what all the headlines and the television shows and the white kids said.

Written by me.

When I was young I had a paper round. Every morning I rode my bike to the newsagent's which, from memory, was run by an Asian couple, to my not very worldly-wise mind possibly South Korean or Vietnamese. I knew there were lots of Vietnamese in west London where I lived because a couple of children had started at my school, 'The Boat People' they were called and we were told not to stare and to be friendly because they had had a lot of problems in their country to do with something called communists.

The newsagent couple were very nice, especially kind to me because I always arrived good and early in the morning for fear of getting a disapproving look from the man who lived on Belsize Road and who liked his paper before he set off for work. If I was late, he would come into the newsagent's, cigarette drooping from his mouth, and, silently, his eyes full of cross irritation, take his *Daily Mirror* from me as I guiltily and hurriedly crammed my morning round into the canvas satchel which was sometimes so heavy it threatened to pull you off your bike, Raleigh or otherwise. Mr Belsize Road had a dog which of course always made paper boys and girls nervous.

The newsagent couple – I am not sure I ever knew their names – believed I was called Neil. The reason they thought that was because I told them that was my name.

One morning, worried that I was a little late, that nice couple rang my home and spoke to my mother. 'Is Neil okay?' the woman newsagent asked.

'Who's Neil?' my mother understandably responded.

My name is, after all, Kamal.

Lots of us did it – children with funny, foreign names who used short English names in our effort to fit in, particularly with people we didn't know well. We were the generation of black and Asian people who fought for similarity, it was a confidence thing. A lack of confidence thing. The language of being proud of who you are and where you came from had not yet become part of the everyday conversation about race and identity in Britain, that was to come later. Mohammad is now in the top ten boys' names in the country. No one had ever heard of the name Kamal in the 1970s. It means perfection in Arabic. It is also – for a schoolchild – uncomfortably close to camel in English pronunciation. 'You got the hump?' *Ha ha*. Today, a name is a badge of honour, from Azibo to Zyshonne, Aiesha to Yanika. When my son tells me the names of his friends in his rugby team I hardly recognise any, and am glad of it. Young people don't think names are 'funny' any more. It wouldn't cross their minds.

I am happy, now, that my name is Kamal. Glad that my father and mother plumped for different rather than the same. No offence to the Neils of this world, but Kamal fits me better. It joins me to my background rather than divorces me from it. It has been a long journey, from the 1970s to today, 'names' just one small eddy in that big pool of progress that makes this country what it is. This country where a white woman and a black man fell in love and played their small part in changing Britain forever. Trendsetters, my mum and dad. That's what they were.

In 1939, *The Times* described the White City Estate in west London as 'the largest and finest estate of flats which London County Council has yet built'. By the 1980s and the time my mother arrived at the local comprehensive school to teach, the area was only notable for its desperation, another gleaming project brought low by a lack of money and a lack of will. In the huge blocks of flats water dripped down the walls and mould grew in the corners. Outside, the estate was in the grip of crime, drugs and gangs. There was anger, lots of anger. It was home to many Afro-Caribbean families who wondered 'Is this it?' of the life they had been invited to travel across a wide sea to enjoy. Their children, second-generation immigrants like me, saw the hollowness in their parents as they walked the dangerous streets with road names like South Africa, Commonwealth and Bloemfontein, around the corner from the old General Smuts pub, where the hard white men would go to glass the opposition before a football match at nearby Loftus Road, the home of QPR. The bars were segregated along ethnic lines.

'The girls felt angry, hopeless,' Mum said. 'They thought all white people were against them, they thought we were all rich Tories. They couldn't believe "a white teacher" would ever vote Labour. Everything was Us versus Them.'

And Mum set about trying to change some of that, one of many optimistic young women – and men – who rolled up the sleeves on their shirts bought from Marks & Spencer, hired draughty offices at the top of run-down buildings and called themselves things like the Centre for Urban Educational Studies (CUES) and All London Teachers Against Racism and Fascism (ALTARF), photocopying their Letraset newsletters on thin paper probably better suited to making roll-ups, and popping to the Indian canteen upstairs where they did 'bloody good samosas'. They talked about collaborative learning, dismissed that establishment language that described black children as having 'chips on their shoulders' or an 'attitude problem'. They said that racism wasn't for black people to solve, it was a white person's issue, felt hopeful there would be progress, that the strength of their argument would carry all before them, set off on trips to places like Norfolk with good cheer in their hearts, convinced that the local teachers would be keen to hear about their work, important despite there being a vanishingly small number of non-white children in most of the county. They were greeted with nonplussed handshakes.

My mother and her friends made earnest documentaries for the BBC called things like *Racism – the Fourth R*. In the thirty-minute film, young tank-top-wearing children called Kevin explained – with that mixture of care and nonchalance only a six-year-old can muster – that *Going Swimming* by Gill Smith was a bit rubbish because all the characters' faces were coloured grey and 'people are really brown'. This was a time when teachers would ask 'don't you have doors in the jungle' of black pupils who had neglected to close the classroom one. Shahid was interviewed, revealing how he had to 'try and grin and bear it' when the British Movement ('Pakis Out') marched along his street, worried that 'we weren't really wanted here'. Pupils spoke of 'beating up the coloured kids on the bus', just like I remember happened at my school. And CUES and ALTARF were there to help, with educational aids and books, arguing that the only people with chips on their shoulders and an attitude problem were teachers looking for excuses. Theirs wasn't the multiculturalism of steel drums, saris and samosas – they were about the front line, not dancing around in 'national dress' to tabla drums, pleasant as that was.

'Other' to Mum and her friends wasn't the same as many people saw other. Other to Mum was Enoch Powell. Other to Mum were those who didn't hold coffee mornings and jumble sales to support the African National Congress in exile, putting up exhausted arrivals from South Africa before they returned to battle for democracy.

Other to Mum were those who backed the original formulation of the 1981 Nationality Act which could have meant her son – born in Perivale Maternity Ward – was not a full British citizen. It was reformed, in the end, extending the ability to 'pass on' citizenship to mothers as well as fathers. Salman Rushdie described it as a piece of legislation 'expressly designed to deprive black and Asian Britons of their citizenship rights'. Being born in Britain was not enough to be British, the act said, one of your parents had to come from here as well. Rushdie argued that citizenship based on where you were born – *jus soli,* the right of the soil – was being replaced by citizenship dependent on your parentage – *jus sanguinis,* the right of blood. That had only one target.

Other to Mum were those who didn't see it as a particular problem that all the 'disruptive units' in the education system were full of black kids.

Other to Mum was Ray Honeyford, the bearded and bespectacled headteacher of an inner-city Bradford school where the pupils were 90 per cent non-white. In 1984 he created that most British of events, the periodic blow-up about race, by 'saying the unsayable' in the libertarian *Salisbury Review.* Honeyford, who was eventually paid off after acres of coverage and controversy, said multicultural teaching – an attempt, where it worked, at respecting different traditions and, where it didn't, a route to separatism – was producing 'Asian ghettos'. He also attacked 'an influential group of black intellectuals of aggressive disposition, who know little of the British traditions of understatement, civilised discourse and respect for reason', pausing to describe one parent speaking English at his school 'like a Peter Sellers' Indian doctor on an off-day'. That made Mum – who was white and knew plenty about British traditions – cross.

Other to Mum were those teachers in an audience she had – as an expert – been asked to come and speak to about being in a mixed-race relationship and what that meant for her mixed-race child in school. The audience members at Ealing Town Hall asked how on earth she had got herself into such a mess.

Other to Mum were the pessimists.

The attainment gap between pupils with an immigrant background and their native-born peers is significantly smaller in the UK than in other economically developed countries.

However, they are relatively less satisfied with life compared with their classmates.

4

Zoo time

Big School was very different to Little School, and mine was a couple of miles down the road from my house. Every day I met up with some of my friends and we walked the thirty minutes together, bags slouched over shoulders, discussing the homework we hadn't done and the girls we hadn't managed to become boyfriends of. Big School was a sprawling comprehensive, 1,200 pupils and a huge jump for all of us from the small neighbourhood primaries that fed this education megalopolis. Eleven-year-olds cried in their over-large blazers as parents said final goodbyes on the first day of the first year. We were a mix of every background, white, black and brown, and every class, from the 'manor houses' of north Ealing with their wrought-iron lanterns hanging in the porch and their Saabs in the driveways, to the council estates of Greenford where drugs were peddled on the upper walkways and ice formed on the inside of the windows. When it was cold.

This was the 1980s. We were young, awkward and still, as we grew older, never spoke about race or identity, not ever. My school was Every School, that London mix of teenagers that bred strength and tension in equal measure. The air along the parquet-floored corridors crackled and fizzed, sometimes with fun, sometimes with anger. Shouts and jostling, flare-ups. 'You got a problem?' 'No.' 'YOU GOT A PROBLEM?' Teachers, stretched and mostly knackered, tried that most difficult-to-achieve mix – learning with a modicum of control. There was little time for other indulgences.

Comprehensive schools in big, complicated cities are an amalgamation of tribes. In-groups and out-groups, winners and not-so-winners. It doesn't matter at what level you think about tribes, across the world, across the country or across the playground, the reasons for their existence are the same. Grouping people allows us all to make sense of chaos, make sense of a set of variables too wide and complicated for individual understanding. We have ten meaningful relationships in our lives. And live in a world of billions of people.

Big School was London with a fence around it. Teachers operated just like we all operated, looking for and using visual clues, allowing our brains to connect those clues to a set of templates it has created to make order out of mess. The black kids, the white kids, the Asians. Posh kids. Poor kids. But be wary. What if the templates you are using are based on falsity, assumptions, prejudice? And, of course, they always are because those templates are shortcuts that allow us to function. What boxes are you creating to put people in? What box would you expect the white children to be in? The black children? The brown? Me?

I deployed one technique to get me through school. Noise. I was a performer. Loud, sometimes ridiculous, a show-off, an irritant. 'Zip it up, Ahmed,' one teacher, the head of year, would regularly shout. 'You've got a voice like a foghorn.' Or, if

I was, as often the case, the last to come to attention. 'Ahmed, you've got a bum, you've got a seat, now put the two together.' Such an irritant that at one stage a whole class 'sent me to Coventry' – the silent treatment, the girl sitting at the next-door desk whispering under her hand that she wasn't allowed to talk to me because of some misdemeanour I was guilty of. They had all had a meeting and decided it – a guy called Tim the ringleader. I cannot remember what my bad behaviour was but it was certainly serious enough in the minds of thirty other teenagers to produce the response: 'Kamal, why don't you just shut the fuck up?'

The clown. Hell, I would make stuff up if I thought it would get me noticed, stories about my father flying Concorde and other tall tales, a cover for all that stuff swirling inside, that idea that I didn't quite fit and that if I didn't quite fit some bugger in charge of everything was going to put me in the Wrong. Bloody. Box. I performed for the teachers – worked hard, took part in school plays, played in the orchestra, ran on the athletics track until my heart burst. I wanted praise, to be top of the class, elbowing my way around. I performed for my mates, the sly comment at the back of room, the screwed-up bit of paper flicked at some spod who didn't have many friends and sat in the corner. The heavy school bag flung off the connecting bridge between two school blocks, narrowly missing one of the deputy heads walking below. The detentions. Once, walking past the front desk where the history teacher, a lovely, young guy who had all our best interests at heart, was marking essays, I stopped, turned my back towards him, lifted up my blazer and farted straight in his face. It was comedic and horrific, school life in microcosm. There was a stunned silence in the classroom. And then a collective intake of breath – hang on, did that just happen? The teacher was furious. I mean, he had to be furious. A pupil, gangly, a bit stroppy, but who also studied hard and was interested, engaged, one-on-one, had just farted in his face. But what must that fury have been mixed with? Apart from the smell of that teenager's fart. Bafflement, upset at the rank disrespect he had just been shown in a school always on the verge of being out of control, being overwhelmed by the craziness.

Now, wait, wait. Am I saying that because I am mixed-race I farted in a teacher's face? That my fear of racism, of prejudice, meant that I was obliged to lift the back of my blazer and proffer my backside? Throw bags off bridges? No. But there are a lot of dotted, connecting lines here, as well as a child psychologist's PhD project – 'Possible Reasons for Kamal Ahmed's Very Odd Behaviour'. The dotted line of the techniques we use to overcome the hurdles that may be put in our way. What those hurdles look like. And are those hurdles peculiar to you, or a group of you? Are there more, or fewer, than other people face? And what happens if you don't get over them? If the system contrives a set of hurdles so high that getting over them is not the point. Surviving is.

I was lucky.

I wasn't the kind of brown – Afro-Caribbean brown – that meant expectations were set low to the point of oblivion. I was the kind of brown that looked Asian, and that mattered in the 1980s. In the league table of prejudice, I was middle ranking, between the white folk at the top and the black kids at the bottom. The school was divided, certainly; 'apartheid' some described it. Black children owned one playground, white children another.

Being a black child was different. You rarely saw a black teacher. There were few role models, markers of status, figures to emulate. It was different for me. My mother *was* a teacher. Now, things were changing slowly through my decade at school – young, positive teachers were starting in education, that first cohort of the newly trained who had a different attitude about what could make a difference for young people and would, eventually, with the help of a new headteacher, transform my creaking school, long after I had left. One friend, Andy, was once taken aside by a member of the new, young cohort, a black female teacher, after the latest rumpus had resulted in the usual, a row of black boys sitting outside a senior teacher's office awaiting punishment. 'Many will expect you to fail, Andy,' she told him. 'No one will respect you. It's different for the white kids.'

And the mixed-race kids, she could have added.

Andy was a funny guy. Smiler, we called him. But, just like so many thousands of young black people, he laboured under the banner of opportunity lost. As the school years went by something changed in him. Smiler grew up and grew cynical. His is a common story, shared by so many Afro-Caribbean children turning up in those early high school years, hopeful, expectant, and leaving five years later with nothing very much apart from some vague notion that the 'careers teacher' might like them to become a car mechanic.

A year before we arrived at our high school with new books in our bags and uncommon trepidation in our stomachs, a man none of us had ever heard of published a report for the government, then led by Margaret Thatcher. Commissioned by the Labour education minister, Shirley Williams, in the late 1970s, Anthony Rampton sifted through the evidence and spoke to expert witnesses. 'We are convinced that West Indian children as a group are indeed underachieving in relation to their peers. This should be a matter of deep concern not only to all those involved in education but also to the whole community,' he said in Command Paper 8273, 'West Indian Children in Our Schools' (1981), cost £5.30. 'Virtually all these children are *British born*. They are therefore in no way "immigrants".' In English, he found, 9 per cent of 'West Indian children' received the highest grades in O Level or CSE – the exams we all took at the time – compared with 21 per cent of Asian children and 29 per cent of 'other leavers' – white. There was no category labelled 'mixed' or 'somewhere in between'. Did we get 'racism-lite'? A decade earlier Bernard Coard wrote a book, fifty-one pages long, called *How the West Indian Child is made Educationally Sub-normal in the British School System*. He was from Grenada, like Andy's parents – although Andy's parents never launched a coup in their country or became president for three days, both of which Coard did. Andy's father was a tailor, not a revolutionary; his mother a nurse.

Some old, rough data from my school in the 1980s – the exam results from a couple of forms put together 'on the back of a fag packet' by one of those positive young teachers worried by what he was seeing – revealed the problem. Number of children who received grades A–C at O Level: white 28, Asian 19, West Indian, 1 – a girl. Steve McQueen, the artist and director, was the year below me at school. I probably never noticed him, I was older and the young kids were the ones you pushed aside in the lunch queue. But McQueen had an experience similar to Andy's. He was put in the bottom sets at the age of thirteen. Thirty years later he would win three Oscars.

'That inequality – I fucking loathe it with a passion. It's all bullshit, man. It really upsets me,' he said in an interview at the time his film, *12 Years a Slave*, was released (Madonna was photographed with him at the premiere and 'then spent the whole film texting', McQueen said with a laugh). The film also won two BAFTAs and a Golden Globe.

> It was horrible. It was disgusting, the system, it was absolutely disgusting. It's divisive and it was hurtful. It was awful. School was painful because I just think that loads of people, so many beautiful people, didn't achieve what they could achieve because no one believed in them, or gave them a chance, or invested any time in them. A lot of beautiful boys, talented people, were put by the wayside. School was scary for me because no one cared, and I wasn't good at it because no one cared. At thirteen years old, you are marked, you are dead, that's your future.
>
> There were no examples of artists who were like me. When did you ever see a black man doing what I wanted to do?

His father used to urge the young McQueen to learn a trade and would ask friends if 'anyone understood' what his son did.

Different expectations lead to different outcomes, and groups that drift apart, separateness becoming calcified. In my first two years at school, I was in a few lessons with Andy, but slowly he became more distant, as did many of the people with his colour skin, more peripheral, down in the lower sets, like they sank away in the school sea until, looking down, I could no longer sight their faces through the water. Sitting with an old school friend many, many years later, we fell, as we often did, to talking about the sometimes good/sometimes bad old days. 'Not many black kids made it to sixth form, did they?' my old school friend said. And I thought about it then for the first time, really. No, Jon, they didn't.

There were houses at my school, four, all named after Stuart, Georgian and Victorian white men with bristly side-whiskers, top hats and high collars. There were different colours to signify each – Brunel (blue), Coleridge (yellow), Shaftesbury (red) and Newton (green). This was the old local grammar school, hanging onto its 1950s traditions, adrift in a sea beset by the swells of expansion since becoming a comprehensive that left the headmaster clinging mournfully to what he knew, a regimented school half the size which, just ten years earlier, only took the academic victors in the 11-plus lottery. And not many of them were 'other', black or brown. With mortar board and black cape, the head would march into assembly with as much authority as he could muster and the pupils would take turns seeing how much spit they could land on his trailing cloak as he approached the lectern at the front.

Thirty-three years after I last saw Andy – he was sixteen when he left school – we meet in a coffee shop in King's Cross. Like him, the area has changed. In the 1980s people like me only went to King's Cross to catch a train somewhere. It was home to drugs and pimps, violence, the pitiful offering favours for money, polystyrene cups proffered, a few dirty coins in the bottom, addled, crushed faces. It smelled of urine and failure. The pavements were sticky.

This was part of Bad London, made famous in films. It was an essential part of the London I grew up in, the grubby underbelly of home. The enduring image of the 1986 movie *Mona Lisa* – which we all trooped to see with the girls we had persuaded to hang out with us, intently holding hands in cinemas of grand art deco design, seats velvety – was the 'desperate bridge' behind the station. It was where prostitutes walked the sticky pavements, the heels of cheap shoes pretending riches catching in the cracks.

For me, there was one striking thing about the film. And her name was Cathy Tyson, born ten miles down the road from me in Kingston-upon-Thames. The striking thing was she looked a bit like me and it was rare to see anyone, let alone on a twenty-foot-high screen, who looked a bit like me. Her father was from Trinidad, a barrister, and her mother Irish, a social worker. She grew up in Liverpool, Toxteth, and ran away from that blighted place when she was thirteen. She was caught a week later working as a cleaner in a hotel, so bad at her new job she only managed to clean 'a room a day'. A police officer passing in the hotel corridor – forces had been alerted to search for two missing girls in London – asked whether this unlikely-looking teenage chambermaid was Cathy Tyson and Cathy Tyson answered yes, before remembering, damn, her new name, and re-answering 'No, I'm not, I'm Stacey Smith'. The police officer arranged for her to be taken home and she later offered 'gratitude for the policeman, I've never felt that before'. Police in Toxteth, you see, were the enemy.

She dropped out of college at seventeen and took up her passion, acting. Where she lived in Liverpool was 'a vibrant place, but the black people were anti-white and the white people were anti-black'. And she, like me, was stuck somewhere in neither place, location free. One thing Ms Tyson did know, she couldn't really step out with the boys she fancied because 'I didn't look like a Sindy doll'. I didn't look much like Paul, Sindy's boyfriend, either. Although, I would defy anyone to actually look like Paul who, in the 1980s, had an alarmingly orange tan.

The place has changed now, just like my school has changed to be one of the best performing in the country. King's Cross has experienced what so much of the capital has experienced – the facelift, the transformation to Good London, complete with Waitrose, complete with a champagne bar. The pornographic shops selling 'mags and poppers' have gone, their doors with the multicoloured plastic fly screens you more often see protecting butchers' shops – not, here, to keep out prying insects but to keep out prying eyes – replaced with the bright: Starbucks and Five Guys, Leon and Nando's, craft ale pubs, ersatz individualism and delicatessens selling bread at £5 a loaf, sourdough with pedigree certificates. Now it is all concrete and glass, steel-clad offices for Google and the chasers of artificial intelligence. Now it is all executive apartments, starting price £1 million, sitting, like nouveau guests at a manor house party, around the newly resplendent St Pancras Hotel, the Victorian Gothic urban cruise liner, ready for voyage on the edge of the Euston Road. Built in 1868 when the world's maps were painted pink right down to the bottom of Africa, the empire dabbling its toes in the Cape of Good Hope and the Southern Atlantic. Now, all that pink has gone.

I have a beer. Andy has water. They cost more than someone on the minimum wage earns in an hour. We talk of the 'corridors' at our old school, laughing as we reminisce, the passing of the years rendering all those historic pains and disjunctures with a patina of healing time. Wounds long forgotten, comedy acting as the curative. There were three corridors which children congregated along at lunchtime, itself an assault course as too many people tried to buy bad food in too short a timeframe. The black corridor, the white corridor and the Asian corridor. And, each lunchtime, groups of boys on the corridors would fight, usually black against white, until there was a break in hostilities, and black and white would put aside their differences and decide to rough up the Asians, who were often working, Andy mentioned in passing. Academic stuff.

He reminds me of a moment at school I had long forgotten. 'You used to try and trip up the Asian kids on that corridor, where there were the fights.' This was showing-off Kamal, make a noise, be noticed. Showing off to the cool, black kids, pretending a little to be one of them. Just like writing that piece of graffiti on the front of my exercise book was an offer to the white kids. But still making sure, despite all that misplaced bravado, that after school I was with my Asian friends – friends who invited me round for food and cups of tea, their parents welcoming me with smiles and jokes – trying to understand why their homework was so much better than mine.

A jealousy was, Andy said, how he first felt it. White people had all this history, kings and queens, pomp and pageantry, inventors of the modern world, the iron and steel that built King's Cross, the medicine at the nearby ear, nose and throat hospital, the science and art and culture resplendent in the museums on Exhibition Road – these are your forefathers. Me, Andy? Slavery. 'That's you in history.' Nothing else until

Dr Martin Luther King Jr and a story about America. And slowly you lose that very simple and powerful weapon which can take you through so many of those challenges of life and make the difference between success and its often too close sibling, failure, or, maybe more accurately, not achieving your true potential. And that weapon is confidence. Andy laughs, but it is not the laugh of the school room, the Smiler laugh. This is a 'well, there you go' laugh. I look at my beer glass. There are a couple of mouthfuls of drink left at the bottom.

I am not Andy or Steve. But I am affected by what affected Andy and Steve. The most important thing, here, is colour. That brings the solidarity of experience, even if those experiences are different, not as rough for me, not as brutal. The mixed-race child is Janus, facing into the 'disgusting system' and held by it. And also facing the Elysian Fields, the link to the country that invented everything. Part slave, part conqueror. Part rootless, part rooted, tracing a family tree deep into Britain's history, my family, the farmers from Yorkshire, as well as the wealthy from Omdurman. Part victim ('Go home, jungle bunny'), part perpetrator ('Keep Britain Tidy, Kick Out Pakis'). Part confident that I could be what I wanted to be, part questioning, why was I made to feel different, what did that mean for who I was. Should I, maybe, just be a car mechanic?

Andy only knew one of his grandparents – quite normal, he said, for people from the Caribbean. Slavery was recent in his history, so it was not a lack of a family tree that held him back, it was that someone had chopped his family tree up. No grand grave marks where his relatives are buried. No official record in a country obsessed by official records. His parents didn't go to parents' evenings, either working or exhausted or frankly so far off understanding how this British schools system worked, they simply didn't know how to engage. My mother went to parents' evenings all right. Every single one of them. I never heard the end of it.

'Slavery was a weapon for other children. Something to use in the playground. I felt inferior. We all did,' Andy said.

Yes, we all did. Even those of us who didn't have all the pain of that experience. But could relate to it. Enough of it, frankly.

Andy's home was near the school; you caught the E1 bus to get there, sitting on the top deck in a fog of cigarette smoke because only uncool – and healthier – people sat downstairs. There was one guaranteed good night of the week in West Ealing: Sunday, when National Front supporters selling newspapers outside the parades of shops – pint of milk 23p, *Daily Mirror* 18p – would be confronted by young black people up for a battle. A bit of a rumble. Andy remembers it was Sunday night, because that was the night *Roots* was on TV, a series about slavery that became a phenomenon in America and was watched by 130 million people – 100 million tuning in for the two-hour finale. Only the last episode of *M*A*S*H* and the great reveal – Who Shot JR? – in *Dallas* were more popular episodes of American television dramas. More than 80 per cent of households with a television in America tuned into the series at some point during its eight-episode run, broadcast on eight consecutive nights so that, if it was a flop as some television executives feared, the pain would soon be over. People organised television sets at parties to ensure guests would turn up. Businesses lost trade as customers stayed at home.

Everyone who is not white remembers *Roots*. And a lot of white people remember it as well. In the UK, more than 19 million tuned in, *Coronation Street*-type figures. You watched it, thrilled by the story of black people ruined by white people, the great 'face of adversity' morality play, pitched from the other side, the side not reflected in the history books, not slaves as victims but slaves as people who could and would fight back. When you were a young, brown boy whose experience of black people on television was that bloke who read the news, you did not care that the critics attacked the series as historically simplistic, caricatured and 'puerile'. What I loved was a story, this story that was not the usual stuff of family viewing schedules. The BBC bought the rights and broadcast the first part of the series over an Easter weekend and then on the following three Sundays. It took off. Not just in its viewing figures, but also for what it did for the people who watched it. What it did for Andy. And me. 'You knew when *Roots* had finished,' Andy said. 'All the black kids would come out of their houses and look for the skinheads to fight. ' "This one is for Kunta Kinte!" Whack.'

It was the same in Detroit where young black people ('toughs' as they were described by that week's edition of *Time* magazine) chanting 'Roots, Roots, Roots' took on the white pupils at one of the local high schools. The underdog fighting back, the traditional fairy tale repainted in literal black and white.

Roots effects rippled outwards. They were ripples that affected an eleven-year-old boy called Ian Roberts, who decided as he watched black actors bring to life Kinte, Chicken George and Kizzy that he would trace his ancestry, back to Africa and a bit of pride. Ian Roberts is now better known as Kwame Kwei-Armah, the actor and director. 'What made *Roots* so difficult for many people with Caribbean heritage was that it confronted them with the fact that their families originally came from Africa,' he said in a piece written in 2007. 'Growing up in West London, Africa was something you saw in Tarzan movies where savages were beaten up by our white hero. We felt no kinship with Africa.' It affected the theologian, Dr Robert Beckford, who said that watching *Roots* 'became more important than church'. It affected Doreen Lawrence, the mother of Stephen Lawrence, who said that going to work after a night watching a dramatisation of the horrors of a slave life 'you looked at people completely different, you'd begin to have a mistrust of white people and that took a long time to go, we were completely shocked'. Lenny Henry's mother 'called all the black people she knew' to talk about the series. 'I remember going to school on the Monday and people somehow didn't mess with you that day because all the black kids had this look in their eyes that said you better back off.' In America, *Time* magazine quoted Clifton Jones, a sociologist at Howard University, Washington DC: 'To see the spirit with which their much-maligned ancestors survived slavery is a great corrective to any lingering inferiority that blacks feel.' He put *Roots* on a par with the Black is Beautiful movement of the 1960s. As *Roots* reached its finale, Kizzy told her son, Chicken George, about Sam, her lover, and why she couldn't marry him: 'Nobody ever told him where he come from. So he didn't have a dream of where he ought to be goin'.'

Andy finishes his water and I finish my beer. We pledge to keep in touch and Andy says he will email me examples of 'good black history' that he has found out about since leaving school. Material that has made him rethink his school life and wonder what might have been.

'So, what is your background anyway?' Andy says as we shake hands outside. 'I never did know where you fitted in.'

The world is round. This is a headache for map-makers who need to produce representations that are flat, either on paper or on screen. In the sixteenth century, a Flemish cartographer, Gerardus Mercator, produced a representation of the world which we all recognise today. It later became known as the Mercator Projection and is still the staple of classroom walls and Google searches.

The Mercator Projection has a problem – as do all maps. It is a problem of distortion, created by moving from a three-dimensional sphere to a two-dimensional surface. Imagine a beach ball with a global map on it. If you cut it around its diameter and then try and lay it flat in two pieces next to each other, you can't without stretching and pulling and squeezing the plastic. The countries on the globe change shape, flat on the floor – perspectives alter, straight lines bend. You have to make decisions on which bits to expand and which bits to squeeze, which bits look big, and which smaller. There are choices to be made about how you want it – the world, your map – to look. And that confers power.

As well as explaining the world to a curious audience, Gerardus Mercator's map had to be of practical use so that his royal sponsor, Duke Wilhelm of Cleve, could see the value, as well as the beauty, in it. Its parallel lines of longitude and latitude had one slam-dunk application. They allowed navigators, travelling the world in wooden boats with brass compasses and the fickle stars to guide them, to reliably plot north and south axes and therefore sail to places – and trade – in the knowledge that at least the direction was correct. The towering seas could still kill them, but the fog of where they were was less thick.

Those vital, straight lines on a flat surface had one marked result, particularly when Europe was put – slap! bang! – in the middle of the world. As it would be, understandably, in 1569 by a cartographer schooled in that continent's grand seats of learning. It exaggerated the size of northern hemisphere countries and reduced the size of land masses closer to the equator. Europe looked bigger. Africa, China, South America looked smaller. The 'Greenland problem' – as it became known – was stark; on the Mercator Projection, Greenland looks larger than China, although it is a quarter of the size. Europe looks the same size as South America, a continent almost twice as big. The Soviet Union, as it still was, just, during my school days, looked twice the size of Africa, a continent nearly 3 million square miles larger. I used to receive incredulous looks from school friends if I insisted that the United Kingdom would fit into Sudan ten times. Yes, even including Northern Ireland. Size of country of homeland could confer some bragging rights in the playground, particularly if your country was no good at cricket, football or seemingly any of the important things in the world.

In the 1970s a German historian and cartographer, Dr Arno Peters, published a new world map which was 'area correct', building on the work a century earlier of the Reverend James Gall, a Scot and expert in mapping the stars. It became known as the Gall–Peters Projection and there was Africa, huge and in the middle, with Britain, Germany, France pushed up towards the top, less prominent, less visible. South America had its rightful place, in terms of size, twice as large as Europe. Greenland shrank. Yes, this new map had its own distortions, elongating countries on the equator, messing with shape, but it made more than a cartographer's point. It made a point about pride. 'History will be kind to me, for I intend to write it,' Sir Winston Churchill said. Dr Arno Peters had done the same for the geodesy of the Third World, as our geography teacher used to call countries that in those days didn't have a McDonald's. When you've always looked at the world in one way – the way you were shown it – changing viewpoints can help.

I remember my mother proudly showing me the Gall–Peters Projection when it was first produced in Britain in the 1980s. Just to give her son another tool in the box marked 'managing the trials of life'. It became a totem for those of us who liked to imagine we could strike small blows against the establishment view, so famous there is a joke about it in that great liberal depository, the television series, *The West Wing*. 'You're telling me that Germany isn't where we think it is?' a baffled Josh Lyman, chief of staff to President Josiah Bartlet, asks the Organisation of Cartographers for Social Equality (sadly fictitious). Yes, the victorious might have the first go at defining our image of the world – with a large Britain and dominant Europe – but we can take another look. I hadn't really thought that much about the Gall–Peters Projection, until Andy Sampson mentioned it more than thirty years later. No one had shown him the map. He had found it on YouTube. It was the first link he sent me by email.

I support Liverpool Football Club. I live nowhere near Liverpool and never have done. None of my family come from anywhere near Liverpool and I am not sure many of them have ever been there. At the age of ten I cried when 'we' lost in the FA Cup Final to the arch-enemy, Manchester United. Jimmy Greenhoff scored their winner, a deflected shot looping off him into the back of the net, beyond Ray Clemence. That was a bad day.

Football is important for tribal identity. We might all be different colours, different classes, but sport creates a bond where, at least for a time, such differences are less important than the other 'other' of this ninety minutes. The other team. What's the fastest way to unite disparate groups? Find them a common enemy.

Liverpool were my team for the same reason they were the team for a lot of young, non-white kids, wherever they came from. 'Why' needs to be explained backwards, temporally at least. Let's start in the near past, 2015, and a story from France.

'We're racist, we're racist and that's the way we like it.' The Chelsea fans are on their way to watch a match against Paris St-Germain. The metro train in Paris is more crowded than usual as thousands of supporters make their way to Porte de St-Cloud station on Line 9, ready for kick off. It is the evening rush hour. Souleymane Sylla is a salesman in the French capital, making his way home to see his four children, as he does every working day. He has a leather bag slung over his shoulder, a dark coat. It is cold, February. He walks to the centre of the train, which is crowded, maybe a little more than usual. But there is room. He is pushed back, back onto the platform, by someone on the carriage, a man, white with a dark jacket. 'Chelsea, Chelsea, Chelsea', chanting fills the air. The carriage is hot, there is the smell of alcohol – a beery, burping, tannin texture to the air. This sea of faces is recognisable to anyone who has been to a football match; expressions angry, fixed, ready to take up arms. Standard-issue short haircuts, jeans, the atmosphere heavy with suggestion, aggressive suggestion. Men who need to show other men that they are not to be messed with. If you want trouble, then, boy, are we ready. Even if, underneath, who knows what soup of fears afflicts each and every one of them. The external shell here is all that matters. Defiant eyes. Jaws pushed outwards. Sylla tries again. The push back this time is more forceful and Sylla nearly loses his footing. 'We're racist, *la, la, la, la, laaaaa.*' A third time. Push. '*La, la, la, la, laaaaaa.*'

And that might have been that – just another incident on a city train around the time of a football match. Except that a fellow traveller, Paul Nolan, also on his way home like Sylla, filmed it – shakily, nervous – on his phone and sent it to a newspaper in London. The footage made it onto the television bulletins and I watched it, over and over again. 'It was very crowded, the train stopped and it was clear there was some trouble, some people shouting, and it was clear these were English people,' Nolan wrote. 'I was ashamed of their behaviour, as a fellow Brit.'

Four men were tried and found guilty of racist violence. They were banned from football matches for five years (Chelsea Football Club banned them for life, saying their behaviour was 'abhorrent') and given suspended prison sentences of between six and twelve months. They denied racist behaviour, one saying that the first time he realised that Sylla 'was black' was when he saw the video footage played back to him. Two boarding-school friends gave glowing character references.

'Not only am I humiliated, but most people with black skin feel humiliated,' Sylla said after the case finished. That hot flush, singled out for what you look like rather than who you are, not in your control, going about your own business when others want to make you their business.

Before it was knocked down and rebuilt, complete with shiny new offices, flats and a hotel, I only went to the old Shed once – Chelsea's famous stand where the most diehard fans would mass and sing their hearts out to each other and to the team in front of them. A father of a friend was a season-ticket holder and Chelsea were our local, big club. I don't remember who played. I don't remember the score. All I really remember was fear; abuse and chants, the smell of alcohol and men, white men, with fixed faces, ready to take up arms. If you want trouble, then, boy, are we ready. In the 1970s fans whooped and grunted like gorillas when a black player was on the ball. In the 1980s one image encapsulated modernity and ancient attacks on 'otherness', on the enemy, the different tribe, in one shutter click: John Barnes, black, mercurial, brilliant – almost Brazilian in his footballing elegance – back-heeling a banana off the pitch during a match between Liverpool and Everton. A banana thrown by someone in the stands, as they regularly were when black players were on the pitch. 'Here, have that, you black bastard.'

Ron Shillingford, the black sports writer, has been a Chelsea fan since 1968. On the Shed they had their own song for him: 'Oh Crombie Ron is colourful, Oh Crombie Ron is colourful. He's a coon, he's a wog, he's a nigger. Oh Crombie Ron is colourful.'

What was Shillingford meant to do with that?

He did indeed wear a Crombie to matches – over a Ben Sherman shirt and Sta Press trousers, the outer attire of the average skinhead – because he was cold. I think skinheads thought such coats vaguely military, with oxblood Dr Martens and yellow laces for effect. Shillingford was braver than me, who, after that one experience of the Shed, sat at home watching football on the television where it was much safer and no one had a special song for Kamal Ahmed about my coat or the colour of my skin.

And that's how I ended up becoming a Liverpool supporter, a Plastic Scouser, as my London friends who do actually support Chelsea and Arsenal and Spurs, like to describe me: a glory hunter, not a real fan. But, if time is anything to go by, at least I'm a proper Plastic Scouser who has supported Liverpool for over forty years because if you watched football on television in the 1970s the only live club matches were the FA Cup Final and some European Championship games. And then you had the recorded highlights of the league games on the weekend's 'must never miss, ever, ever, ever' programmes: *The Big Match* with Brian Moore (ITV, rush of excitement when the theme tune started) and *Match of the Day* (BBC, rush of excitement when the theme tune started) with Jimmy Hill, David Coleman and Des Lynam, whom I felt I knew better than my own father. And in the 1970s and '80s only one team – to my young mind – played beautiful, romantic, artistic football and dominated the sport, and that was Liverpool.

I remember once writing on my exercise book (maybe even that same exercise book stained by 'Keep Britain Tidy, Kick Out

Pakis') 'Howard Gayle: Black Magic in the Box', after Gayle, not a legend at Liverpool of the status of Kenny Dalglish or Steve Heighway or Kevin Keegan, had played a magnificent sixty-one minutes against Bayern Munich in the European Cup of 1981. That was the season Liverpool – 'we' – went on to win the trophy for the third time in five years. A sixty-one minutes so good, his autobiography is named after it. Of that banana incident when John Barnes tried an elegant back-heel, Gayle said he would have picked it up and 'thrown it straight back'. Gayle was a black football player who played for my team. That would do me.

Sadiq Khan, the London mayor, knows how I feel. And probably how a lot of non-white people felt growing up in the 1970s and '80s when the National Front saw football Saturday as one of their best recruiting days. 'My first experiences of football were two of my brothers going to Stamford Bridge to watch Chelsea and being racially abused in the Shed, chased away by the National Front wearing Dr Martens and green bomber jackets,' he said. 'Back then it wasn't safe for somebody looking like me to go onto the terraces so in the 1980s I'd watch my football on TV, on *Match of the Day* and the other programmes, and I became a Liverpool fan because they were playing such great football at the time and winning.'

Andy has a similar memory: 'I was a Liverpool fan and still am today. I wish Chelsea, West Ham and Millwall bad luck in their games as I have never forgotten them being the most racist clubs. Chants of "There's no black in the Union Jack, so go back" is why I find it hard to claim those flags, or the St George's Cross, as being for me.'

People sometimes ask me why I support Liverpool, coming from 210 miles south, from Ealing, not known as a key Scouser enclave. 'It's complicated.'

My mother has never spoken much about what it was like bringing up a brown child in a white world. She was more worried about being a single mother, proving to her family that she could cope with what life had served up. But if you were going to do it anywhere, mixed-up London was about as good as it was going to get. Fewer looks on the bus.

This wasn't just about geography. There was something else that gave Mum and me an advantage. That peculiar British advantage. What people considered to be our 'class'.

> As soon as I came here, the people next door saw I'd got coloured children and they put a fence up, after that they were alright and some other neighbour came on and said that at first when they saw the coloured children, they thought they'd get some right dirty people in this house.

Mrs Jagger lived in Huddersfield in the 1960s. She might never have come to the notice of the wider world until she was contacted in 1965 for a study funded by the Joseph Rowntree Foundation into 'fatherless families'. Joseph Rowntree was a businessman who made chocolates, a Quaker who preached peace and a social campaigner who in 1904 launched the charitable organisation that bears his name. Its purpose was to investigate, and attempt to tackle, the causes of poverty. Dennis Marsden, the son of a Methodist mill worker and eminent sociologist, was tasked with researching the first-hand experiences of single mothers – more commonly neatly boxed up as either sinners, scroungers or saints. It wasn't a study of ethnicity, but of the women asked if they would like to take part by the National Assistance Board (one criterion for the research was that the women had to be on state benefits), just under 10 per cent had children who were mixed-race. Mrs Jagger, who had a 'West Indian boyfriend' and three children, was one of them.

> If you've got coloured children, they'll class you as if you were a prostitute. In shops sometimes, when you go in and you'll see the salesgirls all dolled up, well, they look at you as if you were going to pinch summat, and I don't like them to do that because I've been as good as them, and then on the bus sometimes, you get these old women looking at you from head to foot, but they stop looking when I start looking back at them, and then one woman was walking past me on the bus, and I heard her say 'Disgusting'.

And there's something I realise as I am reading the study's findings and talking to my mother about attitudes 'then' and attitudes 'now', reading the account of Mrs Whiteman who, like Mrs Jagger, was asked about her experiences of growing up with a mixed-race child in the 1960s, questioned by a benefits official.

> She said: 'Don't come here with your coloured children and your half-caste children. You go back where you belong. What will the children think when they grow up and their brother's half-caste?' They say at the National Assistance Board we shouldn't go out with coloured men, we should go out with our own.

Mum and I had the protection of something, not quite money because we didn't have much; more of 'social capital', of living in a style that was in no way glamorous but was also not exaggerated, spiced up, by that extra prejudice, class, or brought into sharper focus by poverty. I should 'check my privilege' when commenting on the world around me, understanding that my personal experience is not everyone's personal experience.

Just as Andy's mother and father never went to parents' evenings, so Mrs Jagger and Mrs Whiteman experienced a different world from my mother. Provincial where my mother lived in the world of the metropolitan. We shopped at John Lewis. The sofa and armchair in our small front room were from Liberty. A good night out for Mum was at the Royal Opera House, in the cheap seats in the gods, to see her favourites – once queueing outside the artists' entrance in the 1970s to try and grab a signature from Plácido Domingo for the cover of her vinyl record. While I was in the bath as a little boy, Mum would produce flashcards with words like 'happy' and 'book' in big clear letters. 'What does that say?' she would ask, teacher voice. When I didn't get the word right she would bring down her hand, splash, on the water. 'No!' Those flashcards were scary. But when I started school I could read better than most.

In April 2010 the equality think tank, the Runnymede Trust, researched again the question of single mothers and this time Dr Chamion Caballero and Professor Rosalind Edwards did factor in ethnic background. The names are now first names, twenty-first-century names; the recollections are not as harsh, maybe, as decades earlier. But a sentiment remains, a sentiment that runs deep in Britain, whether it was in the 1970s or today.

Chloe: 'I think there's a stereotype around white women with black children. And we are perceived to be a bit rough, a bit common, a bit like we don't care who we sleep with, even if they are black! I think that people always expect your child to be behaving badly when you have a white parent with a black child because you're a bit loose and feckless.'

Lucy: 'Society does portray such a bad image … that basically you're a slag who went out one night and went with a black man because he had a big willy!'

Zoe: 'Being white with a mixed-race child, I am judged. I feel like I am judged.'

Are we shaking off the fear of the other? Would Chloe or Lucy or Zoe hear, any more, 'that's disgusting' on the bus? Should we give thanks that no one, mainstream, would now argue as Marie Stopes did a short ninety years ago that 'half-castes' should be sterilised? So that, according to a 1934 interview in *Australian Women's Weekly* with the lauded pioneer of the right to birth control, 'painlessly and in no way interfering with the individual's life, the unhappy fate of he who is neither black nor white is prevented from being passed on to yet more unborn babes'? The eugenics movement had many advocates, from John Maynard Keynes to George Bernard Shaw to William Beveridge. The world has suffered Adolf Hitler since then and the movement sits in disgrace. But, for someone who is mixed-race, those names, that recent history, are still close enough. In 2008 the Royal Mail put Ms Stopes on a stamp as a 'family planning pioneer'. The same year as they also honoured the civil rights campaigner of the 1950s, Claudia Jones, seen by many as the 'mother of the Notting Hill Carnival'.

Are we shaking off the fear of the other? Marie Stopes wanted me stopped. That, truly, messes with your head.

If you had a £1 note in the 1980s you bought a record, a vinyl one, flicking through the hundreds of singles in the local shop to find the right one, rushing home to play it at a sound level one notch below 'Mum shouting up the stairs that it was disturbing *The Archers*' level. I had lots of records because I saved up lots of £1 notes from my paper round and, later, from driving a white van around the home counties delivering computer parts. I had a silver Aiwa hi-fi stacking system that had graphic equalisers and a twin-deck cassette player as if I was some sort of budding DJ. It was a step up from Mum's era. All they had was treble and bass.

Music was a good thing because it was a mixed thing. And it was a rare thing because it actually spoke about being a mixed thing all those years ago. It was more than rare, it was unique. Marie Stopes might have wanted me stopped, but Pauline Black and Neville Staple and Terry Hall were willing to put me on the map and sing about stuff that I understood. Welcome to Two Tone.

'Black, white, unite – don't fight.'

Pauline Black was the lead singer of The Selecter. Like Cathy Tyson, all of us mixed-race kids zeroed in on her because she was one of the gang, the secret club. She didn't worry too much about being called 'jungle bunny', and I'm not sure she fought the kids who called her names. As a child, to her it seemed a silly insult. As anyone who had watched Desmond Morris's *Zoo Time* programme on the television knew, she said, rabbits didn't live in jungles, they lived in fields in Britain, under hedges. So, what, are you saying a) you don't know where rabbits live? Or b) that I live in Britain? Which I do, so there. Black had a golliwog as a favourite toy, given to her by an aunt who was white. I also had a golliwog. Its eyes fell off.

There are lots of interesting things to know about Pauline Black. She changed her name by deed poll from Vickers to the literal descriptor 'Black' at the age of twenty-six. It was an identity thing. She was brought up by her adoptive white parents in Romford, Essex, in the 1950s, the only black child in a family where racist jokes were common and it was drummed into her that she had better be careful about ever going out with 'black men', what with their dangerous ways and propensity for infidelity. In her thirties she found out about her birth parents – her Nigerian father died a year before she tried to make contact – and met her Anglo-Jewish mother who was living in Australia. The experience made her feel 'whole again'.

But, to me, a teenager slowly building a sense of self, Pauline Black was interesting, no, important, because of her music. The Selecter were a new model music group in a new model genre that was making the clubs of first the Midlands, and then all over Britain, jump up and down in chaotic, sweaty abandon. Even Ealing got the groove.

Two Tone was a bringing together of Jamaican ska and reggae with an added slick of punk. It was, literally, mixed-race music. The Selecter had Pauline (a woman in an industry of blokes), five other black artists and one white guy. Their home was Coventry. Which was also the home of the Specials of Staple and Hall which joined them on the 2 Tone label I fell in love with, complete with the chequerboard motif and Walt Jabsco logo, a smokingly hip dude rendered in graphical black and white with pork-pie hat, dark glasses and sharp-tailored suit, white shirt, narrow black tie, white socks, black loafers. I bought pair after pair of white, towelling socks to wear with my black tassel slip-ons around the suburban streets I called home, edgy as a circle.

On stage, Two Tone stole the skinheads' paraphernalia from right under their angry noses and made it their own – Fred Perry T-shirts, red braces, crew cuts, Sta Press trousers. The Beat came from Birmingham, Madness from London. We all followed, dancing madly, arms flailing at parties to 'Too Much Too Young' ('Keep a generation GAP, try wearing a CAP'); here at last, something cool for Brown People – Rude Boys and Rude Girls who were sending a message. 'Stop your messin' around'. 'Better think of your future'. 'Time you straightened right out'. Because of course, when black and white people came together, that's where I was.

I had a Harrington jacket with checked red lining. My drawers groaned with Fred Perrys – white, black, yellow, pale blue – which my mum cleaned and carefully ironed so you could see the crease in the short sleeve. I listened over and over again to 'Do Nothing', 'Tears of a Clown', 'Man at C&A', 'Blank Expression', carefully shielding my mother from the lyrics of 'Rat Race' which shouted that education was a waste of time ('I got one art O level, it did nothing for me'), because, you know, being a revolutionary had its limits. The Specials' 'Ghost Town' spoke of urban decay as the television news bulletins were full of fires in Toxteth, Bristol, Handsworth, Moss Side, Brixton, police vans pelted with missiles; mass unemployment, desperation. 'Ghost Town' was resplendent with diminished chords ('The devil's chord', as Jerry Dammers, the driving force behind Two Tone, described it), wailing vocals, dystopia. This was the 1980s rendered in vinyl.

I had badges celebrating Walt, 'Three Minute Hero', 'Mirror in the Bathroom'. I wore them proudly everywhere I went, even when I was shoved into puddles by the white kids and stood, soaked, carefully picking those badges out of the brown, filthy water, still convinced that I had discovered the blueprint for a new, integrated Britain; that belief, just like my mother in the 1960s, that all that was necessary was a well-honed argument, a bit of shared experience, some minor chords and everyone who was not like us would see that they had been wrong all along.

When some in the crowd performed *Sieg Heil* salutes at Two Tone concerts, Pauline Black thought the power of persuasion would 'show them the error of their ways'. 'Rather naïve', she admitted in an interview thirty years later. Red Saunders, rock photographer, campaigner, and one of the first to conceive of the idea of Rock Against Racism, summed up the feeling as we jumped and choroused towards what we imagined was a brighter future. 'There were very few black and white musicians playing together,' he said. 'Suddenly, there were the Specials. I thought, fuck me, this is job done.'

Eric Clapton might have been saying on stage at a concert in Birmingham that 'Enoch was right' and 'I think we should send them back' – them being 'the wogs'. (Saunders wrote to the *New Musical Express* and *Sounds* after the gig at the local Odeon in 1976: 'Come on Eric. Own up. Half your music is black. You're rock music's biggest colonist.')

David Bowie might have been telling *Playboy*, 'Britain is ready for a fascist leader'. (Later putting his statements 'Adolf Hitler was one of the first rock stars' and 'You've got to have an extreme right front come up and sweep everything off its feet and tidy everything up' down to his cocaine-wrecked state living as the Thin White Duke, much as Clapton put his 'fascistic' comments down to drink and drugs.)

We had this.

(And our lyrics were better.)

Two Tone didn't last coherently for very long. Dammers, a political fighter and musician, was a juggler of ideas and the bands all had their own, a combustible mix. For the Specials, always to me the first among equals, there were fights on stage with fans, smashed keyboards, copious drinking, arguments about whether 'muzak' licks really were necessary on the *More Specials* album (their second and last that I queued up to buy at the Our Price record store on Ealing Broadway). Maybe the people involved, wrestling each other to the floor over musical differences, didn't understand how important they were, how desperate the fans were for One More Tune.

Because they taught Britain a lesson. Taught Britain that there are ways to gain that confidence, that solidarity. Dance together. Sing together. The mood may not last long, you may all be linking arms and simply talking to the converted, it may just be a way of making a lot of people feel a bit better. But it is no less important for that, no less important in a world where the slights were – are – ready to pounce at any moment. Black described it as 'exhausting', learning 'how to manoeuvre through the many micro-aggressions which are keenly felt on a daily basis'. That I felt on a daily basis. In a world where I wished my name, sometimes, was Neil, and my Indian friends called themselves Tony and Ian rather than try and explain what their actual first names were – Two Tone was an antidote.

Two Tone was our safe space.

Jumping around late into the night, high on R. White's lemonade and small, warm cans of Heineken, believing that tomorrow belonged to us.

I have never had a serious, long-term relationship with a woman who is not white.

A friend, who has a similar history, said it was all about our screwed-up notion of status.

I said it was coincidence.

5

Happy face

Go on the 'b' of the bang.

BANG! The crowd releases a roar.

'This time they GO. Christie got a good one, also going well is Dennis Mitchell ... and Fredericks ... and Christie COMES STORMING THROUGH and it's LINFORD CHRISTIE ... the British captain is Olympic Champion, the GREATEST PRIZE IN BRITISH SPORT...'

It took 9.96 seconds for Linford Christie to win the Olympic 100 metres final at the Barcelona Games of 1992.

Go on the 'b' of the bang.

BANG! The roar. Again.

'They get away first time! Christie got a good one ... Cason going well as well ... and it's Christie and Cason ... with Cason on the nearside and CHRISTIE COMES THROUGH ... TO BECOME CHAMPION OF THE WORLD...'

It took 9.87 seconds for Linford Christie to win the World Championship 100 metres final in Stuttgart a year later. The time was one one-hundreth of a second outside the world record. Less than the time it takes to blink.

I watched the Olympic race – commentator David Coleman – on a flickering, black-and-white portable television on a kitchen sideboard. I lived in Scotland where I had gone for love and work. My girlfriend was from the Ayrshire coast. We had met at college in London and agreed that whoever found a job first, we would go there to live. I think she always knew it would be her, she was more successful and more focused, better, simply, than me. So we ended up in Glasgow and here we were, at a friend's flat in Edinburgh, on a night that was more important for me than it was for the other people in the room.

I felt more nervous than Christie looked. He was serene, an engine of power. His eyes did not blink, just stared, absolute, hooded, down the lane in front of him – 1.22 metres wide and 100 metres long, a tunnel of twitching muscle, owned by those who are fleet of foot, kinetic energy bouncing through those light, gossamer trainers, neck tense, straining, blood thick in the veins, heart engorged, pumping oxygen, oxygen, to propel fourteen stones and six foot two inches of human body, breath held for the explosion of the start, the crowd's clamouring noise, time passing in slowed-down motion, like that moment before a car crash, the world touching on the brake, 1 second ... 2 seconds ... 3 seconds ..., no one ahead of you, just the breathing, the breathing and the pop, pop, pop of seven other black men's shoes on the track, behind you, getting closer, 4 seconds ... 5 seconds ... 6 seconds, hitting top speed, top cadence, are they getting closer? No, maybe further away, no matter, that line, that line must come, the finish, run through the line, and win and put your fist in the air, one finger extended, Number 1.

He won. Dammit. He won. The man who arrived in Britain from Jamaica the year I was born and ran for the same running club I did next to Wormwood Scrubs, west London – a prison where black people were over-represented in the cells. He won. In those 9.96 seconds of supreme physical effort Linford Christie embodied the start of something – the black meaning good decade. This, he, was the new Two Tone. The new start, the next 'here we go again'. The hope, the belief, the same fervent belief my mum had in the 1960s, I had in the 1980s dancing with abandon, that in a moment, a movement was launched that would change things for good. A new future that would soar, borne skywards on the updraughts of its own glory, a great hulking power of argument and obvious evidence, sweeping all before it. When Linford Christie ran through the line and raised his finger it meant much more than the gold disc they later hung around his neck. I had to turn away and look at the floor for a bit. I didn't want my friends to see the tears, ridiculous, in the corner of my eyes. He had won for all of us. The out-group.

Do you remember where you were when John F. Kennedy was assassinated, or Neil Armstrong first landed on the moon or Margaret Thatcher resigned or Princess Diana was killed or Prince died? I remember where I was when Linford Christie won Olympic first in Barcelona. I sat as close to that flickering television screen as I could, knowing this wasn't particularly the way I would have chosen to watch this most important of events. It was 7 p.m. and everyone was talking and messing around with the cooking. 'Ssshh, please, just for this,' I pleaded. They were all white people and not that interested in sport. But we – we, those of another colour – had our man, he was British, black, a bit angry. And bloody fast.

School and university were over. We had just started in the world of employment, that generation of Thatcher's children who had it instilled in them that if you worked hard the market would provide, reward you, whoever you were. My mother was the generation where the state provided, the great fixer after the horrors of war. We didn't need any of that, didn't want any favours or handouts (neglecting to remember that we were the last to leave university debt-free). Our merit, our talent, was going to allow us entry to any castle we cared to storm. Out of the way, old country, we are coming through. In athletics (CHAMPION OF THE wORLD), in music (Soul II Soul, the Young Disciples, Tricky, hip hop, trip hop – hell, white people even wanted to be black, Yo, Wigger!), in culture (the Africa Centre, Chris Ofili).

Between 1991 and 2011 the percentage of the population identifying themselves as 'white British' fell from 93 per cent to 80 per cent. The proportion identifying as 'non-white' grew from 7 per cent to 14 per cent, more than doubling from 3 million to 8 million people. The 'mixed' ethnic category – that's me, folks – doubled to over 1 million people a decade later, a trend that was certainly evident in the 1990s before a 'mixed' category was added to the census. This was it. The future was brown. We were an approaching wave, crashing over that privileged beach which, we thought, was protected by little more than a few flimsy deck chairs. This was going to be Our Decade.

Going on the 'b' of the bang summed it up, Linford Christie's comment that to be first in a race you didn't just launch yourself when the starting pistol went Bang, you launched yourself when the starting pistol uttered the first whisper of B. Go quick and hard and no one can beat you.

It became such a famous quote, Thomas Heatherwick designed a sculpture called *B of the Bang* for the Commonwealth

Games in Manchester in 2002. It was fifty-six metres tall with 180 large metal spikes, a steel firework reaching into the Mancunian sky. Heatherwick's team fabricated it in Sheffield. It was a thank you, in a way, to Christie, a person whose relationship with the country that was his home became a metaphor for Britain and race. He was a hero for many black people, a signal that the 1990s were going to be different, that we would all go on the 'b' of the bang and success would be ours.

Now, no one was wet enough to think that race as an issue was going to be washed away. We all knew the statistics about educational attainment and employment rates and wondered why there were so few non-white chief executives at Britain's biggest companies. Or any sort of executives. Or even senior managers. Christie himself was described by fellow athlete Derek Redmond as 'perfectly balanced, he's got a chip on both shoulders', there were comments about his 'lunchbox', the tetchy appearances on television, the clashes with that other Olympic hero, Sebastian Coe, cultured, middle class, white – the man who once accused Christie of making himself 'deliberately unintelligible to all but those who had a passing knowledge of jive'. Lord Coe opened the London Olympics 2012 as chair of the organising committee, smooth and confident, the man who delivered the successful games. Linford Christie was not at the ceremony, banned for a drugs offence he has always denied. Linford Christie does not have a peerage. Linford Christie does not have a knighthood.

'People say 100m is not that far. They should try running it. It's a long, long way.' Linford, I understood where you were coming from.

When I was young I was a reasonable runner. At school, the athletics coach would start me ten metres behind the other boys in the 100 metres to see if I could catch them, giving me a target rather than have me running out ahead. I never did sprint fast enough to reach their shoulders, however hard I tried. As my teenage years passed, I kept my 'reasonable' tag in the 100m, 200m and 400m and trained, twice a week, for Thames Valley Harriers, never quite good enough to make the team for the main events and asked to fill in for the 110 metres hurdles because no one practised that very much. I jumped over the barriers with all the grace of a newborn giraffe.

Linford Christie also ran for Thames Valley Harriers and sometimes we would see him, a rangy, slim guy, down by the start line, surrounded by the serious coaches, a sign that he was a serious runner. He was so proud of his GB tracksuit he would wear it to the shops in Shepherd's Bush ('How do you get to Shepherd's Bush? Up the shepherd's leg' was the playground joke). If I had been good enough I would have worn my GB tracksuit as well. What so few people understood about the 1990s and many non-white people was how bloody patriotic we were, given the chance. We were British and we were proud of it, and we weren't looking for reasons not to be. So, Christie wore his British uniform and what happened? A passing police officer wondered aloud what 'a nigger like you was doing in a tracksuit'. On some other everyday when Christie was hanging about, being black, he was arrested for that offence well known to any young non-white person of 'being in charge of a nice car whilst the wrong colour'. The police stopped him, convinced that a young black man driving a Ford XR2 was not the happy recipient of a Budget Rent-a-Car sponsorship deal but a thief.

When the police originally called him over 'to have a word' Christie thought they wanted his autograph.

So, what was the response of this supposedly chippy, thirty-two-year-old when he ran, that single finger in the air, through the 100 metres finish line in Barcelona and on, beyond the geography of that running track and into history? It was to find a Union flag in the crowd and drape it over his shoulders, speaking, in that one moment, to a million second-generation immigrants like me that this was our country, we were not guests, we were not a preventable evil, we had every right to reside where we were and that fear of other was no more legitimate than fear of UFOs – that other type of non-existent alien that H. G. Wells spoke of. On the podium receiving his medal Christie said the 'moment when they played God Save the Queen' was his proudest, representing his country.

And, Linford, it was one of mine. I know you held back on the emotion, not wanting endless clips of you in tears to be used in those Olympic best moment television rundowns, like they use those pictures of a crying Michael Johnson, the American 400m world-record holder who ran in gold Nikes. And I held back the tears as well because I was in Scotland crouched around a black-and-white television with people who were only watching you that night as a side event to the main show, which was a discussion about where we were going to go for supper. I loved that you carried the flag, a counterpoint to *There Ain't No Black in the Union Jack* – that night there was a big, black B in Britain. I loved it that when you were invited to Buckingham Palace that you 'felt the Queen knew who I was, and that was better than all the medals.' You were the team captain and more important than you can imagine.

And just as seeing you win meant pride, seeing you hurt distressed me as well. All the jokes about your 'lunchbox' and 'prize-winning bulging', having to explain – during that libel case on drug-taking that you won – to Mr Justice Popplewell (who asked with establishment bemusement 'what is Linford's lunchbox?') that it referred to your genitals and that trigger point for a thousand myths and fascinations, enthusiasm mixed with fear over black sexuality, and that nod to the age-old narrative of the 'other' being emotionally hot-blooded, the savage, thereby intellectually suspect, because brawn and brains don't mix. I watched you on the sporting programmes, surrounded by quizzical white men telling you 'no, no, I don't accept that...' when you protested that this joke of a hundred headlines was racist and stereotyped the black man. You, on your own under the hot lights, the thoughts hard to construct under the pressure of disbelief. The disbelief of those who haven't had to think overmuch about the political and sociological connotations of what was being said.

At work, not long ago, a colleague whom I like and get on with and is helpful and all those things you would expect from someone you see more often than most of your friends, came over to my desk to tell me a story. Other staff were sitting around chatting, and quietened to listen. It was one of those stories that starts off with a tone that suggests it is all going to end in praise, and you need to deploy your well-practised 'oh, that's so kind, really, but I'm not that good ...' – your very British response. My colleague spoke about a family lunch party he had attended at the weekend and a relative who would often see me on television and, apparently, found it mesmerising. I could hear an alarm bell, faint in the back of my consciousness.

Economics – which I cover for the BBC – is rarely described as mesmerising. 'When they look at you in your suit, they can really see that there's a massive, you know, cock ... down there!'

He laughed, looking around the office for approbation.

I sat in silence.

My colleagues sat in silence.

It is rare that I have nothing to say, that a situation is so profoundly off-piste you are simply not sure what to do with it. Like asking for a pen from the person sitting next to you and they hand you a grapefruit. In part the situation was so bizarre it was funny, funny for someone who is fortunate enough to hold a relatively senior position where he works. 'You are joking, right?', I could have responded. In part it was shocking – 'I'm sorry, what did you just say?', I could have responded. But I didn't say anything because in part, the major part and the part that is hardest, suddenly there I was again, a little boy suffering the flush of embarrassment, the 'other' who will never really be accepted in a country that is his home.

'I sit in my house minding my own business, and it is people like you who bother me that make me have to do all this,' Linford Christie said in that court case to clear his name.

Which about sums it up.

'Keep on movin'. Don't stop, like the hands of time. Click clock, find your own way to stay.'

A moment, this time in music. A soundtrack next to the race track. An album, as important as any 100-metre battle. Ten songs with names like Happiness, African Dance, Fairplay, Feeling Free, Back to Life, Keep on Movin'. Chords and poetry, beating out a rhythm, a tattoo marching towards a better future. The music of black – brown – meaning good.

And you have to thank Margaret Thatcher, Norman Tebbit and Britain's propensity for 'doing a foreigner', for the man behind it, the collective behind it. That group of musicians, hustlers, marketeers and pin-sharp groovers called Soul II Soul, led by Trevor Beresford Romeo. Now, that's a name to conjure with.

We eased out of the eighties in pain. Unemployment was high. Prices were up. Strikes were up. The miners fought the police. And I marched against the next nuclear holocaust with rainbow gloves and long shaggy hair. The economy was juddering, squealing, as it moved away from the traditional business of making things to the service business of selling things. Of making the consumer king and queen. Among this grubby mess, a new economy was born, an economy I and millions like me were to give thanks for. A shadow economy of cash-in-hand businesses as the 'Gis a job' generation sought any opportunity to earn, to keep hunger at bay and the bailiffs from the door. The trick was making money whilst remaining on benefits handed out by the government of £26 a week. Moonlighting was not just an American detective drama starring Cybill Shepherd and Bruce Willis.

This burgeoning grey economy tiptoeing on the borders of legality bothered David Cooksey, an Oxbridge-educated former venture capitalist working for the Centre for Policy Studies, a think tank full of right-wing intellectual vigour and the germination point for many government policies. His idea was to formalise the new mood of entrepreneurialism with what became the Enterprise Allowance Scheme. EAS recipients could earn an extra £40 a week and still claim benefits. Crucially for the government it encouraged the unofficially self-employed – the cash-in-hand brigade – to become officially self-employed. It is not clear whom Thatcher assumed she was helping with the policy, but Trevor Beresford Romeo from Hornsey, north London, was probably not high on her list.

Trevor ran a 'sound system', a collective term for what is, loosely, an uber-hip travelling disco. Complete with 'box boys' to carry the huge stack speakers, the selector to pick the tracks, the DJ who played the records and the MC who juiced up the crowd with his or her silky words, Trevor was making a name for himself as he plied his mix of underplayed, often US, songs around the reggae and soul clubs of the capital. And that name was Jazzie B and the Soul II Soul posse. If you produced a scatter map of where Jazzie B and his collective appeared, it would pretty much match the route of the Number 14 bus to Roehampton in south-west London, because that was the one that went near his house. He used to push his equipment to the bus stop in a shopping trolley.

Jazzie B applied for an EAS and was successful, as were a whole range of creatives, fashion designers, musicians, artists, white and black and any other colour you like. The thing about this grey economy was that it was multicoloured. It was meritocratic. If you could find customers you had a business. And people looking for a break, second-generation immigrants, alternatives; those who were different, other, flourished in a climate originally not built for them because, boy, when you are struggling at the margins and no one is set to give you a break, *you gotta do something*. Alan McGee, the anarchic founder of Creation Records ('the mission was not wanting to have a real job'), Alan Davies, the comedian ('what really saved me – even though I was a Leftie and a Labour voter and a CND person – was Thatcher's Enterprise Allowance Scheme'), Julian Dunkerton of the fashion label Superdry, Tracey Emin, and the visual artists Jane and Louise Wilson, all were beneficiaries. It was a most odd conjunction of interests: the wild world of the arts meets the civil-service grey suits. And it worked. Jazzie B described the privations, desperations, the rank battles of the 1980s – the battle to survive – as 'opening the door to the 90s', Our Decade. That's how I felt. We would have a happy face as the thumping bass made our dancing boots tremble. *Jouissance* was on our side, this was an eruption of real joy.

'It's our time, time today. The right time is here to stay. Stay in my life, my life always. Yellow is the colour of sun rays.'

The lesson? That individual endeavour was the way out of any situation. That the market will provide, if you give us – that other lot – a fair shot at it. 'Technically speaking, she [Thatcher] legitimised people like me,' Beresford Romeo said in an interview twenty-five years later. 'We set up a small business in an institutionally racist environment where it was difficult to get a job you wanted.'

And this one album became the hymnal to that endeavour, the effort that good people can make to better their position. *Club Classics Vol. One* by Soul II Soul became the soundtrack of my life, played at full volume (admittedly not a level to worry noise pollution officers) in my mother's Nissan Micra (light blue), which she lent me to drive my student detritus up to and down from Leeds University via an ever-drizzly M1 as this new decade of hope dawned. This collective, along with Young Disciples and the Brand New Heavies, were the new Two Tone, black and white people coming together to sing and dance and just bloody well cool their way to some kind of victory. Draw a line through the decade and you arrive in 2001 at Mike Skinner and the Streets with his rapping riffs on 'fit girls' and 20 Benson, a nod to the Specials. It was 1979 all over again.

The *Club Classics* album cover is brown, with a silhouetted Jazzie B dancing. One fist is loosely raised, the image redolent of the Black Power salute at the Mexico Olympics of 1968 by Tommie Smith and John Carlos, the 200 metres gold and bronze medal winners. The two were expelled from the games, Smith saying wearily: 'If I win I am an American, not a black American. But if I did something bad then they would say "a Negro". We are black and we are proud of being black.' Jazzie B was proud of being black. We all started to be proud of being other.

His hair on the cover of the album is in the 'Funki Dreds' style which became a marker of 1990s fashion. It was a nod both to Rastafarian dreadlocks (which Jazzie's mother, a firm Christian, would not allow in the house) and the shorter look of the soul boys. The designer behind the broader Funki Dreds brand, Derek Yates, also wanted to bring in the short back and sides of the 'trendy white crowd'. He could have also spoken of the trendy mixed-race crowd, people like me who never quite made it into reggae because we weren't black enough, with our skinny arses and all.

On that cover, Jazzie is wearing a waistcoat that could have come from Savile Row, but loosely, taking the W1 of central London to NW1 – messily trendy Camden Town where Soul II Soul had its 'headquarters' which also doubled as a shop. It was the establishment meeting the hip. He is wearing dark glasses. The Soul II Soul name is brought together inside two interlocking circles, the II captured in the middle of this harmonious Venn diagram. It is a very British take on being black, on bringing different groups together – the music, with that urgent, soulful, classic R&B drum rhythm, the words of optimism and the need for focus ('I'm on this mission to achieve'), the style that would engage a whole generation who, like me, went out and bought full-length black parkas and John Lennon spectacles.

And inside this album, oh, the songs. Caron Wheeler singing, her beautiful voice calling us all to arms, to keep on moving, don't stop. Like the Beatles and the Rolling Stones were to a young generation in the 1960s, Soul II Soul and their fellow travellers summed up the sense of a decade. But where the Beatles and the Rolling Stones, Bob Dylan and Lou Reed were about the freedoms of young white people, making their way in a decade that was not so much a time as a point of view, they rarely spoke to or for people like me. The resonances were more distant. Popular culture, a phrase minted in the 1960s to denote a certain type of modern, young person, morphed in this later moment, this 1990s moment, into a popular culture I could finally understand. Soul II Soul were the vanguard for a new approach to race and Britain in the 1990s. 'Collective' was used advisedly. Work together, be optimistic. Trevor Nelson, the DJ and friend of Jazzie B, said it was the start of real multiculturalism.

This wasn't about seeing and respecting and tolerating other cultures in a big mixed-up pot. This was about creating a new way, not asking for permission to be here, but building our own narrative. Black, British, diverse and proud. Just dig out that video once more, the one they played on *Top of the Pops* when 'Back to Life' (track nine of *Club Classics*) made it to Number 1 and tell me it doesn't make you feel happy. Go on, do it. Put this book down ...

You see?

After the 1980s, we were entering a new era, but it wasn't the 'Dawning of a New Era' the Specials had sung about in 1979, all angry and demanding about a society fraying at the seams; this was an era of, as Jazzie B would put it, 'positivity'. His business was the Funki Dreds, a whole brand, a mix of reggae, soul and hip hop which produced its own distinctive drum and bass foundation. And Jazzie's rap, with a voice low like an old-school Southern preacher, was a Paul Robeson for a new generation.

'Well it's like dreaming of your goals, ambitions and feeling free. I'm on this mission to achieve. Achieve what? What's in your mind's eye.'

It was a very British tribe, a move away from, as Jazzie once described it, seeing ourselves as 'aliens with passports'. The fact is we were Black and British, and suddenly there was a breakthrough. We were heard. We had found a story, a role in this nation's narrative that wasn't about conflict or failure or racism, a new, uplifting story of home, even if it was via, as Paul Gilroy dismissively called it in *There Ain't No Black in the Union Jack*, 'the shiny arena of the infotainment telesector'. Linford Christie had run us into the headlines. And Jazzie B had sung the soundtrack.

I always wondered how much of a bubble we lived in, I lived in. This was an era of solid economic growth and I had my middle-class defences of education and, though not wealthy, the certainty of employment. Being out of work never crossed my mind. I moved steadily upwards, from job to job, nearly always the only non-white person in the office and aware I carried a certain issue for some, a lightly worn suspicion about my 'ambitions'. Did I really fit the culture – was my ethnicity the wrong shade, my background a little too far below the salt? When you are not one of them, them find it hard to wholly cover it up. But, no matter, we beat on against any current that washed against us, convinced the tide was flowing in our favour. When Tony Blair said: 'A new dawn has broken, has it not' in 1997, it seemed not just the smart phrase of a salesman politician, but the sense of an age, whether you supported New Labour or not. No one had had it this good since the 1960s.

In this new decade good things happened. I married a wonderful woman in a Cotswold church in the springtime, which was all very English and sunny and the bells pealed out and we had our reception in a stately home with the owner brandishing his walking stick at anyone who dared throw confetti on the gravel drive. I wore tails and a waistcoat. My new father-in-law was Irish and didn't mutter to his wife 'that's a funny kind of name' when I was introduced to him. Which had happened before. He was an immigrant himself, a doctor, and well understood the English nuances of identity, the slight temperature drop when you walk into the wrong kind of pub. His response to life was to throw his arms out wide in a grand gesture of welcome, glass of good wine in one hand, the other proffered forward, ready to shake in a trusty and trusting hello.

My wife and I had two children (Maud, named after the great Irish feminist and actor Maud Gonne MacBride, and Noah, a respectful nod to the prophet who appears in both the Quran and the Bible – and at least not 'Ziggy' as my wife added with a shudder, which was the name I first suggested, more in hope than expectation) and thought we were well on our way to a post-racial future. In conversations long into the night with people more sceptical than me, I insisted that this stuff just didn't matter any more, black and white and blah, blah, blah; that when Maud and Noah were old enough to go on marches and vote and snog the right (and often the wrong) kind of people, the heritage, the background of those around them would only be interesting for what they gained in talking about them, not for the barriers that might be thrown up between them and others.

But maybe a lot of us confused gloss and partial victories and very fine music and fast runners for changes of substance. I've thought a lot about that Gilroy phrase, and wondered how deep those new roots really ran. We had lots of nice tinsel, but what did the underlying tree look like? Sometimes you need to look at the aggregate, the trend, to understand that the specificity of an individual's experience – mine, my friends, my circle – does not equate with a general move of substance.

Yes, on average exam scores at school for black and Asian pupils did improve, an improvement particularly notable for those from Indian or Chinese backgrounds. But African-Caribbean and Pakistani-origin children were still a long way behind the average attainment for white pupils. A young Andy might still have been asked if he wanted to be a car mechanic.

Yes, in the labour market, prospects did brighten. But on average British-born ethnic minorities were doing little better than their parents when it came to employment rates and earnings, despite levels of unemployment halving over the decade. A study by the Commission for Racial Equality found that, when sent fabricated CVs where the only difference was ethnic background, white candidates were three times more likely to be asked for an interview.

Maybe I should have changed my name to Neil permanently.

Education and jobs, two of the most vital indicators when it comes to assessing how a society is treating its citizens, its subjects. There is a third – the system that protects a society from itself and brings those guilty of the most grotesque transgressions to justice. How was that faring?

On 25 February 1999 the British narrative on race changed, and we abruptly realised that Our Decade was not really our decade at all. The date was publication day for a government-commissioned report into the stabbing of a teenage boy at a bus stop in south-east London. It changed how the country looked at race, at itself and at the largely previously hidden anchors of discrimination, deep beneath those deck chairs we thought we were going to wash away with such small bother. Little did we know that beneath the sand were blessed rods of iron connecting the chairs to granite. And that February we were given a new phrase for those anchors, the structures you couldn't see beneath the sand – 'institutional racism', the pervading atmosphere, the muscle memory in organisations which causes them to fail ethnic minorities because of ignorance and bias, 'unwitting' it was said, being wrong, doing wrong, without even knowing it. I was dancing to Soul II Soul, smiling, happy, while the system was going about its subterranean business, out of sight.

'Stephen Lawrence's murder was simply and solely and unequivocally motivated by racism. It was the deepest tragedy for his family. It was an affront to society, and especially to the local black community in Greenwich,' wrote Sir William Macpherson in the foreword to the inquiry into the stabbing of a son, a brother, a friend and a student at a bus stop in 1993. The police investigation into the death was shambolic, factually flawed, defensive and infected by an attitude that somehow Stephen Lawrence, his parents, Neville and Doreen, his friend Duwayne Brooks and all the local people who wanted to achieve that most basic thing – catching the killers – were somehow *suspicious* and should not be accorded the fundamental right to respect, due care and the best service from those we pay to guard the castle walls. *Quis custodiet ipsos custodes?* Who, indeed, will guard the guards?

I covered the publication of the report for the *Guardian*, where I was working, dutifully trooping to the morning news meetings to be asked – along with the other non-white staff – how the paper might consider its opinions on the matter. We, the group of us who fulfilled that description, were never quite sure that our opinions on, for example, education policy, were quite as keenly sought. I went to the press conferences on the day the pink-covered report was unveiled. I listened to the voluminous arguments. I read the report in grim silence in the media room, turning page after page, each one taking a single leaf away from that book of improvements we had all been eagerly adding to over the decade before.

And this is what struck me then, and strikes me now. The inquiry report was 335 pages long, a miserable read of missed opportunities, bad practice, venal attitudes and incompetence. And there was a whisper in my mind. Haven't we been here before, with our exhortations to do better, to be better? To identify a problem and be resolute in our determination towards change?

Presented to us journalists alongside the Macpherson report was a pack of information from the Metropolitan Police including a 'Diversity Strategy' complete with 'practical changes that benefit Londoners'. There was also a Home Office folder, plastic, containing 'Initiatives on Race Equality' and detailing ten projects the government had launched to combat this scourge that had apparently crept upon us and shouted Boo! There was the introduction of targets for the recruitment of ethnic minority officers, the development of race equality grants, even mention of European Union directives to make the world a better place and sing hymns.

I paraphrase.

All noble, well-meaning attempts at change from people who could then look themselves in the mirror and say: 'We're trying.' When Sir Paul Condon, the head of the Metropolitan Police, made his first public comments on that same day, that day of judgement – for that is what it was, a judgement on the state of race in our country – behind him was the force's crest and the phrases, picked out in large blue letters, 'protect and respect' and 'policing diversity'. Outside, eager officials pressed sheaves of paper into willing hands. There were diagrams. Reported racial incidents? Up 68 per cent. The number of racially motivated crimes solved? Up 73 per cent. I wrote at the time: 'Each had a little rising blue and red arrow ending in a starburst, a bit like a supermarket special offer.'

And later that same day in a room at the Home Office, there was Doreen Lawrence, the mother who had campaigned with her husband, Neville, with Duwayne Brooks, with friends, with lawyers, with anyone who cared, for years to get to the truth. She read a statement out in a halting voice, three pages of A4 text. There weren't any copies to hand out because Mrs Lawrence didn't have a press office.

'What I see is that black people are still dying in the streets and the back of police vans.'

The events of that day happened in a triangle of roads in Westminster, the homes of our grand establishment. The House of Commons on Parliament Square where the then Home Secretary, Jack Straw, the very man who had agreed to an inquiry in the first place, rose to say his piece: 'I think I can speak for the whole House when I say that Mr and Mrs Lawrence's campaign for the truth has been pursued by them with enormous dignity, courage and determination. I pay my personal tribute to them today.'

Sir Paul at New Scotland Yard, 10 Broadway: 'We feel a sense of shame for the incompetence of that first investigation and how the family was let down. We felt we could and we should have done better in this case. Stephen's brutal and racist murder has already brought about significant change and the legacy of his tragic death will be enduring reform.'

Doreen Lawrence at the Home Office on Marsham Street: 'This society has stood by and allowed my son's killers to make a mockery of the law. To me institutional racism is so ingrained it is hard to see how it will be eradicated out of the police force.'

A triangle of streets that had been – has been – tramped around many times before. We had tramped around them in 1981 and the Scarman Report into the horrific events in Brixton that year ('Urgent action is needed to prevent racial disadvantage becoming an endemic, ineradicable disease threatening the very survival of our society'). That was going to be the watershed, just like William Macpherson was described as 'the watershed' eighteen years later. Other inquiries would come, into racism against Muslim people, Jewish people, the others in our world. Drip, drip, drip, patter, patter, patter.

A triangle of streets that did not just define a geography, but defined power. Those who have it and those who do not. Doreen and Neville Lawrence lived in south-east London with their son. The report into his murder revealed the decade for what it was. The icing sugar on the cake looked good. There was still something rotten inside.

Ten years after that wearing day and I was divorced and living in a flat in Wandsworth. Neither, sadly, were to do with my ethnicity. That wonderful woman stayed wonderful. Me, not so much. You can blame lots of things on brown stuff. My own emotional failings are not among them.

I had also changed jobs, deciding that given that my marriage had broken apart and I had moved home I might as well add the third line of those 'most stressful moments of your life' lists and quit the career that had nurtured me for more than fifteen years. Until 2008 I had always been a journalist, reporting on others, their mistakes, their triumphs. I had risen high enough at the *Observer* to lead a team of people doing the same thing. I wondered what it would be like to be an actor rather than a critic and, sensing that a marriage break-up, house move and job abandonment might be the gentle signals of a midlife crisis, a change in direction could be just what I needed. That or a Maserati.

What could I do? What was uniquely mine to offer, a mixed-race kid who was called 'Geek' at school and shoved in puddles? What could bring together all those strands that run so deep in many of us? The struggle to belong. The wondering, the gentle currents of insecurity that float in our lives. Do you quite fit? My wondering – was I black enough, white enough? What could I do to help the new generations of Andys who would be at school right now, happy at eleven and disillusioned by eighteen, the people I wanted to live in a world different from mine. If this is a journey from the negative to the positive, what small cog had my name on it?

I set off with purpose. A new body had been set up in 2007 which envisioned a bold approach to equality – that thing which I clung to as the lifeboat away from the reefs of Enoch Powell. This was all about opportunity and bringing down some of those barriers, cutting some of that rottenness out of the cake. It was a shiny, twenty-first-century thing: the Equality and Human Rights Commission, built to bring groups together. Literally so. It was an amalgamation of the Commission for Racial Equality, the Equal Opportunities Commission, the Disability Rights Commission and also had responsibility for gay, lesbian and transgender rights, as well as age and religion and belief. Well, that touched everyone, one big pot of 'we're here to help you all just get along'. And, get this, it had a duty – written down in the legislation – to promote good relations.

Good relations. What two better words were there to finally honour the legacy of Stephen Lawrence?

The commission was constituted as a solution to the age-old problem of 'other' – how to balance the need for different groups to have their own voice with the obvious desire that, ultimately, it would no longer be necessary to have such a body at all, not in the new post-other world we were still busy building. The commission, like Neanderthal man, was a staging post between primates and *Homo sapiens*, Planet Bad and Paradise. Our success would mean our extinction.

Walking into the office for the first time, it was different. Years earlier, with a girlfriend who had, fortunately for her, avoided marrying me, I had been on a road trip to America. We visited Atlanta, the home of Dr Martin Luther King Jr. We went to a restaurant, possibly to order Po-Boys with shrimp and lots of dressing. I don't quite remember. But I do remember walking in and experiencing a unique feeling. We were welcomed by a black woman. Taken to our seats by black staff. The chefs in the kitchen glimpsed out the back were black. And all the customers. Black – buying stuff, shushing kids, with bejewelled hands, to quieten down, laughing, rowing over what to order, talking about houses and holidays and schools and the ordinary stuff of life. My girlfriend was the only white person in the place. Turning to me, she said: 'This is the first time I have been aware of my colour. This must be what it feels like for you every time you walk into a restaurant in Britain.' Where the customers are white and maybe the black guy is out back cleaning the toilets.

The Equality and Human Rights Commission had a black chair. The chief executive was a woman. Staff were gay and straight, there was a high percentage of brown people, of people with disabilities, of people who had long known what it was like to feel other. I wasn't the only brown in the village. In fact, my otherness seemed piddling, inconsequential, a weak moon among the brighter lights of real discrimination, the cases we fought on behalf of victims of police brutality, disabled people trying to use everyday public services the rest of us take for granted, those fighting pay gaps, discrimination in work, sacked for being pregnant, transgender people looking for simple acceptance. Not much to ask.

And I thought back to Doreen Lawrence and that day a decade earlier and I was resolute. I was no longer a critic, but an actor, I reminded myself. When it came to the police, had things changed for the better? Or would we have to tramp that same triangle of streets in London at some point in the as yet undetermined future, listening to the authors of and respondents to yet another report which revealed the failure of the criminal justice system, for example. We could find out, should find out. This new commission with the power to investigate and to winkle out answers. So, we agreed. The commission would produce a report, ten years on from Macpherson.

We knew – all those good-hearted people who worked with me – it was a big test. Anecdote, and probably a lot more, was working against us. Yes, on Merseyside the killers of the bright, focused A-level student Anthony Walker (they drove an ice axe into his head so deep paramedics struggled to remove it) had been found within days and put behind bars for most of forever. The local force declared the crime racist the night it happened. No Stephen Lawrence repeat this time. But, two years earlier the BBC's *The Secret Policeman* documentary had revealed, via undercover recordings, that racism was alive, well and kicking at the police's Bruche National Training Centre in Cheshire. Sir William's demand that his report mark a 'watershed' appeared to have passed fresh-faced recruits to Her Majesty's Constabulary by. One was recorded saying that 'Stephen Lawrence deserved to die' and that his parents, who had fought the battle against an establishment careless of its responsibilities with such dignity and grace, were 'a fucking pair of spongers'. Another wore a homemade Ku Klux Klan hood and said he was ready to 'bury' an Asian under a train, that Hitler 'had the right idea' and that an Asian colleague 'will regret the day he was ever born a Paki'. After the investigation was broadcast, ten officers resigned and twelve were disciplined. I remember watching the programme in disbelieving silence, just as I had read the Macpherson report, each minute of that documentary, like each page of Macpherson, slapping us in the face, those of us that insisted on remaining so bloody optimistic.

The programme raised the usual questions. Boringly usual. If a journalist was able to unearth such evidence, why hadn't the official regulatory bodies that oversee the police managed to? How did the holders of such extreme views manage to glide through the recruitment process, supposedly overhauled after Sir William's report? If this was happening at one training centre, what on earth was going on elsewhere?

The commission's role was to uphold equality and human rights law in England and Wales and provide evidence of progress or otherwise on whether the country was improving its 'good relations'. We had a very small unit looking at the police – two people, slogging through spreadsheets and reports, ringing around forces and asking for statistical breakdowns. They started to sift the data, always a sensible place to start.

The answers revealed something significant about the country in which we live. We make progress and we fall back in equal measure. And that is what makes us so uneasy about race, about otherness, and gave me, back then, the first inklings of something which maybe I had been ignoring for too long. The complexity – my mother's constant quiet encouragement to understand that the first answer to a question is not always the right one. That the nature of prejudice is that it is ingrained, that very odd thing in our heart that brings a reaction to what we consider strange, or have been told is strange, that even we do not like. The thing about that ingrained nature? It is not always there to be changed, sometimes it is there to be revealed and understood. For every positive statistic I can point to, someone else can point to a negative one. Good and bad, not in equal measure but certainly a proportion of each. That is the proper picture of our country. The police were not some unusual part of society, separate from us. They were us.

Some parts good. On employment, the targets for new ethnic minority officers hired, the commission found, had been exceeded. The proportion of Asian and black officers had also doubled. Good work, pushing to be different.

Some bad. Large parts of the police's work – such as specialist squads dealing with armed crime – were still seen as the exclusive preserve of white, middle-aged men and home to an uncomfortable 'canteen culture' of ribaldry and insults laced with racism. Non-white officers tended to resign from the police more quickly than their white counterparts.

Some more bad. On stop and search, there had been no significant change in the high number of black and Asian people stopped over the previous fifteen years, well before the horrors of Anthony Walker and Stephen Lawrence, back to when Linford Christie was still lighting up the winner's board and being stopped for driving a quite flash car. Some forces were stopping nine black people, nearly all men, for every one white person.

And that bled into another issue, the consequence line that embeds our response to 'otherness' deep in the system, a system that therefore monotonously spews out the same answers. Nearly a third of all black men appeared on the DNA database for possible crimes committed, compared with just 10 per cent of white and Asian men. Such a skewed set of figures can lead to 'ethnic profiling' as the database delivers high numbers of 'black suspects' for all crime categories. Raids and arrests then follow, driven by statistics that are built on slanted foundations.

And so it goes around, one step leading to another, you have to retain your wits to keep up.

Some more good. On racist incidents police had taken on what was known as 'broken windows theory', imported from America. The theory is simple – leave a broken window in a building and more windows will be broken. Fix the window and the rest will also stay intact. What's more, if people expect the window to be fixed – revealing high levels of trust in your neighbours and the authorities – the first window is less likely to be smashed at all. It becomes self-regulating.

In an experiment in the 1960s a car with the bonnet up and no licence plates was left on a street in the Bronx, New York. A similar car was 'abandoned' on a street in the comfortably middle-class Palo Alto in California. The car in the more anonymous, low trust, low-chance-of-conviction Bronx (suffering from the 'no one cares' effect) lasted precisely ten minutes before it was vandalised and valuable items such as the radio and the radiator removed. In Palo Alto the car lasted a week until one of the researchers, Philip Zimbardo, took a hammer to the vehicle and smashed a window himself. The car was then overturned and trashed within twenty-four hours. The main perpetrators in both cases, the Bronx and Palo Alto, were described as 'clean-cut and white'. Just in case your prejudice had led you to think otherwise.

Police in the UK appeared to have learnt the lesson of psychology – and we should too. Since Stephen Lawrence's murder they focused on stopping low-level racial harassment in the belief that would stop escalation – to the brick through the window or the burning rag through the letter box. Here's an example. An Asian member of staff told the Equality and Human Rights Commission's police team that his son had accidentally thrown a cap into a neighbour's garden. The neighbour had refused to return it and, during the subsequent argument, had been racially abusive, words that were heard by a number of local people. The police were called and warned the neighbour that he was possibly guilty not just of theft but also that, under new laws, if he was prosecuted it would be considered 'racially aggravated'. The cap was returned. The Asian man said that he was 'surprised and impressed' by the officers. He probably told his neighbours the same. And his family. And his friends. And the next time low-level harassment occurred, local people would be more likely to pick up the phone again. To the cops.

And they did. Figures from the British Crime Survey revealed the proportion of incidents being reported to the police rose. In the 1990s, about one-in-twenty racist crime allegations were reported. That figure went up to one-in-five. At the same time, the total number of racially motivated incidents fell from 390,000 in 1995 to 184,000 in 2007. The Home Office set one central target for the police: increase public confidence. This seemed a pretty good way of going about it.

Go on the 'b' of bang. So good, so important, they made a sculpture in honour of the idea and placed that grand metal structure, with the 180 naturally rusting iron spikes bursting 184 feet towards the sky, right in the middle of Manchester, home to the 2002 Commonwealth Games. A sculpture to Linford Christie, to Trevor Beresford Romeo, to Stephen Lawrence, to Doreen Lawrence, to Anthony Walker, to anyone in the police who wanted to improve things, to show that they were not the problem, a sculpture to the 1990s, to improvement, to getting along, to good relations, to running, to music, to me, to a country that wanted to show that it was not institutionally racist, that the curve was always upwards, whatever the naysayers said, to the future.

The sculpture was unveiled in 2005. It was a year late. Four years later it was gone, suffering from metal fatigue, the spikes falling off, creating a public hazard. Health-and-safety railings appeared and flapping tape cordons closed it off to the public. *B of the Bang* cost £1.7 million to build and Linford Christie was at the opening. In the end the spikes were put into storage. The core was melted down for scrap.

Sudan has twice as many pyramids as Egypt.

6

Dear Sudan

My mother comes from England, my father from Sudan. Now, in straightforward terms, my father living in Britain was the victim. Was the victim of all the slights and pains of living in a country where you are not in the majority, as a black man. And are not in power, as a black man. And, of course, that is true. My father believes that he never rose to the highest ranks of the NHS or ophthalmology in Britain because he was a first-generation immigrant. Now, his colour and Muslim background may have had nothing to do with his lack of ultimate promotion – maybe he was a bit rude, a bit mediocre, a bit all the things that, if you are white, are not necessarily a barrier to rising up the ranks. Black people are quite capable of being lazy and not very good, just like white people. Just don't imagine it to be a group trait.

My father may have been bad at lots of things. But I knew him. I saw him working past midnight and up at 5 a.m. to complete his projects. I knew that he was working in his scientific field in a language that was not his mother tongue. And, we may never know how much his colour mattered, but know it mattered in some way, the data have to push you towards that conclusion. Not just for him but for many like him. In the labour market, non-white people are over-represented at the lower end – the cleaners and the carers – and under-represented at the upper end – the managers, the executives. Black African unemployment in the UK is running at about 16 per cent, white unemployment at about 4 per cent. Only 6 per cent of British Muslims are in 'higher managerial, administrative and professional occupations' compared with 10 per cent of the overall population. Try applying for a job with the name Abubaker Ahmed and try again with John Smith. Mr Smith will receive more interview requests and employment offers than Mr Ahmed. My father faced that tiring, always upwards, climb throughout his life, the slope millions of non-white people wake up to every day. The black tax. To arrive at the same position you have to work twice as hard.

Whatever the causes, and this is where it becomes more interesting, my father also had an explanation as to why. What would happen, he suggested to me once as we sat and chatted about life in Britain, if a white, first-generation immigrant to Sudan had come to Professor Seddig Abubaker Ismail Ahmed at Alzaytouna Specialist Hospital on Sayed Abdul Rahman Street near the airport in Khartoum and applied for a job? And what if that applicant, good as he or she was, was up against a Sudanese doctor of approximately equal talent? Well, Professor Ahmed would probably plump for the Sudanese doctor, now wouldn't he? 'He would understand him, where he came from, his family!' my father would say with that sharp, high-pitched laugh that often accompanied comments that cut against the expected but that, to him, were blindingly obvious (Dad had a fine nose for the controversial). You look after your own, you see. Whether you are a Hindu in India or a Chinese manager wondering about that Japanese applicant. Try searching 'Nigerians in South Africa' and see how quickly you discover comments such as 'they are the seed of Satan' and 'we don't want them polluting our land'. In Chile, high-status Castilian Spanish names earn around 10 per cent more than those with indigenous names, even after controlling for levels of education.

Does that make Dad less of a victim? Or, maybe, a racist? No, because his simply-put belief played no role in the career of another doctor. My father never did become Professor of Ophthalmology at the Alzaytouna Specialist Hospital, even if they had such a position. And he never had the chance to turn down a white doctor's application. He didn't have that necessary second element to turn a prejudice into an 'ism': power.

What his opinion does do, though, is open up a possibility that we might understand prejudice, an instinct against the 'other', from the point of view of reconciliation. 'I could be like you' is the starting point for a far better conversation and the possibility of change. My father understood this.

And I have come to understand it. And part of the reason is my very own link by blood to a different country. My British self knows well enough about our colonial story, the suggestion that it was a global wrong. But what of my 'other' history, the other mix in my mixed race? What could that tell me about racism and identity? Rather a lot, as it turned out. Not all of it comfortable. And much of it putting Britain's travails in a rather more benign light. There are better alternatives, yes. There are also far worse ones.

We can all agree, apart from those on the margin with which this book is not concerned, that *racism is a bad thing*. But it is not a peculiarly British or American affliction, a bad thing with unique, Caucasian characteristics. And neither is gaining from slavery, not in my history at least.

This matters because confining our debate on race to a battle between white people, black people and the history of the Western world restricts our ability to find a path, however gropingly, towards solutions. One group is on the defensive, the other takes the position of the justifiably angry victim. The gulf between the positions – a gulf too wide to be traversed by those ever wobbly bridges of understanding – makes progress impossible. The two sides sit, one shading its eyes from attack, the guilty; the other ready to launch, pushed too often into the role of the aggressor. White people are worried. Black people are angry.

Reconciliation requires an understanding that within each of us are the seeds of the other's malady. 'He that is without sin among you, let him first cast a stone at her,' Jesus said to those who sought to punish an adulteress. Are we all prejudiced, somewhere deep inside? To understand, I needed to take a journey 'home' – that place of which I knew little but had such a major impact on who I was, its existence visible, manifest, in the very colour of my skin. Apparent all day, every day, of my life.

Khartoum airport is in need of some tender loving care. And money. Bulbs and neon strips are missing, leaving the light inside the terminal dull, a little listless. Signs suggesting which line to queue in whether you are from 'home' or 'abroad' have fallen and are propped up by a wall, pointing to nothing very much. Heat creeps under your clothes, the air is dense, motes dance before your eyes. Airports were once seen as a window to a country, a suggestion of development, like launching a space rocket, building motorways or having nuclear weapons. They are the first thing foreign travellers see. Khartoum is not like Heathrow. I feel a stranger and am a stranger, a first-time visitor. I hold my children's hands firmly.

There are no direct flights from Britain, and the journey has been a long one via Abu Dhabi. My auntie, Asma, has sent a fixer to ease Maud, Noah and me through immigration, which he does, slowly, with much smiling and some rather more animated gesticulations at men in uniforms wielding passport stamps. Outside in arrivals, there is a scrum of people and more heat. Sudan is not a country that can afford air conditioning.

'Sorry, sorry,' Asma grimaces tightly as we meet, the children shaking hands with a woman they have never met before, sister of a man they only vaguely remember, if at all. 'It is very lovely to meet you!' she says, her smile warming, her arms open. She pauses, looks around, hands on her hips. A sigh escapes her lips, like a dinner host receiving guests and suddenly realising the carpets in the dining room have seen better days. 'It is so chaotic. We are waiting for a new airport. We have waited for a long time.' She waves her hands at the dirt roads. 'It will be a long wait.' The place reminds me of a ramshackle Delhi airport on a trip twenty-five years earlier. Delhi airport now wins awards for its slick, modern upgrades.

Professor Asma Elsony is director of the Epidemiology Laboratory for Research and Public Health in Khartoum. I have met her maybe twice in my life, when she came to the UK to visit her brother. That's how I met many members of my 'other' family, fleetingly and without depth. Asma is also a member of the technical review panel for the Global Fund, the multi-billion-dollar medical organisation which fights that tripartite of attackers in the developing world, AIDS, malaria and tuberculosis. She is an expert advisor to the World Health Organisation in Geneva and was formerly president of the International Union Against Tuberculosis and Lung Disease in Paris. When she left, Dr Nills Billo, the executive director of the union, said 'for more than a decade, Professor Asma Elsony has been a driving force to advance and expand the union's portfolio from TB control to other areas of public health importance'. Staff stood and cheered at her final meeting in Lille in 2003.

When she was a lot younger, Asma studied in Moscow and was proficient in three scripts: Latin, Cyrillic and Arabic. She knows a lot of doctors across the Middle East because, she explains in precise English, Sudan produced most of them. Its university system was once on a par with Oxford and Cambridge. Asma is very proud of Sudan. Education is the ticket to greatness.

She ushers us to a large white 4x4 and it is clear my family here can avoid at least some of the punishments of poverty. We are in a bit of a hurry. Asma is keen to show us the confluence of the Blue and the White Nile, the different-coloured waters coming together, mixing. It is a tradition for first-time visitors to Khartoum. 'We need to be there before 6 p.m.,' Asma insists. 'Why,' I ask, wondering if it is something to do with the timings of prayers, a significant moment in the city's day. 'It gets dark,' she says, wondering if her guest is a bit simple.

I get into the back with Maud and Noah and watch their faces as we drive away from the airport, past men sitting on their haunches on street corners selling watermelons, the green flesh made rosy by the sun. Maud and Noah's mother is English, someone with fair skin and grey-green eyes courtesy of her Irish background, her immigrant father. A casual glance at my children and you would not imagine that their grandfather was from what was known in the nineteenth century as 'The Sudan' – the land of the blacks.

I am mixed-race and it is stamped on me, in me, by my colour, sometimes a sword, sometimes a shield, sometimes a hindrance, a stone in my shoe. Maud and Noah are mixed-race as well. But not the visible mixed-race of the second-generation immigrant like me. We fret about our own adult and distinct experiences as 'non-white' in a white country, but what of my children who say that 'ethnicity' is not what troubles them, is not what they talk about in those lessons on 'self' that are bundled together under the curriculum title 'Personal, Social and Health Education'. That race and discrimination is not the priority at school. Bullying, that is the thing. And online safety. And gender fluidity.

I ask Maud if she feels anything very emotional, as we bump along dusty roads in the country her grandfather was born in. 'Not really,' she says. When they were younger I spoke to both my children about why their surname was Ahmed, a bit about their grandfather and the journey he had made. But that was just parent noise, useful, maybe, at some point in the future, but less important now when the focus is reaching the next stage on the latest Xbox game or the politics of the classroom, perfecting a ballet step or a phase in rugby. In London, that wild, great, mixed-up pot, complicated ethnicity is taken for granted. A change from my day.

Do I feel anything very emotional? Trepidation, possibly, about the Elsonys I will meet for the first time – and there are a lot of them. If I'm honest, I am more concerned about whether the hotel will be okay, the sheets clean and my children will manage and be polite. This might be a long journey to find my roots. But I'm still a dad.

Now, that seems like a big admission. Surely the homecoming is *the moment*. Excited friends asked me on my return to relay the feeling, hope and expectation on their faces. I mean, who hasn't watched *Who Do You Think You Are?* 'Yes, wonderful,' I replied, but I wasn't quite sure. Nothing inside had really moved. No tears had prickled my eyes. That could just be me of course. Or the Yorkshire bit of me. They don't really do emotion there. Unless it's about cricket.

Or it could just be distance, geographical as well as that measured in the heart. When I went to America and stood by the monument to Dr Martin Luther King Jr, I felt an affinity. It was a colour thing, the historic story of struggle, that same story that left me in tears as I watched *Cry Freedom*, the movie about Stephen Bantu Biko, the South African fighter against apartheid who preached black pride and consciousness ('Being black is not a matter of pigmentation, being black is a mental attitude') and was beaten to death in a prison cell by South African Army guards. I remember my girlfriend of the time took my hand in the cinema.

But I realised as we drove along Africa Street, past the Sheikh Mustafa Elamin High School for Boys and around Khartoum Sports City, that it is the British story that has won in my life, and that is because I did not have a tale to tell of where I came from.

And that was because no one told me it.

I was jealous about that, jealous of my schoolmates who could speak Punjabi, knew about where their parents came from in India. So jealous that I learnt some of 'their' words so I could kick around with them and join in some of their banter. 'Alright', 'mother-fucker', the numbers one to five, 'bastard', 'breasts', 'white guy' and 'goofy' just about covered it as far as schoolboy vocabulary was concerned. I could use each proficiently.

Without language, a narrative, you cannot tell stories, or listen to them. It is the first question I am asked by Arabic speakers in Britain: 'Do you speak the language?' No, I don't, I would answer, embarrassment clear on my face, disappointment clear on theirs. I tried, pathetically, once to learn it when I lived in Glasgow but only felt the awkwardness of how ridiculous it all was when the Egyptian teacher pointed out that my pronunciation of my own name – Anglicised throughout my life – was appalling. He tried to teach me how to say it correctly, and at home in my flat in the swanky Merchant City I practised again and again, *A-heh-med*, the middle *heh* a soft sound in the back of the throat, a breath, not the harsh, throat-clearing *Ak-med* much loved of a certain type of Britisher keen to show, in their efforts with foreign names, their cultural credentials. I would tell the *Ak-med* pronouncers, 'No, really, I've Anglicised my name to *Ar-med*, and pronouncing it like that – *Ak-med* – is wrong anyway.' They always looked a little crestfallen, before briskly moving on to tell me they had once visited Libya and 'met a bloke called Kamal' who appeared invariably to work in oil.

Turning away from the main road, we bump across a rough piece of land and draw to a stop beside the semblance of a wall. And there it is, over the top of the rocks. The Nile, just north of Abdul Gayoom Gate, past the Al-Ninin Mosque and Omdurman Teaching Hospital, where the blue and white waters meet, the latter heavy with the pale clay sediment carried on its thousand-mile journey from the south. The light is starting to fade. The air still. We stand, the four of us, looking at the water. Family. Strangers. Linked by the intangible.

I'm not sure my father liked Sudan very much as a country, or, more precisely, didn't like how those with power behaved. It was a country that backed Saddam Hussein's invasion of Kuwait in 1990 and was home at various times to Osama bin Laden (who funded a number of companies and agricultural projects in the country, as well as terrorist training camps) and Ilich Ramírez Sánchez, otherwise known as Carlos the Jackal. In the 1970s it had a university medical school in the capital described by the Anglo-Indian academic, Dr Mukesh Kapila – who did so much to expose the horrors of Darfur – as 'well on a par with anything at Oxford'. In 2003, when he returned to the University of Khartoum, Kapila was 'shocked by how much it had declined', 'like a kindergarten' standards had sunk so low. Kapila worked at a hospital in Peterborough, eighty-five miles north of London. Many of his colleagues in Britain were Sudanese doctors.

It was, and still is, a country struggling with the stains of war, brutal conflicts which have had race and racism – prejudice plus power – playing incessantly in the background. The devil's chords. The country my father lived in stretched from Egypt and Lake Nubia in the north to Uganda and the Nimule Park in the south, a distance of over 1,800 miles. He didn't live to see South Sudan secure its shaky, ugly independence from the rest of the country, but knew of the battles that ebbed, poisonous, through the nation he once called home. At its simplest, the Arab north saw itself as superior to the 'black African' south.

In his book, *Sudan: Race, Religion and Violence*, the South Sudanese writer and academic, Jok Madut Jok, talks about a country where the state targeted 'the non-Arab and non-Muslim groups for violent absorption into the "Arab race" or for exclusion from state services if they insist on asserting their perceived racial or chosen religious identity'. Race was a more flexible concept in Sudan than in the genetics-plus-colour-plus-culture-obsessed West. It was not based simply on the hue of your skin, and could be 'mitigated', for example, by economic standing or a clear devotion to, and compliance with, the various forms of Islam which held sway with whoever was the governing force at the time.

But, despite the fact there were paths away from the unchangeable facts of skin colour and ethnic heritage, inequality with a thick, racial gloss ran deep. This was an initially uncomfortable and then sobering fact for those, and I include my naive self, who had always argued the 'colonial rulers bad, self-determination good' playbook. The dirty practicalities of the facts on the ground kept pulling, urgently, at my sleeve. Jok quotes a Dinka tribe leader, Makwec Kuol Makwec, in 2003:

When you visited the north, you must have noticed the differences between the Arabs in the north and us here in the south. They are red-skinned and we are black. Their names are Ali, Muhammed, Osman etc., and our names here are Deng, Akol, Lual etc. We have no shared ancestry, they pray differently but they want to force us to believe in their gods, they try to impose their language upon us and they have killed our people in the process over the years. They chop off women's breasts during the raids; they have taken our people and forced them into slavery. Their climate is arid and hot and ours is cooler and vegetated, and they want our land.

Their economy is more advanced and we have nothing here because they have extracted our resources for their own use. Their entire way of life is different from ours, they are dishonest, they have no respect for kinship, they take their own cousins in marriage, and now you are asking us if we can live together with the Arabs as one people, where we, the black people, do not have a voice? If you really want to bring peace, my suggestion to you is that you treat this country like a piece of cloth and you take a knife and cut it in the middle. I assure you, the Arabs are not a people we want to share anything with.

I read that and breathed out. The enforced changes of names to those decreed 'Islamic', the slaughter by the Janjaweed ('devils on horseback') militias in Darfur, much of which was justified by a warped belief in the subhuman despicableness of the 'other', the victims (in this case farmers from the Fur up against nomadic tribes); the destruction of homes, burning of land, genocide.

I am part Sudanese, half, maybe, depending on how you split the cake between 'blood' – who you were born to – and 'soil' – where you were born. After hearing many tales of black people being the bad guys – that's what you grew up with in Britain – I wanted nothing more than to hear a different narrative. At school I only remember learning four things about Sudan: that it was a desert, that there was nothing much of importance there, that it was a country once run by the British, and that Lord Kitchener in 1898 came and kicked the 'fuzzy-wuzzies" arses after the Mahdi army had the temerity to overthrow the Governor of Khartoum, General Charles Gordon, sticking his head on a spike for good measure. Pictures in the history books showed spear-wielding black people advancing on the pistol-holding British army officer. A more Victorian sense of the savage versus the civilised would be hard to imagine.

I sat in class, always desperate for better news, something to bring a little pride, a little resilience. But it never came. Kitchener's British forces and their new Maxim machine guns had 'mowed down the mass tribes of the Mahdiya in one of the most one-sided encounters in modern military history'. It left 11,000 Sudanese dead and 16,000 wounded. There were fewer than 500 casualties among the British forces.

Just another story of Africa's incessant failure. I wasn't taught about the noble history of Sudan and its Kushite kingdom, equal to the Egyptians, a thousand years before Jesus Christ was born. Their power stretched to the Mediterranean. I wasn't told about the remarkable collection of fourteenth-century Christian frescoes at the National Museum in Khartoum, relics of the country's early kingdoms which lasted for 700 years, and could sit alongside anything in Venice. Or that the fuzzy-wuzzies were actually Beja nomadic tribespeople rather than a joke deployed by Lance Corporal Jones in *Dad's Army*. Ha, ha. Or that the Gezira irrigation scheme a hundred miles south of Khartoum is one of the most successful in the world and, in its pomp, allowed for the production of up to 6 per cent of all the cotton on the planet.

I wanted General Gordon to be the one in the wrong. Wholly. I leapt on the fact that he had originally been ordered to vacate Britain's colonial lands by London which saw too little upside in keeping hold of a country that was 'mostly desert'. And he hadn't. I leapt on the fact he took it upon himself to set up his own fiefdom in the capital. Another negative mark. Officials in London wondered whether Gordon had gone slightly mad in the sun, and even his supporter, Winston Churchill, said that 'mercury uncontrolled by the force of gravity was not on several occasions more unstable than Charles Gordon; his moods were capricious and uncertain, his passions violent, his impulses sudden and inconsistent'. I stuck my hand up in class. 'Miss, Miss...'

The full picture was different, nuanced, complicated, like us all, others or otherwise. Just like the history of race in Sudan is different, not binary, not good guys versus bad guys. Just like the history of race everywhere. Including Britain. Gordon was a man influenced by different, swirling currents, battling at times to bring rights to slaves in Sudan, at other times trying to set up alliances with slave drivers. He stuck with Khartoum because he believed he was doing the right thing for the local people and for British interests. He neither fitted the jacket of 'colonial enemy' nor 'liberator', and the letters he exchanged with the Mahdi, Muhammad Ahmed ibn Abdallah, reveal a human tone of friendship rare in colonial discourse. Each man tried to convince the other of the righteousness of their faith.

We all like to have heroes in our life. And having a hero often means defining an enemy. One view is that Britain is the enemy, a colonial master that ruined what it touched. There is truth in the narrative that our country gained far more than it ever expended on the colonies, particularly when it comes to the economy. And that slavery was a cornerstone, a dirty foundation to the wealth of the nation. But life, history, is not a choice between where we are and Shangri-La. It is a choice between Shangri-La and the alternative. And the alternative for Sudan has been a post-colonial history marked by racial conflict, an elite power base in Khartoum jealous of its position and unwilling to yield to 'peripheral' interests in the south and east. And it is that fact that provides some perspective to those that complain about statues of rich, white Victorians in university grounds. Sudan, Rwanda, the Balkans, Armenia, the latest warnings about the plight of the Rohingya Muslims in Burma, being landmined out of their own country. Ethnically cleansed. If white people should feel guilty about this country's colonial past, should I feel guilty about Sudan?

Yes, the connections are tangled. Colonialism is the denial of democratic rights and self-determination. If I want to make mistakes as a country, let them be my mistakes, not yours. Colonial powers deliberately stoked tensions to retain control, and the echoes of that are still being felt. At the time of the First World War the British had a policy of 'under-developing' Darfur in the Sudanese south to keep it from supporting Turkey, an ally of Germany. Education, the British feared, would increase calls for dangerous emancipation and provoke problems among a 'discontented class of semi-literate trouble makers'. For Marxist historians read by my mother, such as Walter Rodney, Europe and the capitalist system could be blamed for the 'under-development' of Africa – colonialism and all ('Imperialism was in effect the extended capitalist system,' Rodney wrote).

If your economic system sets you against each other, then the necessary definition of an 'other' beneath you will surely follow.

Some use this argument as a neat way of avoiding responsibility for unleashing hell.

> Armed conflicts continue between government forces and armed opposition groups, particularly in Darfur, Southern Kordofan and Blue Nile states. Government forces have attacked, killed, and raped civilians and looted and destroyed their property in violation of the laws of war, and forced hundreds of thousands to flee their homes. Authorities arbitrarily detain political activists and subject them to ill-treatment and torture; use unnecessary lethal force against anti-government protesters; and censor the media. Despite these abuses and the International Criminal Court warrant for the arrest of President Omar al-Bashir for crimes in Darfur, the United States and European Union pledged renewed support for the Sudanese government citing cooperation in counterterrorism and migration control.

It does not take long reading into the history of Sudan to trip up against the barbs, this one from the front page of Human Rights Watch's online section on the country, partly my country. Around it, a garland of thistles, snippets of stories building a picture. 'Obstruction of aid denies women life-saving health care.' 'United Nations condemns enforced return of Eritrean refugees.' Indiscriminate bombing. The violent breaking up of student protests. Detention without trial. Mock executions. Torture.

Enough already?

No.

Six years before he wrote *Race, Religion and Violence,* Jok Madut Jok wrote another study. *War and Slavery in Sudan* was published in 2001. It delivers a cool analysis of Sudan's story, a story that is partly my story. 'Arab slave-takers pick their victims based on race, ethnicity and religion and consider the blacks in the South to be inferior infidels,' he wrote. But there is something in that sentence. And that something is the tense, which is present. This is not a book about history, to be read in order to learn the lessons of the past, as a student would in Britain. 'The capture and sale of Dinka women and children from South Sudan into slavery in the North has been going on since 1983.' This book is full of passion about something happening in my lifetime, still being campaigned about now, touching on a long story of slavery over many centuries perpetuated by Arab groups across North Africa. A year after Jok's book, Human Rights Watch published this on their website:

Human Rights Watch has long denounced slavery in Sudan in the context of the nineteen-year civil war. In this contemporary form of slavery government-backed and armed militia of the Baggara tribes raid to capture children and women who are then held in conditions of slavery in western Sudan and elsewhere. They are forced to work for free in homes and in fields, punished when they refuse, and abused physically and sometimes sexually. Raids are directed mostly at the civilian Dinka population of the southern region of Bahr El Ghazal. The government arms and sanctions the practice of slavery by this tribal militia, known as *muraheleen,* as a low cost part of its counterinsurgency war against the rebel Sudan People's Liberation Army.

I always wanted my father's country to be a hero. Something to boast about. But, as with all things in life, it's complicated. There has been too much war. It is too prevalent. Slavery is still part of Sudan's existence.

I always wanted my father to be a hero, and made up stories about him to cover up whatever failings some would accuse him of. My father never did fly Concorde or make marbles, as I used to boast to my schoolfriends. Maybe I wanted to do the same about the country he came from. And in that way build a better story about myself. Familiar to me was my mother, white English, and my country, white British. Different to me was my father, black African, and the country he was born in, Sudan. What was familiar I was less interested in. There were exotic attractions in what was different.

Now, looking at all this evidence, a thought comes to mind. Thinking about my mother I became prouder of her, of what she has achieved. By realising that so much of what she did was not in fact familiar at all, that seeing somebody everyday is not the same as knowing somebody.

Maybe Mum is like Britain, a little. The country I grew up in is familiar. I see it every day. But do I know it? Do I appreciate it? And know what it has given the world beyond the Bessemer steel process and Two Tone. Reading about Sudan, visiting Sudan, seeing my creative, smart Sudanese family does not make me feel more Sudanese.

It makes me feel more British.

Maybe I can learn to 'feel Sudanese'. Maybe that is the point, that we all contain different identities, James Baldwin and the flock of starlings, moving from tree to tree. I have pledged to myself and Asma that I will return, although I am not sure Maud and Noah will be rushing back, particularly if Dad takes them again to those museums with the fourteenth-century frescoes and models of herdsmen from times past. Even museums with digital tablets and air conditioning in London are not top of their list of priorities. Or that of many teenagers.

I hope I can learn. Sudan is home to the largest community of Sufi Muslims in the world, a moderate and socially open arm of Islam which sets the tone for the approach of the country – on an individual level – to those who visit it. Welcoming, friendly and calm. Every week in Omdurman at the Hamed al-Nil Mosque up to 500 followers gather to dance to a beat of drums and chanting. Men in patchwork robes spin to the music, spraying water from silver teapots. Everyone smiles, welcomes the tourists with their iPhones and tapping toes. What contrast there is between the people of Sudan and the power holders in Sudan or their proxies.

I should learn. Learn from my cousin Dina, in her early twenties, who is studying medical engineering and wants to stay in Khartoum and help her country develop, one of the millions of women who are making their way in a country where Islam, at least when it comes to gender, has historically been of a lighter touch. Over a hundred years before Dina started studying for her finals, the former Mahdi fighter, social activist and esteemed writer, Babiker Badri, established one of the first private schools for Muslim girls in Omdurman, an institution that started in a hut made of mud, teaching nine of Badri's own daughters and eight from neighbours' families. It is now the Ahfad University for Women.

I should learn from my auntie who wears her scarf lightly on her head and scoffs at those who believe piety should keep women at home. I should learn that though the government may author strict dress codes, it seems the Sudanese have their own ways of circumventing the rules. In his book *Sudan: The Failure and Division of an African State*, Richard Cockett writes of young 'fashion girls' wearing outfits of the brightest colours, and, although superficially demure, underneath will be 'small tops that reveal the midriff; a space that is known, roughly translated, as "the gap between religion and the state"'.

I should learn from my auntie who asks each of my family members to stand and introduce themselves before the banquet she has thrown in my honour begins – which they do with great joy and love. I should learn from the broad, taupe-coloured piece of cloth Asma has bought and lays out on the dining-room table when the plates have been cleared so that all the guests – all the family – can sign their name on a huge family tree with, there in the middle, three names, Kamal, Maud and Noah. I should learn from a woman who puts small cards in our hotel bedrooms to welcome us.

'Welcome Maud, your family in Sudan love you.'

'Noah Maurice. Welcome to Sudan. Your granddad's family love you.'

'Kamal. Welcome. We love Seddig. Your family love you.'

And I hope I can learn that all families have a past, and that all stories are complicated. Sitting in the house that my father was born in, a tray of mint tea before us, glasses and a silver teapot, the dry, warm air blowing through the terrace, an older auntie talks happily about my family's history, of being governors of the cities, significant in politics, proud of standing up for the rights of the local Sudanese, so often subjugated under the twin heels of British and Egyptian power. You do not have to wait long for any conversation in Sudan to turn to the 'problem with Egypt', the country to the north with more than twice as many people – and ten times the space in Britain's history books. Asma translates. The sun beats down outside, throwing its bleached light on the veranda. A cleansing light. The conversation continues, laughing as a family remembers its joint history, the hot-headed son (my father) who went abroad to change the world. Was always wanting to change the world.

And then there is a pause. Asma looks a little uncomfortable. 'Slaves?' Asma asks.

The air becomes a little thicker. Your mind slightly changes gear, the parameters of the conversation alter. What was the history of my family, so comfortably off in a land where any reading of history can raise alarms? Were my family slave-owners? Where did our wealth come from? Those sepia prints, gently browning on the wall, of proud men and women in all their finery: was it possible to be rich and virtuous? Those same questions that afflict nations and the families that make them up, from the Caribbean to the United States, Brazil to Britain. How was our society built?

I sip my mint tea, allowing the fragrant, floral warmth to percolate through me. Like this country is finding its way into me, slowly. So, just like all those white family stories from Britain where wealth is tied back to a grim past, maybe my family too has its share of things that are not spoken about. Asma looks at me: 'That is the first time I have heard that.' There is a wait. Then she stands and prepares to go: 'I am surprised.'

It is a sensitive subject. After speaking to older members of the family – delicately, with respect – it appears that my family certainly had servants and appear to have taken on slaves who had been given their 'freedom'. There are servants' quarters in my family home, the Big House, and that is where Ardo and Asha lived. They were both obedient to the house master and mistress, the heads of the household, my great-grandparents.

'They did not have slaves,' an uncle, Professor Mohamed Nour, says of earlier generations of my family. 'But they had ex-slaves given to them by friends. These women or men had their freedom papers. But they had no option other than prostitution or making and selling *marissa*.'

And so the story of Sudan goes on – war, slavery, wealth and poverty mixed to produce those that win and those that lose. The enslaved brought from the south by the crooked and the violent, those that live, parasitical, off conflict, the traffickers that trade in people. The enslaved, who, if they were lucky, would find a wealthy family like mine to take them in. Others would have to work on the streets, selling sex for food. Or *marissa*, a beer made of dates and sorghum, illegal in Sudan under sharia law but made nevertheless by the desperate, a way of earning a dollar a day which might just feed a family, hungry children with hair turned orange by malnutrition. And, as with so many countries across the world, thereby criminalising the victims of horrors rather than the perpetrators. The Khartoum government decreed that forty lashes was suitable punishment.

The queues through Sudan's main international airport are as bad on the way out of the capital as they were on the way in.

Asma leads, speaking quietly to a few soldiers. We are waved through as those queuing with access to no such resources, none of that Asma magic, look at us, nonplussed. Inside there are the officials with the stamps and the passport checks and the forms in triplicate. Sudan didn't heed too closely its former colonial ruler's liberal values, but it took on its bureaucratic ones with the gusto of the keen apprentice.

We all give Asma a kiss. There is a warmth between us, grown in a few short days. 'Port Sudan,' she says. 'Next time – it's very beautiful there.' Yes, I reply, I am looking forward to coming back. On my phone, pictures. Of Maud and Noah, faces rosy in the heat, smiling under the azure skies of a country that has maybe entered their heart a little. Of my auntie and her great-niece and great-nephew, eating in one of the smartest restaurants in the city: Thai, on the top floor of a building funded by Colonel Muammar Gaddafi, and which would not look out of place in Canary Wharf. And not at all bad, the food.

There seems a sadness to Asma. The goodbyes, maybe, but possibly more because I remind her that her brother, the favourite son, is no longer on this earth to take her calls on a crackling line to London and that she never did see as much of him as she wanted, would have liked. No one in Sudan did.

Two days before, at that banquet my auntie threw in our honour at her home (huge stews cooked in sheep fat – *waika*, *bussaara*, *sabaroag* – all served by the kitchen staff) I met the person I was named after for the first time: Kamal, my father's closest childhood friend. He hugged me close, other relatives laughed and smiled, taking pictures and toasting us with 7-Up and Coke. 'I studied in Britain,' Kamal said sitting in a *thobe* and *taqiyah*, the robes and cap dazzling, white. 'In the 1970s. I would see Seddig and, when I left, I assumed I would see him again, you know, after a few years, God willing. I came back, it was what always happened, it was usual, few years away, then back here to work. Seddig never did. He was unusual.' He held my hand tightly, tears threatening his eyes. 'It is amazing to see your face now.'

There is not long to go before our flight departs, back home, from this sort of home. We wave, a final goodbye. Some thoughts crystallise, some are too elusive to grasp. I am not part British and part Sudanese. I am wholly British, with a Sudanese background. Now, that may not be a surprise, given I have spent more than 18,000 days in Britain, and only a handful in Sudan. May not be a surprise given I was born in the former, and arrived on a plane in the latter. May not be a surprise, given I was brought up on school trips to St Paul's Cathedral, and came to Sudan aged forty-nine to hear for the first time that the country's pyramids are older than Egypt's (a good tale for producing wide-eyed reactions at dinner parties, like hearing for the first time that there are more canals in Birmingham than Venice).

I feel happier as I settle in my seat, offered delicate pastries and some of that fine Sudanese grapefruit juice. I look at my children, already searching for the latest movies from America on the in-flight entertainment. And realise that their experience will be very different from mine, that the notion that they are not quite British enough, that they are 'other' in their own country will seem as ridiculous to them as I always thought, hoped, it would be for me, but never was. It is sometimes only by going abroad – 'back home' as some like to describe it – that you can really understand where 'home' is and how British you really are. Not 'other' at all. Despite what many people may think.

When I visited my father as a teenager, I would often wear T-shirts I'd bought at concerts I'd been to – in the hope my father would ask about them and it might start a conversation.

Because we didn't always have that much to talk about in the local curry house he would take me to for lunch.

He never did.

It wasn't that he didn't care.

It was just that was the type of thing he would never notice.

7

I can't tell you how I felt when my father died

Farewell Dad.

Farewell to the man who affected my life so deeply but I am not sure I ever really knew.

And like a million other sons and daughters, I will carry that through my life as a missing piece. What might have been.

There will be an extra dimension as well. Because you were the link to the other part of my life, the part that gave me the chance to see things differently. Maya Angelou said you shouldn't go through life with two catcher's mitts. You needed a hand free to throw stuff back. Throw some of the stuff back that life throws at you. And when you are 'other', there is always a lot of that, that stuff that people want to pile at your door. I think that's the kind of thing you would have liked to have said to me, if you had been a touch more poetic. And able to talk about life and love.

But your vocabulary wasn't built for that. Stand up straight, you used to tell me. And stop moaning.

We buried you on the side of a hill overlooking Bristol. Relatives from Sudan I had never heard of rang to offer their sorrows. Asma said she would send a headstone to mark the spot. Plot 256 I think it was. A decade ago. I have never been back.

I visited you two weeks before that moment when the breath stops and your spirit leaves, bending over and kissing you on the cheek in your bed as the stale air laboured in your lungs. You had a few, rotting teeth left and hair that was as thin as your grasp on life. I knew it was the last time I was going to see you alive. 'Bye Dad,' I said, before standing outside your room in the nursing home for a while and thinking about all the things I was never going to say to you and you were never going to say to me. All those things I was going to sort tomorrow, or some other time, soon.

When the doctor rang with news of the inevitable – 'Mr Ahmed, it's about your father…' – I was in a pub near my home in London, watching a Champions League football match. I thanked the doctor for the call, talked of a few arrangements I would make the following day, finished my pint, ordered another one, and turned back to the football, the second half. 'Who was that?' the friend I was with enquired. 'Oh, nothing,' I answered.

I loved you, of course, father. Your hair turned white past forty despite your best efforts at 'out of the bottle' help (often leading to odd orange and blue tinges on your scalp and curses I remember coming loud and clear from the bathroom). But you were a difficult man, a man who always kept your deliberate distance, rarely used the words 'love' or 'thank you' and would politely enquire whether I would like to 'stop being a child' when I complained, as very much a grown-up, that maybe Seddig Ahmed hadn't quite provided the loving father–son relationship which I read in books was so important. Ask you what the most important qualities in life are and you would reply hard work and self-sufficiency. When I was a baby my mother changed my nappies. When you were a sick man, as you were for the last years of your life, I changed yours. If we counted up the numbers over the years, I reckon I wiped your backside more often than you wiped mine.

That doesn't matter now. But it did, for a time, to me.

You were probably killed, one doctor who was caring for you told me, by years of hard work for this country's National Health Service. A scientist, you dabbled with – or more precisely in – all sorts of chemicals as you searched for explanations for cell behaviour, looking for cures for bilharzia and later ophthalmic disorders.

'We didn't really have such good protection in those days,' the doctor said, those days being the 1960s, the 1970s. 'Some of the chemicals were pretty corrosive. God knows what they did to people's nervous systems.'

I don't know if God does know what they did to your nervous system. I know that you died of a disorder that was similar to multiple sclerosis, a degenerative condition where the myelin sheath protecting nerve endings disintegrates. I know because you told me. Explained it as if you were reading out of a textbook, a lesson on science that you had to keep simple for your arts graduate son who had failed to heed your sensible advice and study medicine, physics, engineering, chemistry – anything, honestly, other than politics which you described, very definitely, as 'a hobby'. When I announced that I was, sadly, not changing my chosen degree, we didn't speak much for a couple of years. Our relationship was like that. On. And then off for a while. You didn't come to my wedding. Didn't know that you had grandchildren until I came to see you with Maud and Noah. Every day, it was always easier to say to myself, 'I'll call tomorrow'. And tomorrow turned into weeks and months and years.

You were the immigrant father confused by a son who does not take his father's counsel, as he would do if we were in Sudan. Except that you didn't, did you? When you lived there.

I was the son who wanted something from you but also didn't want anything. I was brown because of you. Maybe that just really pissed me off when I was young. You made me different. You didn't call me Neil. It was only with the thoughtfulness of adulthood that I considered your story, how much you had done, and that we all find it hard to explain who we are. I got a bit older and maybe a bit wiser and a bit prouder of who you were. And therefore who I was.

I noticed that something was wrong with you Dad when you couldn't hold your fork properly.

You'll know, Dad, that when I say 'I buried you', I really mean that. The local mosque helped, run by some of the most caring, selfless people I have ever met. They washed you within twenty-four hours of the phone call I took in a pub and prayed over you as I sat at the back of the mosque with patterned carpets, my closest friend sitting to my right, having travelled from London to be with me.

As had my, by now, ex-wife. She had to stay outside.

I am not a Muslim. But, Asma had been in touch, not just about the headstone but worried that her brother wouldn't be buried properly and so I did my very best for you, the man who left home when I was four years old and I hardly recall anything about from those early years, apart from that you were frighteningly strict and could make me cry just with a look or a slight clip in your voice. African strict.

The son has to dig the grave to bury his father. So, with funeral suit and spade I dug and dug on a hillside overlooking the city that made much of its fortune from slavery. And the kind people from the mosque watched. As did my friend and my ex-wife. She read a poem. He said: 'I thought you were going to throw yourself in.'

I am a father now. Which brings some understanding, of failure, of the preciousness of children and also the confusion and the conflict and that your relationship with them is as much in their hands as it is in yours. I am the reason that Maud and Noah are called Ahmed. That link back to you and Sudan. And I am glad of that. Glad to be called your son. Even if I never told you. And I would find it hard, as Toni Morrison said, to tell anyone how I felt when my father died.

In a psychological experiment in 1974, managers were studied interviewing black and white candidates. The candidates were trained to act similarly to each other.

The managers – all white – sat further away from the black candidates, leaned back more often, away from the candidate, and showed what were described as 'speech disfluencies' – they stuttered and stumbled regularly.

The interviews with the black candidates were three minutes (or 25 per cent) shorter.

In social psychology this is called 'self-fulfilling prophecy' syndrome.

8

Prejudiced, me?

Here's why we're all tired. Tired of the Groundhog Day feel to every publication detailing why Afro-Caribbean children are doing less well in school, why Muslims are doing less well in employment and why boards and executive committees of some of Britain's leading businesses are wholly one colour. Tired of the constant request of black and Asian people – often on their own amongst a sea of white faces – that it is they who should account for and explain the issue of 'race' and 'lack of progress' to an establishment where change is always just around the corner. So many corners we have bumped into ourselves coming back the other way.

It's wearying, you see, getting up every morning and having to push the boulder up the hill. When everyone kept promising that they were going to rid us of that hill. That we could push along the flat, just like all the other folks.

A number of people feel understandably bleak and have had enough of trying to persuade the majority that there is a problem at all, or what should be done about it. The argument is a straightforward one, that when talking about racism the majority fail to understand that this is not a conversation of equals, but a conversation between those who have power and those who do not. And that 'vast majority' who have power, as Reni Eddo-Lodge argues in her book *Why I'm No Longer Talking to White People About Race*, refuse to listen and have little concept that change means them giving up their privileged position.

Black and Asian people are expected to be engaged with identity issues. Engaged with racism. White people are not, are only ever visitors to the place us 'non-whites' live in every day. Black and Asian people are expected to tackle the prejudice they face, lifting themselves up by supreme effort, being better, model citizens, model workers, never putting a foot wrong, proving to those set against them that they can go higher, achieve more, than the discriminator believes and thereby change the discriminator's mind – what the American academic Ibram X. Kendi calls 'uplift suasion', a tactic he says has failed. White people are not engaged with identity, they are engaged with a different type of politics, with power, alongside the full gamut of the arts, science, history, society, religion – busy getting on with shaping the world. Black and Asian people are too busy being told to shape themselves, are always kicking into the wind, necessarily experts in what they do and experts in who they are.

I am an optimist. My mother is white. I need to talk to her. And listen. It cannot matter to me that she is one of the 'vast majority' in this country because if 'we' are not engaged with 'them' what progress can there be? Some might complain that all the equality initiatives and legislation, diversity programmes and 'sari and samosa' evenings have failed. But for that complaint to hold true we would need to understand the counterfactual. What would Britain be like if no one had pushed for change, if we had stuck with where we were, say, one hundred years ago? Would Britain have a greater or lesser problem with discrimination? And if your instinctive answer to that is greater, then there is hope. We should not make the failure to gain perfection the enemy of making any progress at all, however stuttering.

Almost every psychological experiment aimed at understanding what might reduce inequality, prejudice, discrimination and stereotyping – the four horsemen of racism – suggests that contact is better than isolation. Isolation leaves the many sides involved in this debate shut up in their own dwellings, curtains closed, glowering behind their respective positions, entrenched in views that, because of their repetition with little external contradiction, become more embedded. If I have some knowledge of the 'other' community, it is harder to demonise. Individual contact helps good relations.

That contact then needs to be put together with another ingredient, understanding. A little less 'you shouldn't be thinking like that', which leads to closed, defensive positions. A little more 'why are you thinking like that?', which leads to more open, conversational positions. Which is where the little rays of hope live.

And then, the most interesting question of all: 'Might I think like you if you were in my shoes and I was in yours, if our roles were reversed, power relationships and all?' What if you were really given the chance to be a racist? Does prejudice lie in all of us, and if it does, does that mean that we can understand the other side a little more?

'There's only one thing I hate more than racism. And that's the Chinese.'

This is a joke and as with all good jokes it has an element of surprise and an element of recognition, we can see ourselves in it. And it is the second element that is important, neatly summing up as it does the problem with defining discrimination. It is easy to be against it and less easy to admit the contradiction of that position when considering your own prejudices. It is common to be wary when presented with a set of cultural behaviours outside your own experience, the experience of your friends and the experience of what you imagine to be your community. Maybe that wariness comes from your personality, you are someone who does not deal well with difference. Maybe that wariness comes from your own society's stories – the ones you have been told over and over again. The stories that tell you to fear difference.

My friend Ro told me this joke. Ro, a British Asian – who when we have supper with a few mates who *are not all white* calls it 'clowning around with the browns' – does not dislike the Chinese. He does dislike racism. The point he is making is that our instinct to agree with the first part of the sentence ('hating racism') is pulled up short by the ability to understand where the second part has come from ('disliking the Chinese') – and I mean understand not in the sense of 'condone'. The comment also gets a laugh and, when it comes to Ro – a funny bloke – that is an important consideration. Maybe it's his Asian genes.

One of the foundation stones upon which racism sits – prejudice – is something easy to relate to. Consider a self-employed plasterer who lives on the Isle of Dogs. He's a white guy, lived there all his life, never really had brown friends. He's worried that the arrival of Eastern European plasterers – who will work for half the hourly rate he charges and nights and weekends because they don't have any family commitments here – means his once nice little business is in danger. Now, he could consider his response to that as an economist might. Immigration is, in aggregate, an economic good for countries where the population is ageing, as it is in Britain. Immigrants tend (although this is not true every year) to pay taxes at a higher rate than they use benefits or public services – and someone has to pay for all those old people, and for schools and hospitals. He might also consider the theory of comparative advantage, which suggests, again in aggregate, that bringing in goods and people from outside a country creates healthy competition and ultimately higher levels of wealth. For everyone. Or he may not have any time for that and just feel a little bit angry about all the Eastern European plasterers living on the Isle of Dogs.

And from there it is not that many steps to the next stage. Developing that little bit of anger with plasterers from a certain part of Europe into a broader 'issue' with Eastern Europeans in general.

This is at least how some of it happens. Building a group dislike from what is perceived as being an individual threat.

Why move from individual threat to a group dislike? Because, disliking a group gives you allies in a way that an individual dislike – that single plasterer who undercut you – doesn't. Other plasterers on the Isle of Dogs become allies. Other people who have been 'undercut' by Eastern European immigrant workers become allies, carers maybe, people who serve coffee, pick cabbages. Parts of the media report that there are lots of these immigrants coming, uncontrolled, into Britain. That makes you feel a bit panicky. The friends of the people who have been undercut – who have never met a person from

Eastern Europe and have never been undercut by anybody 'foreign' but have heard the stories – they become allies. People you have never met in far-flung parts of the country share your pain. The pain of being undercut.

Finding allies in a world you imagine, you are told constantly, is cut adrift on a sea of rapid change, with few anchors to the solid, reliable past, gives you group support, someone to share your anger with, to nurture it. It makes you feel better. And from there it is easy to see how that mix of economic concern and group identification becomes an issue of 'culture', a way of defending where you are by reference to the unfairness of where they are. People receive benefits too easily. They are dirty. They are rude. They are drunk. They do not understand our ways.

We categorise to keep a complicated world manageable. Some of those prejudices can be positive – oh, I just love the French, they are so stylish. Some can be negative – bloody rude, the French. The twenty-first century is full to the brim of what social psychologists call cognitive busyness. That's a world full of work, work, work, social media, social media, social media, globalisation, globalisation, globalisation, information overload, information overload, information overload, emails, more emails, picking up the children, smartphones, more emails, dropping off the children, shopping, counting the pennies, saving for the holidays, the endless internet grasping for our attention with pings and calendar reminders – life, to paraphrase the usually monosyllabic student Rudge in *The History Boys*, is just one fucking thing after another.

Cognitive busyness increases our tendency to stereotype. Academics Neil Macrae, Charles Stangor and Miles Hewstone showed a group of people a video of a woman describing her lifestyle. Half the viewers were told she was a doctor, the other half a hairdresser. Some were also given a distracting task – remembering an eight-digit number – to perform. Those that were 'busy' with the task recalled far more stereotypical information from the video, whether they thought she was a doctor or a hairdresser, and rated the woman using stereotypical shorthand more readily. The doctor was smart, the hairdresser ditzy – even though the actual woman in the video was saying the same thing. As the world becomes more noisy, we increasingly lean on stereotypes to function. Prejudice is a tool of navigation and a comfort blanket, a shortcut to help us explain what can seem chaotic.

To be clear, prejudice and racism are closely allied (the latter follows the former) but they are not the same. When the MP Diane Abbott was flamed on Twitter for saying 'White people love playing "divide and rule". We should not play their game #tacticasoldascolonialism', this distinction was deliberately lost. People who claimed Ms Abbott was as guilty of the racism she has spent her whole political career campaigning against missed the point. Yes, she may have been better saying 'some white people' but the Tweet wasn't racist against white people. To reach that threshold you would have to imagine a world, as the writer Dorian Lynskey argued, which was a 'parallel universe Britain, dominated, politically and economically, by an unshakeable clique of black working-class women [where] two black men have just been convicted, several years too late thanks to an institutionally racist black police force, of the murder of white teenager Stephen Lawrence'. This is not the world Ms Abbott – or you and I – inhabit. Prejudice only becomes racism when it is weaponised by access to the levers of power, the strength to do something with that prejudice, the connections and networks that build an establishment, the majority position which gains succour from its definition of the 'other'.

But it is important to understand prejudice if we are to tackle racism. Is the prejudice process natural? Is it innate, something deep inside us that can be traced back to our time as hunter gatherers when successfully defining the 'in-group' – our tribe – and the 'out-group' – the tribe over the hill – could mean the difference between a successful hunt, life and death? Or is it a construct, manipulated by those in power to maintain their position and the semblance of order? Have those in power been smart enough to understand that the former, natural instinct, can be very usefully harnessed to maintain a hierarchy? A hierarchy that supports them.

The problem is that racism is a big, horrible word. It drips with the imagery of violence, of slavery, of apartheid South Africa, of the segregated southern states of America, of snarling dogs, of flowers laid at the site of another racist attack in a city in Britain, gently yellowing in the sun, of police with batons, of deaths in custody, of a failure of the very system we pay our taxes to support. The thing is, it is easy to be against all that stuff – the sharp end of discrimination that makes the headlines – and then suppose 'I am not part of the problem'. And that might well be true. But by understanding that we can all be prejudiced we can understand some of the routes to racism and therefore some of the ways out of the messes of our own creation. Because we all own this stuff, however righteous we believe ourselves to be. And that brings a responsibility to act.

Here are some easy questions to answer, very easy if you consider yourself comfortable with different types of communities. If you consider yourself a member of the 'I'm not the problem' in-group.

Do you think not giving someone a job because of the colour of their skin is correct? No.

Do you think people should be arrested more often because of the colour of their skin? No.

Do you think people should be given lower grades at school because of the colour of their skin? No.

Do you think it correct that people should be enslaved by Arabs in North Africa because they are Dinka – sub-Saharan, black Africans – and different from those aforementioned Arabs? No – though you probably haven't heard the issue put in that way before.

Okay. Here are some other questions. Do you agree or disagree?

Our country will be great if we honour our forefathers, do what authorities tell us to do, and get rid of the rotten apples that are ruining everything.

A lot of our rules regarding modesty and sexual behaviour are just customs which are not necessarily any better or holier than those which other people follow.

Our country will be destroyed someday if we do not smash the perversions eating away at our moral fibre and beliefs.

In order, did you answer disagree, agree, disagree to those questions? If you did it is unlikely you portray too many characteristics of what is described as an 'authoritarian personality'. Authoritarian personalities – and the questions you have just tried are a test for that personality type – tend to appreciate order and are socially conservative. They also tend to have stronger affiliation to 'in-groups' and are more wary of 'out-groups'. They reach more readily for prejudiced positions.

But, you're not that, so you can still sail on, not being the problem.

Okay, how about these questions:

To get ahead in life it is sometimes necessary to step on other groups.

Sometimes other groups must be kept in their place.

We would have fewer problems if we treated people more equally.

These are questions used to measure people's tendency for dominance, as proposed by social dominance theory, the idea that discrimination is simply the most modern form of a basic human desire to formulate hierarchical structures and then create myths and stories to support that status quo, however unequal. Hierarchical structures are assumed to be more stable than egalitarian ones and therefore tend to last longer and, in the chase of history, are more successful. Do you find yourself starting to lean towards rather more challenging answers to these questions? Are they harder to answer definitively? The edges are becoming more fuzzy, maybe.

You could answer yes to the first question. It might be necessary to step on other groups to get ahead, for example as a trading nation, putting the economic well-being of people here above the well-being of people over there. How did you feel in the 1970s when 'the Chinks started building ships' and producing steel and the yards in Britain closed and plants were shuttered? We lost jobs, they gained them.

How about question two? Might not other groups, without our British values, need to be 'kept in their place'? Our values are worth more than other people's values, surely? Those people without British values – well, it may not be best we treat them equally. Suggesting equivalence with cultures not of our type has been the big problem of Western democracies that has led to their decline – our decline – as moral leaders, that's the argument. It's time to get a grip, to say why we are better. To believe in Britain.

And from this flows the answer to the third question. No, it would not be better if we treated all people more equally. Some people aren't as equal as us.

Though a larger group of people are likely to show a tendency towards social dominance, maybe it leaves you as cold as the less broadly experienced authoritarian personality type. Who is to say that hierarchy is the order of things? Maybe there were matriarchal societies in the past, built on foundations of equality and peaceableness. Is social dominance just a formalisation of patriarchy, domination by men in power which swept prehistoric, women-centred societies before them? The evidence for such matriarchal societies is scant, which doesn't make the story of them any less compelling or important. It's just that it is a motivating myth rather than a factual history. Like Father Christmas encourages children to behave, it encourages us to be our better selves.

Such stories are important, but the problem is that most of the stories we hear are not about egalitarian, matriarchal societies, or even about Father Christmas. Most of the stories we hear are about the 'badness' of other groups, the threat they pose, the fear they should engender. And those stories, repeated time and again, lead to cases like that of Mel Sealy. And an awful lot flows from the case of Mel Sealy that should make even the most 'I'm not the problem' in-group member pause and reconsider.

Mel Sealy was born in Barbados and was one of thousands of people who came to Britain with all its promises of a different life. He left his police officer job in the Caribbean and moved to a house on Prince of Wales Avenue in Flint, North Wales, a few minutes' walk from the beautiful River Dee. Sealy wore dreadlocks and a striped hat, not all that usual on the streets of Flint. Sealy was black.

In 1998 Sealy, a DIY enthusiast, was building shelves in his home when he realised he had the wrong drill bit. He knew a friend up the road who might be able to help, so he set off on the short walk. His drill was in his hand, he wanted to make sure he found the right size bit. A few minutes after arriving home from his trip there was a flurry of activity outside. A loudhailer crackled into life and Sealy was told – as were most of the rest of the street – that he was to come out of his home and lie on the ground. The house was surrounded by armed officers.

Sealy, don't forget a trained officer, did as he was told. He was arrested and had his hands cuffed behind his back. Police officers searched the house, including taking apart his television. They were acting on a tip-off that someone had seen a man walking around Flint with a sawn-off shotgun. Not a power tool.

'Someone had it in for me and called the police,' Sealy said. 'I am West Indian, and because of my appearance they have type-cast me as a criminal.' No evidence was ever brought to court, the case was dropped and Sealy received £50,000 in compensation. That payment came after the police had executed a second armed raid on his home and again found nothing. Sealy did get the drill back: 'It has never worked since.'

Sealy was a victim of something, but what exactly? Police prejudice? Or a resident's prejudice, someone who didn't like the fact that Sealy had arrived at all and wanted to make his life difficult? Or was it a mistake by the person who made the call to the police, imagining that a black man walking around with something which might look a little bit like a gun was actually a gun?

In 2001, Keith Payne, Professor of Social Psychology at the University of North Carolina, published findings of his latest work on 'automatic' responses to various images. Such tests are carried out to see what we do without consciously thinking, an important part of understanding where bias resides. Participants in his test were shown, very briefly, a picture and asked to say whether it was a handgun or a household tool, such as a pair of pliers or a drill. Before the test, they were shown a photograph of a black man or a white man, a picture they were told to ignore. The test had a fascinating, if sobering, outcome. Those participants who had been shown a black face were consistently faster at identifying 'gun' than those that had been shown a white face. They had already primed themselves to see a firearm via the stereotype equating 'black' with 'violence'. They were also more likely to wrongly identify 'gun' when they had been shown a black face than when they had been shown a white face. Sealy would understand the consequences of that.

'The bias requires no intentional racial animus, occurring even for those who are actively trying to avoid it,' Professor Payne said.

His work was built on by Josh Correll and colleagues at the University of Colorado. In the test they carried out, participants played a video game where they saw black or white men carrying either harmless items, such as a mobile phone or a camera, or a gun. They were then asked to press a button marked 'shoot' or 'don't shoot' depending on what they saw. The results revealed that players were consistently more aggressive when it came to tackling black characters in the video game. Black characters with guns were shot more quickly than white characters. Black characters without guns were twice as likely to be shot than white characters. Of those that weren't shot, participants took longer to take that 'no shoot' decision if the character was black than if he were white. There were similar biases when African-Americans took part in the test.

So, at this point, we could all throw our hands in the air and say, 'Well, we're all racist, deep down, so what's the point of trying to tackle it?' But that is not the point I am making here. The point I am making is that we are all likely to exhibit prejudice and that can help us understand where the 'other side' is coming from. Some of this is unconscious, some conscious. It does not mean we are 'naturally' racist, it means that the world we live in, with its myths and narratives built in part to help us navigate the world and in part to maintain hierarchies, has sent very deep roots into our psyche. Roots which affect us all. Our brain is a 'sorter' – it has to be given the millions of pieces of data it receives every day. It creates aggregate pictures, and via that process prejudgments develop, some useful (a big dog not on a lead might be dangerous), some useless and wrong (black people all live in jungles and are lazy). None of us are above the problem. Start a conversation like that with the people you disagree with, the people you seek to change, and see the results. Admitting your own flaws – and that this stuff is difficult, that it needs work – is far more likely to get movement on both sides than everybody shouting at everybody else through a loudhailer, just like the police did in North Wales when they came to arrest Mel Sealy. Few react well to being shouted at through a loudhailer.

Gordon Allport died, aged seventy, the month before I was born in 1967. The Harvard professor wrote one of the definitive books on discrimination, *The Nature of Prejudice*, first published in 1954. Towards the end of the book he writes this sentence: 'No one can be taught that thinks himself under attack.'

For many years when I was young, I went to urgent rallies with other like-minded souls to argue against what I believed was the great inequity of life, racism, and the great threat to the planet, nuclear conflagration. I was so worried about the latter I would often lie awake at night listening for the air-raid sirens which would tell me I had approximately three minutes to achieve I was not sure what precisely, apart from going downstairs and hiding under the table. The 'Protect and Survive' leaflet, which I religiously read just in case any of its homely government tips were helpful, suggested putting masking tape on the windows and hiding beneath a door leant up against a wall. I was not convinced that Mum and I were capable of getting a door off its hinges. We had struggled for hours, I remember, to even put up a curtain rail.

I wore rainbow jumpers and had two earrings in my left ear. I think having earrings in your left ear was meant to signal that you were not gay even though I had no problem with people being gay. I queued for hours on the Embankment by the River Thames where marches invariably started, ready to vent my anger at the enemy and shout 'attack, attack, attack' with my friends when we thought we spied a racist (usually a member of the public in a pinstriped suit or a police officer). The problem was that the enemy (probably not the person in the pinstriped suit or the police officer) wasn't listening, or if they were they were doing so only to harden their opinions against what we were shouting about. Some of them leant out of their office windows as we marched behind our colourful banners and bellowed insults, waved Union flags and played Rule Britannia on the stereo. As a way of feeling better, marching could not be beaten. And there is some value in that, the solidarity of action. As a way of changing minds it was useless.

I remember a poster from the Campaign for Racial Equality which had a picture of three large brains and a small brain. Beside the first three were the words African, Asian and European, their brains all being of the same size and stature. Beside the small brain was the word Racist. I loved it, and felt empowered – no small victory in a world where confidence can carry you a long way. But looking again at that advert now, there, in those pictures of brains, is the fundamental flaw that runs through much of the debate about 'otherness'. At the time of the original advert, 1996, the head of a rival agency to Saatchi & Saatchi, which produced the advert, identified it, saying that it was 'counter-productive' and 'strategically dumb'. 'The commercials are hectoring. They put racists in boxes,' Mark Tomblin argued.

His agency's advert was rather different, showing a black man's life flashing before him to the tune of 'What a Wonderful World' before pulling back, the audience only then realising that the man is lying in the street dying, stabbed by a racist gang. That black man could be anybody's husband, anybody's father, anybody's work companion – 'relatable' is how it would be put now. Better to connect with the other side, pull on emotions that transcend race and ethnicity, culture even, than tell the other side how wrong they are. Or stupid.

This rather simple notion is at the heart of contact theory. Bring groups together to share everyday stories and prejudices can be tackled. People who live parallel lives, live in isolation with only their own culture readily apparent, will find it harder to overcome prejudice, both their own and any prejudice they may face. In-groups and out-groups suffer the same fate.

Allport wrote: 'To be maximally effective, contact and acquaintance programmes should lead to a sense of equality in social status, should occur in ordinary, purposeful pursuits, avoid artificiality and if possible enjoy the sanction of the community in which they occur. The deeper and more genuine the association, the greater its effect. The gain is greater if members regard themselves as part of a *team.*'

So, if we are not simply going to sit around pointing our fingers at each other in increasingly diminishing circles of understanding, what are we going to do? Do I mean literally we should be sitting around on chairs and talking to each other? All the evidence suggests this would be a very good thing to do, talking and then getting on with something practical, like building a children's playground. A grand, very British, conversation which will make us feel a mixture of embarrassment, joy and a great sense of the ridiculous. Each one of us deciding to do one thing every year that puts us in touch with people one wouldn't usually meet.

The question is why? Why would anyone bother in their busy lives? People tend to act when the cost of inaction becomes too great. We can put up with a dripping tap for a long time. If water is gushing out and hitting the ceiling, we call a plumber. On race, it's time to call the plumber.

What are the definable costs of prejudice that will motivate action, for both the in-group and the out-group? That something is simply unfair could be motivation enough, a high enough cost. 'Fairness' is seen as a quintessentially British value, a value if adhered to that can make societies function better, more equitably. But it is also a vague and malleable concept, a mercurial noun whose meaning is often in the eye of the beholder. We consider the phrase 'It's not fair' to be one peculiar to children who have yet to form a more sophisticated view of the world they inhabit. 'Life's not fair', is the adult response to the enquiring child, one deployed regularly by my mother to toughen up her little boy, all angry-faced and clench-fisted over the latest calamity society had foisted, unbidden, upon him. It is a word so slippery that it is without legal basis.

An appeal to fairness is also difficult to execute with groups of people who may already consider the world to be unfair – unfair against them.

The 'in-group', in this instance white, who may believe that the 'out-group', in this instance the ethnic minority, receive feather-bedded treatment, the protection of legislation and government funding for everything from Diwali night celebrations to council leaflets in every language under the sun. An in-group who already believe that the out-group have – by some mystifying hoodoo power they do not understand from an out-group that everyone claims *is the victim* – changed the country's schools, changed the language, changed the institutions, taken up employment that the 'settled communities' used to do, undermined tradition, brought in crime, brought in terror, brought in values that in-groupers do not understand and insist that everyone lives by them. An out-group that achieved all this even though they were invited here, to this great nation, as the in-group's guests. So, whose fairness are you talking about?

And the out-group who believe that the in-group have no concept of the pain it is to live in a country where the colour of your skin or the tenor of your culture can keep you back in education, in work, in family life. Where you are more likely to be poorer, more likely to be arrested, more likely to be in prison, more likely to be unemployed because of the treatment meted out to an out-group who have come here to work hard and support the economy and bring growth and cultural richness because, if we're honest, the in-group are not very good at all that, are they? The out-group has made this nation great, put it back on the world stage. So, whose fairness are you talking about?

Let's leave fairness at the door. It's not going to work.

What other cost of prejudice can we appeal to? What about sense of self? Prejudice undermines the sense of self – very few people are comfortable self-identifying as prejudiced. So an appeal to an increase in the sense of self – being a 'better' person – could be a strong motivating factor for change. The sense of ourselves as reasonable and smart, rational beings, able to use, in Jonathan Swift's phrase, the 'artillery of words', is part of our liberal, democratic tradition. A tradition that also rests on the values of equality, freedom of speech and mutual respect, an understanding of different faiths and beliefs. For the in-group, that is why we are successful, British. For the out-group, that is why we arrived. We like to believe ourselves thinkers, rational beings, thoughtful and not prone to superstitions, irrational reactions. Make an argument and I will not respond like a savage, I will respond like a gentleman, a gentlewoman, that is what makes us different, after all, from the 'other lot'.

Do you think not giving someone a job because of the colour of their skin is correct? Do you think people should be arrested more often because of the colour of their skin? Do you think people should be given lower grades at school because of the colour of their skin? You can reasonably, rationally, answer no to these questions even if your irrational self says something different. You have to take issue with your irrational self, argue with it. Sense of self as reasonable leads to contentment, the great connection made by the Enlightenment philosophers, the route to Voltaire's 'happy ages'.

Some may argue this is the age of irrationality. We have no need of experts, I do not require an artillery of words in a world where I can live in my filter bubble or my conservative community, appeal to my illiberal reading of religious texts, watch the flickering flames on the cave wall with no need to travel outside to the wider world, no need to make the great Platonic effort and stop being a prisoner of my surroundings, the cave.

But this is a transient phase if we believe – as surely the British do – that we are the crucible of modern thought, we are the home of David Hume and Francis Bacon and Isaac Newton and Mary Wollstonecraft and John Stuart Mill. That in a battle of ideas, rationality, thought, logic will overcome instinct, gut. That the great wave of progress cannot be stopped, and that it is powered by educational excellence, the provision of the tools of life, for everyone, regardless of creed or class. That not being prejudiced is better than being prejudiced, and that it is pointless to condemn the prejudiced because deep in all of us lurks the disposition. Condemnation, as we know, gets us nowhere.

What does get us somewhere is sense of self, what is right and the journey towards general social happiness – a country at ease with itself. In *The Spirit Level*, Kate Pickett and Richard Wilkinson argue that the more equal a society is the better it is for the poor, maybe obviously, but also the wealthy. It is better for happiness for everyone, for health and for dealing with the modern ills of depression and anxiety. Higher levels of well-being act in opposition to prejudice.

You have to nod towards economic performance, of course, that it is all very well talking about happiness and well-being but if you haven't got food on the table or shoes on your feet then all else fails. Contented workers whose incomes are rising faster than prices (not true for many developed countries in the ten years since the financial crisis) tend to outperform discontented, angry ones. There is an economic case for equality. If black and Asian employees progressed through the workplace at the same rate and speed as white employees, then £24 billion of extra value would be added to the UK economy. Extra value via economic output and taxes for everyone. Black and Asian employees tend to work in lower-paid sectors despite being more likely to have a degree – under-employment (being in a job you are overqualified for) is a problem more prevalent among ethnic minority groups than it is among whites. That is an opportunity cost. A government report in 2002 found that the net fiscal contribution of immigrants to the UK economy is about £2.2 billion. That is, immigrants contributed in taxes £2.2 billion more than they received in government expenditure – benefits, schooling and health services.

But economic betterment is a by-product, it is not the central argument: £24 billion is not an easy figure to understand, and who really goes marching with *Gross Domestic Product increases are a right!* written on their banners, shouting about opportunity costs or under-employment? On immigration the numbers waver and change. After that 2002 report, a subsequent report by the Institute for Public Policy Research found that by 2005 the fiscal boost figure had fallen to a net fiscal cost of £0.4 billion. Taxes collected and spent are fickle beasts, and using numbers that are ultimately rounding errors given the size of the public accounts are a fool's errand. There is an economic case for equality. I just don't think it is very good at convincing people. This is a human conversation, not one carried out with a spreadsheet.

It is contact that can help reconciliation. Start, maybe, with the sharing of sorrows – each side telling the other of the privations they feel they labour under. Catharsis can be important. Not as a claim against the ledger of fairness but simply as a way of putting your sicknesses on a plate and saying, there, take a look at that. But tread carefully, both sides here will be bristling, each a hair-trigger away from the storm out, the flounce, the altercation. Understanding and listening are two very necessary words here. If we want to be successful – and we do, don't we? – no group should feel 'under attack', there should be no structured identification of victim and perpetrator. Contact only works when both groups enter the conversation on a par: what are known as equal status conditions.

The sharing of sorrows is not ultimately enough. 'Catharsis alone is not curative,' Allport said. 'The best that can be said for it is that it prepares the way for a less tense view of the situation. Having had his say, the aggrieved person may be more ready to listen to the other point of view. If his statements have been exaggerated and unfair – as they usually are – the resulting shame modifies his anger and induces a more balanced point of view.' Ethnic minorities meeting white people to simply tell them how difficult their lives are – correct though that may be – will generally increase feelings of guilt and resentment among the people who – if not feeling challenged – are open to change. That guilt and resentment becomes a barrier. If the minority group feels itself under attack from the white majority, it is likely to withdraw into its own area of comfort, the shell of isolation which is a visible reality, for example, for some Muslim communities in Britain.

Although the sharing of sorrows may initially be necessary, soon groups will move on, the conversation will move on – if the process is working. Move on to what? The similar stories that we all experience, the ordinariness of life rather than the extraordinariness of discrimination or resentment. The stories of parenthood, work and hobbies, sport, who won at the football, the Olympics, the cricket. Cooking – what spices work well together, how do you make the perfect pot of rice (coconut milk, I suggest), perfect chips? Research by the data scientist Seth Stephens-Davidowitz found that people in America reacted far more positively to prompts to their curiosity about everyday experiences (following a terrorist attack President Obama asked them to consider the military and sports heroes of America who were Muslims, describing Muslim people as 'our friends, our co-workers, our neighbours') than appeals to the values of tolerance or freedom or the 'American way'.

Coming together means coming together as individuals, as mothers and fathers, as teachers, as the employed, the unemployed, the disabled, the young, the old, as people who want to build that new urban garden for the local community to enjoy, to repaint that graffiti-laden wall, to fix that fence, launch that sports project to bring schoolchildren together who may be living separate lives. Each one becomes a small tendril link, knitting together to make something stronger.

Isn't this all a bit back to the future? When I was at school in Ealing, Asian children from another part of the borough, Southall, arrived in buses every morning. The thinking behind this policy was that contact was better than separation, the local education authority taking heed of the government's view that no school should have an 'immigrant population' above 30 per cent. Sir Edward Boyle, the Minister for Education when the bussing policy was first outlined in the 1960s, argued that beyond 30 per cent, 'native parents' would understandably move their children to other schools, fearful of the costs of language teaching and 'social training' for the children of immigrants.

Schools in Southall were above this 30 per cent figure and so every morning coaches arrived, across the playgrounds of the whiter bits of Ealing where I lived, full of brown kids.

Was this policy helpful, based, as it was, on contact theory? And should it be repeated in those areas of Britain where schools have disproportionately high numbers of single ethnic and religious groups compared with the local population?

No, because the policy did not recognise how contact theory works. And it's quite simple to understand why if you imagine the policy reversed. What if every morning, children with white parents in Ealing had been obliged to put their children on buses for a journey to Southall to join majority Asian schools? This would have caused an uproar, just as the bussing of Asian children caused conflicts in the 1960s and 1970s to the extent that some local authorities, such as Birmingham, refused to implement the policy. Parents were left miles away from their child's school. The policy felt enforced, not voluntary. The children on the buses experienced very little 'contact' with the rest of the school because they were from the 'Paki bus' and often put in separate classes for fear of a backlash from white parents. This was not a meeting of equals, a key determinant of good contact policy.

Many years later, Shabina Aslam, who was a 'bus kid' in Bradford, was interviewed about bussing, looking back with the benefit of time. 'We'd walk in late in a group and we'd always have to leave early. The bus monitor used to come round and say: "Can we have all the immigrants please?" and all the black children would stand up. I didn't really have any friends in the classroom, nobody ever spoke to me. I was always looking at the others thinking: "How do I become like them?"' Bussing schoolchildren did not stop me laughing along and playing 'spot the whitey' with the other kids from the top deck of the 207 bus that travelled down the Uxbridge Road, through Southall. No one explained to me that the 'Paki Bus' should not be called that. And who were these kids, anyway, who couldn't stay on after school and play football?

Better is the experience of my daughter. She joined the National Citizen Service, the government-funded project to bring sixteen- and seventeen-year-olds together and engage not only in the adventurous – kayaking and rock-climbing – but in the socially useful, helping to clean up parks in areas suffering deprivation. Maud was a volunteer, worked with other young people across west London – from all backgrounds, but predominantly Asian – and came home invigorated. Ethnic minority young people are over-represented on NCS. And there are not many institutions that can claim that. Unless they are prisons.

We know the young tend towards idealism, a sense that can be lost as they grow old and grow cynical. But the foundation can be laid there, by a million NCS volunteers making friendships with people who are not like them. Studies in America have shown that white pupils who experience low levels of intergroup contact are more likely to use stereotyped assumptions about why, for example, black children might be 'different' or 'cause discomfort'. One reason that 'black and white kids don't have much in common' was 'because black kids like different music'. Students who had higher levels of intergroup contact, measured by the number of non-white friends, might agree with that sentence but would add 'but that's not a reason to exclude someone'. They saw difference, but they didn't see it negatively.

Contact can lead to better understanding. It can lead to greater opportunities. Better economies. It can lead to better schools and better police forces, better public services and better businesses. Diversity on company boards and among executive teams has been shown to have a direct impact on profitability. A company functions better if it looks like its customers. A company functions better if it has opinions tested by many different points of view, is able to hear from those outside what may have previously been considered the set parameters. Diversity is not about hiring someone who looks different but essentially isn't. Diversity is about hiring somebody who might make you feel uncomfortable and not feeling threatened by it.

This debate on contact has its challenges because the street needs to be two-way. Now, for me and people who look a bit like me and have suffered and been bumped around because of the colour of their skin, this raises a difficulty. It means that I have to understand the other side, the side that hasn't experienced the world as I have, the metropolitan world of London. I have to engage with what white people outside my world are worried about. The people who make me feel uncomfortable.

In 2013/14, there were 47,571 'racist incidents' recorded by the police in England and Wales. On average, that is about 130 incidents per day. By 2016/17 that figure had risen to 62,685.

9

Reconciliation

It would be nice if Britain was post-racial. It would be nice if all the laws passed and policies pursued and conferences held on 'doing better' had finally rid us of systemic prejudice. It would be nice if we were always on a path to progression, that understanding and reconciliation meant all the sides in this debate had moved towards each other. It would be nice if, every time you lifted a previously undisturbed trunk of wood, an ugly echo of the past wasn't revealed. But it keeps happening. And while it keeps happening we have to keep trying.

Bijan Ebrahimi was born in Iran in 1969. He lived there for the first thirty-one years of his life, looking after his parents as they became older and more infirm. His sisters, Mojgan Khayatian and Manizhah Moores, describe an unfailingly polite and diligent brother who as a boy would studiously research games the family played to ensure all the answers were right and the rules followed. Ebrahimi moved to Britain in 2000 after his parents died, living in Bristol to be near his sisters. The three of them were finally together again and free from the constraints of living in the Islamic Republic. Ebrahimi was granted 'indefinite leave to remain' a year later by the Home Office, a refugee welcomed to this country.

He went to college and studied carpentry, plumbing and information technology. Maybe he had dreams of being an entrepreneur, fixing sinks, putting up shelves and troubleshooting your PC all in one visit. Britain, after all, was the country that rewarded effort, expected you to 'pay in' if you wanted to get anything back. Like our appreciation.

But that route to riches, to our appreciation, closed off for Ebrahimi – chronic spine and knee problems meaning he became increasingly immobile and couldn't work. He received disability support and lived alone in a flat on a council estate. He had a cat called Mooshi and tended the pots of flowers outside his front door. Some of his life may well have been happy. Much was not.

By 2013, Bijan Ebrahimi was dead.

Drawing a line between the moment he arrived in Britain and the moment a local resident called 999 and said there was 'a body' lying on the street near where Ebrahimi lived, tells a story of this country. How individual, racist violence – which we can all easily condemn – needs fertile fields in which to grow. First an individual needs a group with like mind, the people who reassure, tell you it is okay to behave with aggression and anger and do not restrain that response. A group of individuals who have abandoned self-regulation. A group of people who do not see themselves as sufficiently vested in their own community to protect all the members of that community. That group then needs institutions which also fail to challenge, fail to disrupt growing, extremist behaviour, are infected by some of the very prejudices they have been built, in part, to tackle.

It is easy to sound, appear, like you want to do the right thing. In offices around the country, bureaucracies produce thick documents called 'Hate Crime Policy' and 'Procedural Guidance' and 'Anti-Social Behaviour Gold Strategy'. These are documents which sit on shelves and which no one remembers at just the moment they should be remembering them. Staff will have done the online course – not face to face with anyone who can look into their eyes because that is too expensive. But it will not have sunk beneath the skin of those who need it to. And then, finally, there is the government, society, all of us, who want to get on with our lives and not be concerned too much with what is going on outside the citadel's comfortable walls, the comfortable walls of privilege and economic security. All it takes for evil to flourish is for good people to be too busy doing something else. And too rich to worry.

When I was at school there was a boy younger than me that, thinking back now, was likely to have come from a Quaker family or similar. He would say in a tremulous voice when cornered in the playground that fighting was wrong, pointing his finger as defiantly as he could in the face of the ring of schoolchildren standing around him laughing. 'Bad', he would say as strongly as he could. He cannot have been much older than nine. We pretended he was an idiot, soft as shit, when in fact his bravery marked him out from the rest of us, the rest of us too keen for the applause of the bullies and thankful that some 'other' was being picked on. Rather than us. Many of us have a little strand of mob mentality, deep down.

Ebrahimi was foreign and disabled, living in an area short on hope and long on boredom. Where unemployment, alcohol and drugs ruined the senses of many. Where blaming the other was easier if everyone told you to do that. What was the alternative? Economic pessimism is toxic.

Ebrahimi's neighbours circled his flat. They kicked the cat. They ripped up the flowers. Children baited him with racist comments. In 2007 there was an arson attack on Ebrahimi's home. He was moved. In 2009 a neighbour threatened to kill him. The assailant was identified but no action was taken. Between 2007 and 2013 Ebrahimi contacted the Avon and Somerset Police force 120 times to explain politely and insistently that his neighbours were making his life some sort of hell. Insults, rocks thrown at his windows, chanting outside at all times of day and night, threats to firebomb his flat. Police thought he was the problem, the troublemaker, the irritant, with his endless calls, describing him as 'a pest' and an 'absolute idiot', someone who was 'using the race card'.

When officers were called to Ebrahimi's house in July 2013 following an altercation (some pushing and shoving) with a neighbour who claimed there was a 'foreign man looking at my kids' and that he was ready to 'fucking kill', they arrested Ebrahimi for breach of the peace. Local people clapped and cheered as he was led in handcuffs to the patrol car, shouted 'paedophile'. When Ebrahimi said the police had only arrested him because of the colour of his skin, one officer said he 'was being racist towards us because we were white'. Ebrahimi cried in the police station and asked if the police could guarantee that he would be safe in his home. One officer admitted that it did appear the 'pitchfork and burning torch brigade are after him' but no meaningful risk assessment was made. Ebrahimi was sent back to his flat the following lunchtime to face the people with the pitchforks.

That afternoon he called the police four times. That evening eight times. He was scared, people were outside his house, shouting again, racist abuse. Could the police come? The following day he called five more times, he even went to the police station. No help arrived, with one officer joking that a colleague was busy 'stuffing their face with Pot Noodle'. At twelve minutes past midnight on 14 July, Ebrahimi picked up his mobile phone and tried again. It was to be the last time. One hour and eleven minutes later a call was put through to the emergency services from a resident of Capgrave Crescent, Brislington, Bristol, saying there was a body lying in the street. By the time the ambulance arrived, the body was alight. It was Ebrahimi, murdered by the man who three days earlier had told the refugee from Iran who had come to Britain to make a life that he was going to 'fuck you up'. A friend of the murderer had provided the accelerant to make the body burn.

Lee James was sentenced to eighteen years for murder. Stephen Norley, his accomplice, to four. Two police officers, Kevin Duffy and Andrew Passmore, were jailed for misconduct in public office. Two others, Leanne Winter and Helen Harris, were dismissed from the force for gross misconduct. Seventeen officers and civilian staff faced misconduct hearings. Procedures were tightened. The Chief Constable of Avon and Somerset Police admitted that 'we failed Mr Ebrahimi in his hour of need' and that he was 'unreservedly sorry for the pain his family have suffered'. He admitted 'some of these failings were systematic' but insisted 'it's important to acknowledge that the actions of a very small number of individuals had a catastrophic effect'. The Independent Police Complaints Commission's inquiry 'found evidence that Bijan Ebrahimi had been treated consistently differently from his neighbours, to his detriment and without reasonable explanation'. The evidence it had sifted through 'has the hallmarks of what could be construed as racial bias, conscious or unconscious'.

Ebrahimi's family finally achieved some degree of justice, just like Doreen and Neville Lawrence achieved some degree of justice. But the sulphurous smell of 'haven't we been here before' is heavy. Ebrahimi was murdered fourteen years after the report into the death of Stephen Lawrence; thirty-two years after the Scarman Report into the running street battles and burnt-out cars of Brixton, which found that the Metropolitan Police's Operation Swamp had indiscriminately targeted black people for stop and search; thirteen years after the murder of the Walthamstow teenager Zahid Mubarek at a young offender institution, where he had been placed in a cell with a violent racist. Robert Stewart beat the nineteen-year-old British Pakistani to death with a table leg hours before the teenager was due to be released to go home to his parents. The subsequent inquiry, only granted by the government after a four-year campaign by Zahid's family, found 186 failings across the prison system.

'They thought these two sisters were going to be fobbed off with a few words,' Ebrahimi's sister, Manizhah Moores, said. 'We were not the foreigners that they thought. Maybe we can tell them what to believe and they will go away. But we fought for this. We were there all the time. Every meeting they asked us to go to. We read every report.' Just like the Lawrences read every report. Just like the Mubareks read every report.

The sisters read to the very end of the IPCC inquiry on how racial prejudice can still lead to death in Britain. And they may have gained some comfort from the final conclusion of Jan Williams who led the inquiry: 'The most salutary lesson for the constabulary is underlined by the sad poignant fact that Bijan Ebrahimi kept faith with the police throughout. The Avon and Somerset constabulary misconduct panel noted that he remained respectful, cooperative and calm, if at times tearful. He was persistent in arguing his case, but nevertheless polite. Under extreme stress and provocation, at no point did he descend to profanity, to insult, to abuse. He never ceded dignity.'

What are we to make of the case of Bijan Ebrahimi? We know that incidents like these are not one-offs. That simmering tensions can live unchecked in all the corners of Britain. That 'micro-aggressions' can soon be amplified, twisted into something more violent if there is no narrative of hope or self-regulation, local or national, pushing against that tide. When did Lee James start on his journey towards the murder of Ebrahimi? When did Robert Stewart? Was it the people close to them who set the limits, or in these cases, the no limits? The communities they grew up in? The lack of contact with anyone different, denied a chance of realising that 'other' people are, in fact, 'just like me'? Were they just violent thugs, bent on killing? A mixture, maybe, of some and all of these influences. There is no excuse for what they did, but they grew up in a society we all live in. Every racist murder is a failure of us all.

And at this sharp, painful end of Britain's race debate we should also pause and remember the deaths of Ross Parker (a white teenager from Peterborough stabbed and beaten to death by three British Asian Muslims), Kriss Donald (a fifteen-year-old white schoolboy murdered and set alight by Pakistani gang members in Glasgow), Richard Everitt (also fifteen and white, murdered in north London by an Asian gang), Marcin Bilaszewski (nineteen, killed by a black attacker who shouted that 'Hitler should have killed all the Polish people'). A report in the *Observer* in 2006 revealed that between 1995 and 2004 there were fifty-eight murders where the police considered race played a key part. Twenty-four of those murder victims were white.

Every murder is equally horrific, tragic and a soul-numbing mess for the victim's family and friends. But in aggregate the murder of black and Asian people is disproportionately high given the low percentage of the population made up of black and Asian people. And when the police say 'white' they include in that categorisation Jewish people, 'dark-skinned' Europeans and Gypsies. Of the twenty-four white victims, seven were killed by white attackers, four by black, six by Asian, while seven were in cases where the racial background was not identified.

Though we should recognise that all sides in this debate can be affected, let's not get bogged down in the weeds of statistics and Home Office data sets. Racial violence is with us and the failure of institutions is a recurrent theme. It is too easy, however, to blame the singular event, the murder, the racist attack, on a series of singular failures, the individual failing to follow procedure, the institution failing to set the right tone, stumble to the right policy. What is the bigger picture that leaves some parts of Britain dislocated? What divides us? Leads to a sense of grievance? A sense of anxiety? I am not talking about murder here, though that is its ultimate expression. I am talking about the social and economic piece of this big, difficult jigsaw.

We know that economic hardship reduces social capital and reduces resilience – that essential ability to deal with the challenges we face as individuals and as groups. If we can find some succour from defining ourselves against the other, we will take that route if our own position is weak.

And that position is weak. In seven of the last ten years, people were earning less in December than they were earning the previous January. Inflation – the rise in living costs – was outstripping the rise in incomes. Britain has just experienced the longest stagnation in earnings since the 1860s. In the last decade real incomes have fallen more rapidly in the UK than all other developed nations bar Greece, Mexico and Portugal. We are very poor at creating wealth for everyone who lives here.

A fifth of all households in the UK are on relatively low incomes, around £232 a week. That's 13 million people who might be considered to be just about making ends meet. It will surprise few people that ethnic minorities are over-represented in this group, with between 40 per cent and 50 per cent of some ethnic groups, including those of Pakistani and Bangladeshi backgrounds, living on low incomes, compared with 19 per cent of the white population.

It would be easy to study such figures and conclude the problem of low income is an ethnic minority problem. And to an extent, it is. But within the figures lurk other reefs. There is increasing evidence that a growing social class – the white working class – is joining that group of people disconnected from the mainstream. Yes, if you look at the transition from education to employment, the white working class – the subject of much media attention – are less likely to be unemployed and to face social-mobility hurdles than black students and Asian Muslims. But, the shock for many white people is that they never expected to be any part of this debate. Those many may therefore lack the mechanisms to deal with the systematic issues which appear to be discriminating against them, not because of the colour of their skin, but because of their class. The type of mechanisms people like me learnt in the playground.

Part of the historic in-group, the white working class have suddenly found themselves sharing a table – dusty as it is with meagre offerings – with the out-group. They have seen their position in historic decline at the same time as immigration has risen, and risen rapidly over the last two decades. The middle class gained from cheap childcare and cheap workers who could put up their extensions and dig their new cellar rooms for half the cost. The working class watched as something they had never asked for and never been asked about changed their world.

How would you respond to that? By turning inwards, becoming protective of your 'own kind', maybe allowing a little more prejudice to influence your thinking, a coping mechanism. The hollering media, sometimes peddling facts bent with dishonesty, may give easy justification. But the belief that if it wasn't for our raucous press, fear of 'other' would disappear, that newspaper readers are being led by the nose to think bad thoughts, is, to quote the editor of the *Sun*, Tony Gallagher, 'delusional'. It is too easy for the comfortable – like me – to portray those who feel the threat of 'otherness' as people who do not understand their own minds. This is the metropolitans' disease. We are too distant from people who do not think like us – professors looking through our microscopes at a petri dish full of a rare culture, slowly growing mould.

As the effects of the financial crisis a decade ago still wash through the economy, resentment has grown. Trust in politics is at a historic low. When asked to choose between capitalism – the system they live under – and socialism – the system they don't – people plump for socialism, which is seen as for the 'greater good' and 'fair'. Capitalism is associated with greed, corruption and selfishness. A 'brand analysis' of capitalism would reveal a system suffering acute reputational crisis. And as it does so, faith in patriotism has grown. Asked to define words associated with patriotism, people choose 'attractive', 'inspiring', 'satisfying'. A large part of the population is looking for comfort and is rejecting what went before – the European Union or multiculturalism, it doesn't really matter which. If every election, every test of public opinion, comes down to a fight between change and more of the same, people are rejecting more of the miserable same and picking change. Not that 'hopey changey' thing of President Obama and 2008. This is a different type of change.

Cut adrift on economic rough seas they no more understand than they control, anger grows. It can be targeted at those in power. It can be targeted at the rich. It can be targeted at the refugee placed in hard-to-obtain social housing because local authorities have to save money and that means putting people in the cheapest housing available. Yes, it is our obligation as a country, but how much of that is explained to anyone? It can be targeted at the immigrant who has arrived to work, the people of a different colour who live here. Asked if they think there will be more or less racism in five years' time, 50 per cent of people say more, 20 per cent say less. Since 1983 when the British Social Attitudes Survey started asking the question, those answering 'less' only outscored the 'more' camp once, in the late 1990s when economic growth was strong and Peter Mandelson could say without the fear of much contradiction that Labour was 'intensely relaxed about people getting filthy rich, as long as they pay their taxes'.

After the recession of 2008 and 2009, a direct result of the financial crisis, the number of people admitting to being either 'very' or 'a little' prejudiced jumped to nearly 40 per cent, a figure not seen since the 1980s. And given that not many of us like to admit to prejudice, it is a reasonable supposition that the actual figure is higher. As Seth Stephens-Davidowitz found by studying our searches on the internet following a terrorist attack, we are more likely to be looking for 'kill Muslims' than 'Muslim sports heroes'. More than two-thirds of people said they believed 'most White British people' would mind if a close relative married a Muslim. Polled in 2017 on whether they would support higher levels of skilled immigration to the UK following Brexit, 34 per cent of white Britons agreed when told that the skilled immigration would be 'from outside Europe'. That figure fell to 18 per cent when asked the same question, but 'from outside Europe' was replaced by 'from Africa and Asia'. Prejudice of a racial kind has become more hard-baked at the same time as other social liberal indicators such as our attitude to same-sex marriage, sex outside of marriage and abortion have all softened markedly.

Every disconnect, economic and social, means less contact, the danger of more prejudice and worse cultural and economic outcomes, for all the groups affected by this debate about discrimination, including white people. The industrial decline and social change of the 1980s still scars many parts of Britain – the Potteries, Teesside, the former mining heartlands of Yorkshire (where half my family come from), the East Midlands and South Wales, the tourist towns of the east coast that lost their customers to the south of Spain. And however much it is argued that the problems of this great country are not down to immigration, to 'otherness' – and that, in fact, our greatness is allied to immigration, to otherness – it does not alter the debate for those who feel themselves stuck with the crappy end of the stick.

After the Brexit vote – which had little to do with race but did have a lot to do with culture and 'otherness' – I spoke to a number of people about why they voted to leave the European Union. There was the taxi driver in Teesside, a young man in his thirties, who used to work in the mills that sat hard against what was once known as Steel River where they built the struts for the Sydney Harbour Bridge and the new World Trade Center. Most of those factories are closed now and the number of jobs cut from the tens of thousands to the hundreds. Now David drives people like me around for half the money he used to earn. What jobs there were, he said darkly, were 'for Poles'.

There were the Asian voters in Hounslow, west London, who didn't appreciate EU citizens receiving special rights denied to them, to bring family members, to come here to work.

There was the middle-aged, white, evangelical Christian in Rotherham so angry at the levels of immigration she would rather a 'depression' than letting it continue. 'Bring it on,' she told me. She had had enough.

White British and White Other children from low-income homes are the lowest performing groups at primary school. White British pupils make the least progress throughout secondary school, resulting in a worsening in their performance relative to other groups by the age of sixteen. Several ethnic minority groups now outperform White British pupils – 74 per cent of Indian ethnicity pupils achieve a 'good' level of development by age five, compared with 69 per cent of White British children, a figure that falls to 50 per cent for those on free school meals, a common denoter of economic deprivation. That is a far sharper fall than that suffered by Indian ethnicity pupils on free school meals. By the time of GCSEs, White British children are being outperformed by Asian and mixed-race pupils. Only Black heritage children are doing worse. If you are a white working-class boy on free school meals you are less than half as likely to achieve the standard of five or more GCSEs at grades A–C compared with all other pupils. Poor standards of education may have been less noticeable when the white working class could find easy employment in the local factory. But that easy, often well-paid employment has gone, though its echoes are still with us. White children still tend to see achieving a university degree as less important than ethnic minority pupils.

Once in employment, the gaps between people's pay has also been shifting in a way that reveals that 'race' is not the simple definer it once was, with white people at the top of the tree and everyone else further down. Rates of unemployment and low-status employment are still higher for most ethnic minority groups. Once in work, Indian and Chinese men (either born in Britain or abroad) and British-born black people of African heritage earn similar amounts compared with white people. Pakistani and Bangladeshi men tend to earn far less, being over-represented in lower-paid professions such as kitchen staff and taxi drivers (a quarter of all Pakistani men in Britain work as taxi drivers, which is about as sharp a case of occupational segregation as you are ever likely to find). When it comes to women, ethnic minorities tend to earn more than white women, and the pay advantage is notable. Again, Pakistani and Bangladeshi women do earn considerably less, but British-born women of Pakistani and Bangladeshi heritage enjoy earnings similar to white women. In general ethnic minorities have higher levels of qualifications and tend to be clustered in London, where pay is higher. These employment advantages are starting to show in the statistics.

This is not a zero-sum game: you can only win because I lose. It is not about setting up the 'white working class' as a new group being racially discriminated against. It is false conjecture to suggest that white working-class people are doing badly because ethnic minorities are doing well. But there is a structural issue which affects ethnic minorities *and* the white working class, who have as little access to power as the poorer ethnic minorities they are so often told 'are the problem'.

And this is where contact theory comes full circle. How about ethnic minority groups and the white working class coming together to find solutions to where they find themselves? Economic deprivation, lack of aspiration, lack of access to creating wealth via employment, an education system that lets down those that most need it are universal problems in Britain. Sometimes people seem so busy throwing stones at each other they forget that the targets are elsewhere and they need a grand coalition to make 'elsewhere' hear them. The groups so often portrayed as enemies could now become allies. The strength of that voice would be remarkable.

The social critic Terry Eagleton said that the pillar box is evidence of civilisation. That it is painted green in his home country is evidence of culture. His was an Irish story, a country which, on achieving independence from the United Kingdom, painted its post boxes green to match the green in the Irish flag and to make the point that red pillar boxes were British. James Connolly, the Irish republican leader who was executed by firing squad following the Easter Rising, said that the Irish fight against British rule was about more than the colour of the receptacles people put their letters in. It was about freedom. And for that you needed guns, not stamps.

The colour of pillar boxes signifies identity as well as culture. I know I am home when I see a red pillar box. A red bus. When I drink a properly made cup of tea. Identity is that hard-to-define concept which confers power by its very vagueness, the ability to describe it in the way you want, not the way that others want. I am a Londoner and British. It is the second of those two that is open to different uses, to misuse. It suggests great history – the British Museum. The ability of commerce – British Airways, not UK Air or Fly Britain, but *British* Airways. The far right – the British National Party. Its elasticity is its joy and its danger.

I don't describe myself as English, even though I am as much English as British. 'English' has been manipulated to suggest, with its flags of St George and cricket tests, something far more racially distinct, exclusive, even though many of the things I love are very particularly English. I share this trait with many non-white people. Asked to identify their background, two thirds of Bangladeshi-heritage people living in the UK say British. Less than 10 per cent say English. Even the national census recognises it. I can self-identify as black, black British or black Scottish, not as black English. Or Welsh for that matter.

Unlike being English, being British is a brown thing as well as a white thing. It is the ultimate mixed-race descriptor. British is the umbrella I feel most comfortable sitting under. What is it, to be British? Something that is inclusive and reconciled, not exclusive and separate. We all live on the same few thousand square miles of land, which is a good starting point. What is it that makes this land unique? And not French? Or Sudanese? What are the cultural norms that give the nations of the United Kingdom strength? That we can rely on in times of stress?

The opening stanzas of the national anthem. The notes of 'Jerusalem'. The taste, the smell, of fish and chips, sharp with vinegar, the crispy batter bits at the bottom of the paper. The plays of Shakespeare. The music of Benjamin Britten. The inventions of Sir Isaac Newton. The University of Oxford. The game of cricket. The Royal Navy. Constable. *The Archers*. Frinton-on-Sea. Parliament. Sherlock Holmes. Red pillar boxes.

There are many items we might put in a leather case marked 'my country'. Each will reveal something of our values. Codifying it is difficult, deliberately.

'Flower of Scotland'. 'Land of My Fathers'. The songs of the Clash. The plays of Joe Orton. The music of the Spice Girls. Chicken tikka masala. The work of Rosalind Franklin who helped discover DNA. The University of Bedfordshire. The game of football. *The X Factor*. Zaha Hadid. Glastonbury.

Hairdressing competitions. *Mrs Brown's Boys*. Two Tone. The Manchester Ship Canal. Arthur's Seat. Bruce Forsyth. Alton Towers.

That's a different type of imagined country. But it is the same country. My country.

Democracy. The rule of law. Individual liberty. Equality. Mutual respect. Tolerance. Understanding different faiths and beliefs.

That is Dame Louise Casey's list, the woman who produced a report for the government in 2016 on 'opportunity and integration'. The essential British values. Amanda Spielman, head of the Schools Inspection Service in England, said that good education 'takes people on a journey of enlightenment' where if you do not have respect for other people's views 'you won't listen to them'. One of the most important aspects of being British is having a receive button.

There is a different way of course. A different way to use British values. A way that indicates a belief that there are people, groups, who might threaten not just the values but 'Britishness' itself by not understanding them or failing to support them. It is the ultimate definition of 'otherness', the accusation that you might not belong. The use of the word 'British' can be used to suggest exclusivity, only available to members of the club, the in-group. It comes with the whiff of soil, history, place. It is not meant for me, us, the brown group.

In 2007, Gordon Brown, then the prime minister, called for 'British jobs for British workers' in his speech to the Labour Party. What did he mean by that? British workers like me? Or British workers who felt themselves slipping from view, the real British working classes who no longer had it so good? Was Gordon Brown playing to the 'Rule Britannia mindset' as it was once described in a weighty report by Lord Bhikhu Parekh? That theme that runs through the Last Night of the Proms. The then Prime Minister insisted not, but be careful handling dog whistles. When workers at oil refineries and construction sites launched a series of wildcat strikes against the hiring of 'foreign workers' – many carrying placards with Brown's quote displayed proudly – the British National Party called it a great day for nationalism.

'British values' can play this tune, causing the hairs on the back of my neck to rise, finely attuned to fear. Like flags of St George fluttering at the top of a pole in someone's garden or Sellotaped to the back window of a car. Feeling uncomfortable does not mean I am any less proud to be British. I am proud of the common values that tie us together, and am happy to be judged by an adherence to them. Louise Casey's list seems as good a stab at these common values as any. I am proud of the Union flag. But there is a subtle problem with British values which should be understood. Being British also comes with a long list of things we should not be proud of. A schools system that keeps some people of colour back, police who fail too often, prisons too full of black men, the lack of black and Asian people at the top of business and government.

And what of 'tolerance', that tricky little word that Gordon Allport describes as 'flabby'. You tolerate a squeaking door, mess in your garden, a dripping tap. That is, tolerate in the sense of endure. I do not want to be endured, or to feel I have to 'endure' others. We must mean 'tolerance' here in the sense of a warm-hearted tolerance, the type of tolerant personality Allport talks of, rugged, able to get on, allow for ambiguity, not living by strict rules, confident enough to allow for some difference and not to condemn. That sort of tolerance takes effort and is the sort of tolerance I am talking about, that very British idea of conviviality, rolling up our sleeves and making things work.

In order to show I adhere to these common values I also pledge to admit when things about people my colour, my group, make me a little queasy, that it's not just the St George's flags I notice. Such as when the former MP, Oona King, spoke of being shocked when she visited a school in her east London constituency where 'they shared a playground with a fence down the middle'. 'On one side of the fence there were white children playing with a smattering of Afro-Caribbeans and on the other there were brown, Muslim and Bangladeshi children. Perhaps it is because my father was brought up in the segregated south [of the USA] that I was horrified by that; I could not believe it. We read about such things, but when we see them in Britain, we must think that something is seriously wrong.' Research produced in Louise Casey's government review found that when asked to estimate the percentage Asian population in Britain, one school they visited with mostly Asian children presumed a figure somewhere between 50 per cent and 90 per cent. The actual figure is 7 per cent.

I do not want to be part of the panic about an ethnically and racially divided Britain. For every illiberal voice, whether it is white, black or Muslim, there is a liberal voice to counter. The Index of Dissimilarity, which uses census data to measure the spread of ethnic minorities across the country, shows a fall in the levels of segregation for all groups apart from Pakistani, where levels of segregation have levelled off after a fall between 1991 and 2001. Within that figure there are some areas of clustering, wards where there is a high percentage of Pakistani- and Bangladeshi-background Muslims. Why? Because when it is cold outside you tend to huddle together for warmth. Geographical concentration is a natural reaction to hostile terrain and for many Muslims, constantly being told to account for themselves, Britain can seem hostile terrain.

This is the House of Britain. Where we are bound by a sense of values which are not exclusive but are able to flex and be inclusive. Where we understand why so many millions of people from the Angles to the Saxons, the Vikings to the French, the Afro-Caribbeans to the Pakistanis (and a smattering of Sudanese) have come here to make their lives on this small island. Where we listen to each other's problems, not condemn them. Where we realise that talking will achieve a lot more than not talking. Where we are optimistic rather than pessimistic, where the best years are always ahead of us, not behind. Admittedly and understandably the meliorists have had a tough decade. But we still believe the world can be made better by our singular human effort.

VeryBritishProblems @SoVeryBritish

But apart from that everything's fine
10 replies 536 retweets 2,976 likes

Conclusion
In-group

It is a sunny summer morning in Ealing, west London. I am walking through the park with my son, a walk from my mother's house to the main Broadway I must have undertaken a thousand times when I was Noah's age, off to the shops to buy records, off to my bassoon lessons at Ealing Music School, off to meet my mate Jan whose German parents were so on-trend they had painted one of their living-room walls a different colour from the rest, a dark red as I remember. That passed for avant-garde in 1970s suburbia. His mum also let you smoke in the house.

Noah is wearing his Liverpool top with Firmino picked out in letters on the back. He would rather have had Coutinho but they had run out of the letter 'u' at the Anfield stadium shop when we were there. So he settled for the other Brazilian. He wears his top when Liverpool are playing – as they are later that day. It's a good-luck thing. I am taking him for a haircut and we are arguing about the relative merits or otherwise of our shaky defence when, just on the periphery of my vision, I notice a man standing very still.

My job for the BBC means I am on television quite a lot and sometimes I am recognised in the street. People wave and say hello, usually with a cheery smile and a 'thanks for what you're doing' compliment. I look over at the man. He is wearing a jacket, dark clothes, with a baseball cap pulled down to shade his eyes. Odd, I think, to be wearing so many clothes on such a warm day. He is maybe a few years older than me, white.

He starts to raise his arm and, I must admit, I am ready, ready for the greeting. 'Yes,' I would reply, 'I'm on the telly! Thanks so much.' But, it is not a wave. His arm is straight out, not bent at the elbow, the palm flat, facing the floor, fingers and thumb together. At an angle of forty-five degrees from the horizontal this man's defiant Nazi salute is complete, standing in the middle of a park surrounded by neatly tended flowerbeds and local authority water features. He stares at me steadfastly, his jaw jutting slightly, pointing his salute at me. As my son and I pass, and it feels like slow motion, I turn and look at him and he turns to continue his silent protest, his arm aloft, staring. He must have held the pose for thirty seconds.

Noah looks up at me as we walk on around the corner and out of sight of the man in the baseball cap. 'Dad, what was that?'

'God only knows, that bloke seemed to be doing a Nazi salute. That's about the weirdest thing I have ever seen.'

And Noah bursts out laughing. He bursts out laughing because it's nuts and adults are mad and he can no more calculate the reason for a man doing a Nazi salute at his dad than he can imagine the National Front marching along the streets in Southall down the road when his dad was thirteen – the same age he is now.

And we walk under the avenue of trees and Noah takes my hand, which he doesn't do very much now because that's a bit soft for a boy who is approaching young adulthood. And through my mind travel a lot of thoughts about the country we were, the country we are and the country we could become. And why that man raising his arm in a Nazi salute doesn't represent anything very much. Not anything very much that I would consider British.

We are a country that has struggled to understand immigration and its close cousin, race. A country that has never had the conversation involving everyone. A country that has allowed what conversations there have been to be dominated by the worried, not the hopeful. We never did explain to ourselves that immigration was a function of our history, our colonial past, a subject that links our push for the sun to never set on the British Empire – and the riches that brought – with a reciprocal duty to welcome the citizens of the world to our shores. That all differences between the haves and have-nots, the owner and the slave, the black and the white are, to use Yuval Noah Harari's phrase, 'rooted in fictions'. That non-white immigrants have a right to be here as strong as any immigrants on an island which, if you look long and hard enough, is made up of people who are all, ultimately, immigrants. All, ultimately, members of an out-group.

We are a country that has faced a decade of economic stagnation not seen for 150 years. Resentments have grown, in-groups and out-groups have challenged each other, that river I always thought flowed from A to B – where B was better than A – has shown itself a more meandering beast, doubling back, unsure of its route, creating eddies, pools, pauses. We are a country that has hunkered down, decided we want fewer people coming here from outside, need time for us to take breath, for the in-group to regroup.

And through that the country of our future will be born.

And here is a scenario I would like to test on you, the reader who has come this far with me. After Brexit, it is likely that the number of immigrants to Britain will fall. That is what many people voted for. But we will still face the increasing costs of a country full of people who are ageing. The joint forces of medical research and artificial intelligence will push the boundaries of life expectancy. Half of all children born in the year 2000, like my daughter, Maud, will reach the age of 100. We will need to create money, wealth, to pay for that future. And the conversation about immigration and race will change. We will need young people from whatever shore they hail. We will need people like Abubaker Ismail Ahmed – Seddig to his friends – to come here and work hard and help forge a new route for the river flowing from A to B. And at that point the conversation this country needs to have on that complicated, messy, delightful, tough, depressing, uplifting story of race and identity will not just feel right. It will feel *necessary*.

Do you know what? Our decision to leave the European Union might go a lot further towards solving our issues of race and identity than anyone ever imagined.

And wouldn't that be a happy moment? Happy for Maud and Noah who are just starting on their adult journey, third-generation immigrants whose blackness is slowly receding, living in a country that will offer them so much, its beauty, its endeavour, the opportunity to achieve not hampered by the irrationality of discrimination. Maud and Noah's conversations about identity will be very different from mine. The young will carry new standards where the multiple identities of gender and sexuality will be as much a part of who they are as the colour of their skin. 'Mixed-race', categorisations, 'communities' will become increasingly meaningless. The border between those 'in' and those 'out' will change; technology will be the catalytic flywheel for a generation where it is as easy to speak to someone on the other side of the world as the other side of the street. This century will be dominated by the debate about digital haves (smartphones, enhanced realities, artificial intelligence) and digital have-nots (those locked out of the newly networked classes). Race and identity, which dominated the twentieth century, will have to take their place in the queue.

And wouldn't that be a happy moment for Elaine Mary Sturman, a woman who decided that this was a battle worth having – the fight for something a bit better tomorrow than it was yesterday – and is growing old now in a country immeasurably finer for the journey she and a thousand like her set off on fifty years ago. My mother laughs now, laughs about her naivety as a young person in the 1960s, believing as she did that it just needed good people to come together to tackle what they found ugly. That everyone would 'get it'. But naivety can be a great quality, opposed as it is to cynicism and scepticism, the force behind a push for something different because we are able to. We climbed Everest because it was there. We flew to the moon. It may have taken billions of dollars of research money to split the atom and we may never understand the irrationality of human nature. But if we can settle on the conclusion that it is irrational – that prejudice exists in all of us – then that is a place to launch off from because everyone is then included.

And wouldn't it be a happy moment for me, to live in a country where the proportion of people who can count themselves an ethnic minority is expected to rise to nearly 40 per cent by 2050, raising the prospect that 'minority' will be a word facing redundancy for all of us black and brown and 'other' people. And to feel, and to hope, that this is a country comfortable with that. To realise that this stuff is difficult, that we all need to sweat it a little, own it, understanding that it is the very mix of white and black and brown that is the foundation of this great country's history. And is the basis for optimism. That the out-group becomes the in-group, and that in-group is simply British, all the people who live on our small island.

Afterword
Mr Powell and Mr Trump

During my research for this book I looked at a number of interpretations of Enoch Powell's 'Rivers of Blood' speech. I spoke at length to Simon Heffer, a supporter of Powell, and have reflected on many of his opinions, and drawn on his vast wealth of knowledge, for the chapters that deal with that speech. But I also wanted an outside view, a view from someone who would be no natural supporter of Powell but who could deliver a judgement on Powell's speech as a piece of oratory. Cody Keenan, former director of speechwriting in the White House under President Obama, very generously agreed to contribute some ideas to the book, which I have woven in elsewhere. He did so by way of a piece he sent me that I believe is worth publishing in full. Here it is:

Important speeches are ones that endure, that offer something for each new generation to consider and argue. By that test alone, Enoch Powell's 'Rivers of Blood' speech is important. It remains timely today.

But by no test should it be considered a 'great' speech. Its importance and endurance are derived from the basest of human emotions it stirs – fear, division and resentment. One can't really judge a piece of political rhetoric by separating its technical merits from its ideas. Politics, after all, is a battle of ideas, and the ideas contained in this speech I find reprehensible.

Mr Powell begins the speech with a long windup about the role of the state, the fecklessness of politicians, and the corrosive nature of political correctness long before 'political correctness' was coined as a term. Here lies the first flaw of the speech: Powell never truly owns his own opinion. The speech makes it clear where he stands, of course, but he hides behind the opinions of others, claiming the mantle of being the rare politician concerned with the future, an altruist of sorts, a patriot who didn't seek this cause, but rather had it thrust upon him.

The speech really begins to get going as he describes a conversation with a constituent. Technically speaking, this is a good idea. When I was writing speeches in the White House, we would often weave stories from letters that the President received or from interactions he'd had with constituents. We called them 'real people'. We meant it as a compliment, as shorthand to say that anyone from outside the sphere of Washington politics was a real person in ways that we were not.

It's a useful tactic in speechwriting to deploy such stories in order to illustrate what you're trying to do, to gain credibility, to convey authenticity. Any politician can say 'I am one of you', or 'I feel your pain'. But we always found that telling a story to prove the same point forged a better connection with the audience. In essence, it was a real person telling politicians how to solve his or her problems, rather than a politician telling real people how he or she would solve their problems.

We'd also do our due diligence, of course – making sure the 'real person' was an upstanding citizen, that their story checked out, and, most importantly, that they were comfortable with the leader of the free world using their words. We'd also make sure the media knew that the 'real person' about whom we were speaking was, in fact, not a fictional creation, but actually real.

In Mr Powell's case, his opinion – that minority immigrants are ruining the country – is introduced not by him, but by his constituent. And just two paragraphs later, he reveals his motivation to take up the cause is not out of any personal conviction, but the virtue of being a humble servant. 'How dare I say such a horrible thing? The answer is that I do not have the right not to do so ... I simply do not have the right to shrug my shoulders and think about something else.'

It struck me as cowardly. And I confess it reminded me of a quote from the pompous Judge Smails in the American comedy, *Caddyshack*: 'I've sentenced boys younger than you to the gas chamber. Didn't want to do it. I felt I owed it to them.'

In 2017, one would call that 'a copout'. Of course Powell has the right to think about something else. Of course he has the right to choose his own stance on a topic, even at the risk of angering part of his constituency. That's what representative democracy is, and that's how it works in a parliamentary democracy under a constitutional monarchy as well.

By this point in his remarks, Powell has begun by admitting that the topic is considered reprehensible by polite society, and that the responsibility to talk about it has been thrust upon him by posterity. Where is his own agency? Where is his own conviction? What a cowardly note on which to begin a speech about 'evil'. Perhaps he was afraid to be cast as a racist, or perhaps he was afraid to lose an election. Either way, it's a speech that stems from fear – and that's not a speech you want to deliver.

Still, even if he has yet to make any sort of moral or values-based case for his argument, he plows forward, beginning to deploy facts and figures to support his argument. This, too, is vital to a well-argued speech. But he falls short here as well, cherry-picking one data point: that within fifteen or twenty years, there will be three and a half million immigrants and their descendants in Great Britain. It sounds like a lot, which is the point – but is it? What percentage of the British population will that be? How quickly is the native-born population growing?

Without this context, the intent is to make Britain sound like a static society that's being overrun by the unwashed hordes. That, of course, is his point. And from here, the speech accelerates in its disingenuousness, plunging into what actually makes it memorable – not any line or argument or inspirational note – but rather the powerful emotions it evokes.

Eventually, whole towns – maybe even yours! – will be 'occupied' by immigrants and their children. Their numbers will increase as they breed. They are an 'alien element', while the 'decent', 'ordinary' citizens, like the constituent of whom Powell spoke, have 'found their wives unable to obtain hospital beds in childbirth, their children unable to obtain school places, their homes and neighbourhoods changed beyond recognition, their plans and prospects for the future defeated; at work they found that employers hesitated to apply to the immigrant worker the standards of discipline and competence required of the native-born worker'.

At one point, he even claims that dark-skinned immigrants were literally pushing human faeces through the mailbox of a hardworking, responsible white woman.

No thinking person would readily accept the argument that immigrants somehow occupied every single job, school desk, and hospital bed in Britain. But that's not Powell's intent. His intent is to divide – into 'good' versus 'evil', 'us' versus 'them'. The 50,000 immigrants who come each year are 'dependents' who couldn't possibly want to work hard or start businesses, unlike the 'decent', 'ordinary' folks that 'we' know. He uses imagery like 'gathering clouds' and 'throwing a match onto gunpowder' to suggest imminent threats. He blames media elites for their role in ruining society, likening them to Nazi appeasers in the run-up to World War II. And anyone who stands in 'our' way is 'mad' or 'insane'.

It's an effective tactic. Fear, resentment, division and blame are powerful motivators. But he probably should have stopped there before dispensing an array of logical fallacies that only serve to further reveal his own biases.

First, Powell has defined immigrants as lazy dependents who refuse to assimilate. But the first story he shared in his remarks was of a constituent who wanted his kids to emigrate to another country. Will they work hard and assimilate? If so, what makes them different beyond the color of their skin? Or is this just plain hypocrisy?

Second, 'all who are in this country as citizens,' he states, 'should be equal before the law and that there shall be no discrimination or difference made between them by public authority'. Just two sentences later, he argues: 'This does not mean that the immigrant and his descendent should be elevated into a privileged or special class or that the citizen should be denied his right to discriminate in the management of his own affairs between one fellow-citizen and another.'

So discrimination should be illegal, but you can't deny someone's right to discriminate? All citizens should be equal, without assignment to class, but equality for the immigrant or his child constitutes a special class?

Powell then anticipates a counterargument – the comparison between Commonwealth immigrants and 'the American Negro'. It's wise to anticipate and defeat counterarguments, while taking care not to create a strawman. And his general description of the differences between the two struggles isn't wrong, though I take exception to his description of African-Americans being 'given' rights, rather than having 'earned' the rights that we profess our Creator to have given all of us long ago.

This is a speech that's memorable for its content. And when judging a speech, you can't truly separate the technique from the content. Even if technically proficient, a speech is about ideas, about persuading others to work towards those ideas – and these are bad ideas.

There's nothing lyrical about the speech, nothing aspirational about it, it possesses few memorable lines save for the title it inherited. It's cynical, dishonest, cowardly, and actually quite boring. It's a racist dog whistle wrapped in dullness.

It's Donald Trump with a larger vocabulary, and less red meat. In fact, Mr Trump owes a debt of gratitude to Powell. Like Powell, he peddled a vision of what his country had lost, about pernicious changes and dark forces that undermined our way of life. In Donald Trump's America, political correctness and media bias had silenced good, hardworking white people while our borders were overrun by rapists and illegal immigrants (not true, illegal immigration was down), our cities were fiery cesspools of carnage (not true, crime was down), and jobs for hardworking Americans were impossible to come by (not true, at the time of his election, the unemployment rate was a healthy 4.6 per cent, and the American economy had created jobs for an unprecedented seventy-three consecutive months). It was divisive and built on lies. And it worked.

Speeches like Powell's and Mr Trump's can be politically successful. They can give voice to those who feel like they have none, and serve as a powerful challenge to the status quo. But they're rarely the speeches we remember. They're not the speeches we read to our children. And they're never the speeches we carve into marble.

That's why I was surprised to discover that the 'Rivers of Blood' speech is the most memorable speech on race in Britain. By contrast, America's most famous speech on race is one in which water was invoked differently – in which 'justice rolls down like waters, and righteousness like a mighty stream'. Those are the words of Dr Martin Luther King, Jr. And the presence of water imagery is where the similarity stops.

Yes, Powell plundered the 'extreme urgency of action now' from Dr King's 'fierce urgency of now', but for dramatically different ends. Unlike Powell, who argued for separate treatment, Dr King argued for equal treatment. Unlike Powell, who spoke of a looming nightmare for one group of people (one, I might add, that never actually arrived, even if it is still a potent force in British politics and the Brexit movement),

Dr King spoke of a dream – a dream so far denied and as yet unfulfilled for one group of people – but a dream that, once realized, will carry everyone, not just African-Americans, to the promised land. That speech was honest and self-critical; it didn't sugarcoat our failings, but rather looked upon our flaws and dared us to do better.

That's one of the most important differences between the worldview held by people like Powell and Mr Trump, and the worldview held by people like Dr King and President Obama – the possibility of change.

The presence of some upward trajectory to the human story. The persistent notion that self-evident truths are not self-executing, and that through shared effort, we can apply the words of our founding to everybody, and everybody benefits.

The British and American experiences are different, of course. America was built by waves of immigrants, and so we've never had as strong an ethnic nationalism with which to define ourselves. America is an idea, one built on high-minded ideals that we often fail to reach.

But what defines us is that we try. We've been trying for 241 years. That's what makes us exceptional – not that we are perfect, but rather that we are imperfect, and know it, and struggle, relentlessly, to reach for those ideals. When we succeed in that struggle is when we soar. When our leaders remind us of that is when we are inspired. How telling that Powell ended his speech with the same cowardly tone with which he began: 'Whether there will be the public will to demand and obtain that action,' without fully defining said action, 'I do not know. All I know is that to see, and not to speak, would be the great betrayal.' The final line is about him, and him alone – he's been summoned to a task, and he reluctantly accepts.

Dr King closed his own speech on the opposite note – with a dream, but a dream that we can reach together, and when we do, all of us, regardless of race or religion, will know the true meaning of freedom. That's why his is one that lives on not only in marble on the Mall, but in the hearts and minds of our children – and Powell's does not.

Cody Keenan
White House director of speechwriting
under President Obama

ACKNOWLEDGEMENTS

This book started because of the belief of two people. Without them it would never have happened. Alexis Kirschbaum, my editor at Bloomsbury, and Georgina Capel, my agent. Alexis never wavered in her conviction that I had something to say (and helped me say it), and Georgina was the person who urged me to 'write it down' when I told her a little about my life. Both offered endless optimism and routes through those tangled, uncertain moments I am sure many writers experience.

Thanks as well to the remarkable team at Bloomsbury: Emma Bal and Genista Tate-Alexander, for being clear-eyed on what this book was about when I was foggy; Sarah Ruddick for piloting the edit; and Jasmin Elliott for handling the complications of book tours and interviews. To my copy-editor, Kate Johnson, who saved me from myriad mistakes with good humour and sensitivity.

Many people more expert than I gave willingly of their time, for which I am grateful. I would like to particularly mention Simon Heffer who, though knowing that we would be unlikely to agree about Enoch Powell's legacy, read drafts and offered comments without which this book would have been the lesser. Also Jenny Powell, Enoch Powell's daughter, and her daughter, Julia, who very generously allowed me to read and quote from her dissertation. Professor Rupert Brown of Sussex University guided me through the complicated twists of contact theory and prejudice. All errors are, of course, my own.

To my mother, Elaine (who not only patiently revealed much about her own life but proved herself an excellent 'first reader'), my uncles, Anthony and Philip, and my aunt, Marjorie – you are the bedrock of my very Britishness. To my aunt Asma and my family in Sudan, thank you for welcoming me with such open arms. I have learnt a lot about my father and myself.

Maud and Noah have anchored my father-feet firmly to the ground with perspectives – often mixed with side-hurting laughter – only children (and teenagers) can provide. I hope this book tells them something about who they are. To Gemma Curtin, Maud and Noah's mother, and my fellow traveller on that complicated road stamped 'parent'.

To my childhood friends: Jonathan Eva, Jerry Dunn, Pier Lambiase and Andy Sampson. We've known each other an awfully long time. Former school teachers also spoke to me as part of my research but didn't want to be named. Thank you as well.

To the BBC and particularly James Harding, the former head of News and Current Affairs, who reacted with a big smile of congratulation when I told him about my 'mad, book-writing plan' and 'of course' when I subsequently requested a period of writing leave. Colleagues Jasmin Buttar, Piers Parry-Crooke and Simon Jack generously filled the gaps my absence caused. Malcolm Balen was tasked with reading a draft at speed, which he did without complaint, despite it sucking up a good few hours of precious days off.

A thank you to friends and loved ones, the team all of us need to do anything at all. Jane Martinson, Richard Smith, Ollie and Katie Lloyd, Bella Bathurst, D. J. Collins, Martin

Hennessy, Pascale Vogel, James Purnell, Rohan Silva, Fred and Julia Michel, Roger Alton, Catherine Mayer, Andy Gill, Damian Whitworth, Camilla Nichols, Sara Sjolund and Mags Patten have kept me afloat when in danger of sinking. A special mention to Ruaridh Nicoll for having my back these past twenty-five years.

And finally to Polly Glynn, who has calmly taken my hand and agreed, there is much more life to live. I am very lucky to have you by my side.

NOTES

EPIGRAPHS

'It required years of labour': Reproduced with permission of Hachette Books Group, from G. W. Allport in *The Nature of Prejudice*, Kenneth B. Clark, 1979; permission conveyed through Copyright Clearance Center, Inc.

'There is no reason for you': James Baldwin, 'Letter to My Nephew on the One Hundredth Anniversary of the Emancipation', *The Fire Next Time*, Vintage, 1963, p. 8.

'Keep on movin'. Don't stop, like the hands of time. Click clock': from 'Keep on Movin'' by Soul II Soul. All rights reserved. Used by permission.

INTRODUCTION DEAR BRITAIN

'In 1789 the French population': Yuval Noah Harari, *Sapiens*, Vintage, 2014, p. 36.

'sweeping away the last': Adam Nagourney, 'Obama Elected President as Racial Barrier Falls', *New York Times*, 4 Nov 2008.

'In the good old days': Kamal Ahmed, 'After Obama, I can be proud of what I am – black and white', *Observer*, 9 Nov 2008.

'scrambles categories': James Forsyth, *Spectator*, 5 Nov 2008.

'web of ambiguity': James Baldwin, *Notes of a Native Son*, Penguin Modern Classics, 2017, p. 15.

'It's very British of course', 'In America': Ahmed, 'After Obama'.

'The world has shifted', 'Too late for my father': Ahmed, 'After Obama'.

'I think the odd thing': Alain de Botton, American National Public Radio, 31 Dec 2005.

CHAPTER 1 MUM. AND DAD

Sheffield steel development: Astrid Winkler, *Sheffield City Report*, Centre for the Analysis of Social Exclusion: http://eprints.lse. ac.uk/5133/1/CASEreport45.pdf.

'A fifth of that provided by the sun': Michael Pacione (ed.), *Applied Geography: Principles and Practice*, Routledge, 1999, p. 126 (https:// books.google.co.uk/books?id=h5j9EVbMxhwC&printsec=frontco ver#v=onepage&q&f=false).

'Shockingly, British fascism', 'However the Jew': David Kynaston, *Austerity Britain*, Bloomsbury, 2007, p. 98.

'resented being associated': Kynaston, *Austerity Britain*, pp. 270–77.

'I do not think that any scheme': Sir Harold Wiles, quoted in Kynaston, *Austerity Britain*, p. 273.

'many of the coloured men': Ministry of Labour, quoted in Kynaston, *Austerity Britain*, p. 273

'mass movement': Arthur Creech Jones, quoted in Kynaston, *Austerity Britain*, p. 275.

'an influx of coloured people': Attlee, quoted in Kynaston, *Austerity Britain*, p. 275.

'would come and go': Quintin Hogg, quoted in Kynaston, *Austerity Britain*, p. 274.

'profound unity', 'blest by the absence': quoted in Kynaston, *Austerity Britain*, p. 275.

'offal of the earth': quoted in Survey of London, University College, London (https://blogs.ucl.ac.uk/survey-of-london/tag/richard-welton/).

'The most improvident': Dr Duncan, quoted in: http://eprints.lancs. ac.uk/69739/1/Migrants_and_the_media_LPS.pdf.

'in parliamentary debate': Randall Hansen, quoted in Kynaston, *Austerity Britain*, p. 274.

Polish resettlement camps in the UK: see http://www.polishresettle mentcampsintheuk.co.uk/ilfordpark.htm.

Patrice Lumumba: see Gordon Corera, 'MI6 and the Death of Patrice Lumumba', BBC, Apr 2013 (http://www.bbc.co.uk/news/ world-africa-22006446).

The battle of Omdurman: David Shonfield, 'Battle of Omdurman', *History Today*, Vol. 48: 9, 9 Sep 1998: http://www.historytoday.com/david-shonfield/battle-omdurman.

'When in 1941 permission was sought for secondary': M. W. Daly, *Imperial Sudan*, Cambridge University Press, 1991, p. 199.

Sudanese pyramids: see Emma Thomson, 'The Country with Twice as Many Pyramids as Egypt', *Independent*, 14 Feb 2017 (http://www.independent.co.uk/travel/africa/sudan-pyramids-twice-the-number-of-egypt-meroe-soleb-prudhoe-lions-tours-a7579141.html).

'If you want a coloured for a neighbour': see Medium (https://medium.com/@pitt_bob/if-you-desire-a-coloured-for-your-neighbour-vote-labour-the-origins-of-a-racist-leaflet-7978858ddo2f).

'I would not condemn any man': Peter Griffiths, quoted in Stuart Jeffries, 'Britain's most racist election: the story of Smethwick, 50 years on', *Guardian*, 15 Oct 2014 (https://www.theguardian.com/world/2014/oct/15/britains-most-racist-election-smethwick-50-years-on).

'If you want a Jihadi for a neighbour': ITV News, 13 February 2017 (http://www.itv.com/news/2017-02-13/ukip-leader-paul-nuttall-stands-by-aide-after-jihadi-for-a-neighbour-retweet/ John Bickley, 2017).

'How easy to support uncontrolled immigration': Peter Griffiths, quoted in Jeffries, 'Britain's most racist election'.

Islamic nations and slavery: Fiachra Gibbons, review of Ronald Segal's *Islam's Black Slaves*, *Guardian*, 6 Apr 2002 (https://www.theguardian.com/books/2002/apr/06/historybooks.highereducation).

'best country in the world', 'All the white women': Tayib Zein al Abdin, quoted in Richard Cockett, *Sudan: Darfur and the Failure of an African State*, Yale, 2010, p. 74.

'It was, gentlemen': Tayeb Salih, *Season of Migration to the North*, Penguin Modern Classics, 2003, p. 1.

Salman Rushdie writes about the effects of the Nationality Act 1981: Salman Rushdie, 'The New Empire within Britain', first published 1982: https://public.wsu.edu/~hegglund/courses/389/rushdie_new_empire.htm.

CHAPTER 2 PREVENTABLE EVIL

'*Virgil*?', 'That's a funny name', 'They call me': *In the Heat of the Night*, United Artists, 1967, see IMDb (https://www.imdb.com/title/tt0061811/quotes).

'we must secure', 'organised Jewry', 'very civilised': Nick Griffin, quoted in Ian Cobain, 'Nick Griffin's vision for a BNP-led Britain shown in 1990s police interviews', *Guardian*, 6 May 2014 (https://www.theguardian.com/politics/2014/may/06/nick-griffin-vision-bnp-britain-1990s-police-interviews).

'I hope that Hungary': Nick Griffin, 444.hu (see https://www.youtube.com/watch?v=b3PdupzgW7E).

'Whatever we feel about immigrants', 'The real question will be', 'There is creeping resentment': Trevor Phillips, quoted in 'UK told not to fear immigration', BBC News, 20 Apr 2008 (http://news.bbc.co.uk/1/hi/uk/7356993.stm).

'Their problems are compounded': Karamat Iqbal, quoted in 'Enoch Powell's speech doctrine has failed, says race boss', *Birmingham Post*, 21 Apr 2008 (https://www.birminghampost.co.uk/news/local-news/enoch-powells-speech-doctrine-failed-3961715).

'[Mullins] recited Powell's speech in full': 'Enoch Powell's speech doctrine', *Birmingham Post*.

'relatively full': Simon Heffer, *Like the Roman: the Life of Enoch Powell*, Faber and Faber, 1998 p. 253.

'put his hands across his eyes': *Daily Telegraph*, quoted in Heffer, *Like the Roman*, p. 254.

'the greatest parliamentary speech', 'you cannot have a proud and chivalrous spirit': Denis Healey, quoted in Heffer, *Like the Roman*, p. 252.

'these oaths involved such depravity': 'Mau Mau power is built on oaths: vile ceremonies in forests', *Birmingham Post*, 19 Feb 1954, cited in 'A War Between Savagery and Civilisation', the graduate dissertation of Julia Lavin, Enoch Powell's granddaughter, which the Powell family kindly allowed me to read.

'I would say it is a fearful doctrine': 'It is argued that this is Africa', 'sits ill with the accusations': Enoch Powell, quoted in Heffer, *Like the Roman*, p. 254.

'**The right's public justification**': Trevor Phillips, quoted in Sunder Katwala, 'The Enoch myth', *Guardian*, 23 Apr 2008 (https://www. theguardian.com/commentisfree/2008/apr/23/theenochmyth).

immigration polling evidence: see Migration Observatory at the University of Oxford (http://www.migrationobservatory.ox.ac. uk/resources/briefings/uk-public-opinion-toward-immigration-overall-attitudes-and-level-of-concern/).

'**There were many myths about the immigrant population**': Heffer, *Like the Roman*, p. 445.

'**fear of a black planet**': Reni Eddo-Lodge, *Why I'm No Longer Talking to White People About Race*, Bloomsbury, 2017, p. 117.

'**too many immigrants**': British election study, 1964, Migration Observatory(http://www.migrationobservatory.ox.ac.uk/resources/ briefings/uk-public-opinion-toward-immigration-overall-attitudes-and-level-of-concern/).

'**It would be wrong not to acknowledge**': Trevor Phillips speech, 20 Apr 2008, Equality and Human Rights Commission.

'**had to accept that he spoke**': Heffer, *Like the Roman*, p. 457.

'**By the toll of a billion deaths**': H. G. Wells, *War of the Worlds*, Penguin Classics, 2005 (first published 1898), p. 168.

'**wrong in principle**': George Thomson, 'Callaghan: I was wrong on police and race', BBC News, 8 Jan 1999 (http://news.bbc.co.uk/1/hi/ special_report/1999/01/99/1968_secret_history/244320.stm).

'**probably the most shameful**': *The Times*, quoted in Mark Lattimer, 'When Labour played the racist card', *New Statesman*, 22 Jan 1999 (http://www.newstatesman.com/when-labour-played-racist-card).

'**That was why the bill**': Lord Gilmour, quoted in Lattimer, 'When Labour played the racist card'.

'**coloured population**', '**how many years it will take**': Sir Cyril Osborne, House of Commons debate, 1 Feb 1968, Hansard Vol. 757 c373W.

'**There is no prospect**': David Ennals, House of Commons debate, 1 Feb 1968, Hansard Vol. 757, c415.

'**So there was I, a seven-year-old**': Nikesh Patel, 'Life after Idi Amin', BBC News, 'On This Day, 18 September 1972' (http://news.bbc.co.uk/ onthisday/hi/dates/stories/september/18/newsid_3113000/3113720. stm).

'**after the April 1968 speech**': Jenny Bourne, 'The Beatification of Enoch Powell', Institute of Race Relations (http://www.irr.org.uk/news/the-beatification-of-enoch-powell/).

'**gave a fillip**', '**He brought scholarship**': Ambalavaner Sivanandan, quoted in Bourne, 'The Beatification of Enoch Powell'.

'**coloureds for a neighbour**', '**They should live**', '**They're a nuisance**', '**They're content**', '**So far in Britain**': *Smethwick: A Straw in the Wind*, documentary narrated by James Mossman, BBC, 1966. (http://www.bbc.co.uk/news/uk-england-birmingham-36388761), quoted in Rebecca Woods, 'England in 1966: Racism and ignorance in the Midlands', BBC News, 1 Jun 2016.

'**The working-class person**', '**It does raise**', '**[They could have said:]**': Jaswinder Chagger, *Smethwick: A Straw in the Wind*, quoted in Woods, 'England in 1966'.

Druscilla Cotterill: Mike Thomson, 'The woman who never was?', BBC Radio 4 'Document', 7 Mar 2007: http://news.bbc.co.uk/1/hi/uk_politics/6287309.stm; and Fiona Barton, 'Woman in Enoch Powell Speech Really Did Exist', *Daily Mail*, 2 Feb 2007 (http://www.dailymail.co.uk/femail/article-433497/Widow-Enoch-Powells-Rivers-Blood-speech-really-did-exist.html).

'**It is time … they realised**': quoted in Gurharpal Singh and Darshan Singh Tatla, *Sikhs in Britain: The Making of a Community*, Zed Books, 2006, p. 128.

'**If it was any old person**', '**He'd have**': 'FactCheck', Channel 4 News, quoting Mary Beard: http://www.channel4.com/news/articles/politics/domestic_politics/factcheck%2Benoch%2Bpowells%2B1968%2Bspeech/1960847.html.

CHAPTER 3 GO HOME

'**Return, return to Ealing**': John Betjeman, from 'Lines written to Martyn Skinner before his Departure from Oxfordshire in Search of Quiet – 1961', in Kevin J. Gardner (ed.), *Faith and Doubt of John Betjemen*, Continuum, 2005, p. 163.

'**Two hits. Me hitting you**': *The Breakfast Club*, Universal Pictures, 1985.

'**the largest and finest estate of flats**': *The Times*, 1939, quoted in *The White City Estate, Shepherd's Bush* Municipal Dreams, 17 Jan 2017

(https://docs.google.com/document/d/10MHkIiS1N6UkeIcPO12w
fpKoMjmGZGpx41VGgyhdw3w/edit).

'expressly designed to deprive': Salman Rushdie, *Culture Wars in British
Literature*, Tracy J. Prince McFarland and Company, 2012, p. 86.

'Asian ghettos', 'off-day': cited in Justin Parkinson, 'Ray
Honeyford: Racist or Right?', BBC, 10 Feb 2012 (http://www.bbc.
co.uk/news/uk-politics-16968930).

'We are convinced', 'Virtually all these children': Anthony Rampton,
The Rampton Report ('West Indian Children in Our Schools the
Interim Report of the Committee of Inquiry into the Education
of Children from Ethnic Minority Groups'), HMSO, London,
1981: http://www.educationengland.org.uk/documents/rampton/
rampton1981.html.

'How the West Indian Child': George Padmore Institute article on Bernard
Coard's *How the West Indian Child is made Educationally Sub-normal in
the British School System* (1971): http://www.georgepadmoreinstitute.
org/the-pioneering-years/gallery-of-publications/
how-west-indian-child-made-educationally-sub- normal.

'That inequality', 'It was horrible': Decca Aitkenhead interview. 'Steve
McQueen: My hidden shame', *Guardian*, 4 Jan 2014 (https://
www.theguardian.com/film/2014/jan/04/steve-mcqueen-
my-painful-childhood-shame).

Mona Lisa: see http://www.movie-locations.com/movies/m/MonaLisa.
html#.WYgrJNPyui4.

'a room a day', 'gratitude for the policeman', 'a vibrant place', 'I didn't
look like a Sindy doll': Cole Morton interview with Cathy Tyson,
'I tell them to go back where they came from', *Independent*, 9 Dec
2007 (http://www.independent.co.uk/news/people/profiles/cathy-
tyson-i-tell-them-to-go-back-where-they-came-from-763976.
html).

'130 million people': Jennifer Keishin Armstong, 'Viewing figures
from *Roots*, the most important TV show ever?' BBC Culture, 2
Jun 2016 (http://www.bbc.com/culture/story/20160602-roots-the-
most-important-tv-show-ever).

'What made *Roots* so difficult', 'Growing up': Kwame Kwei-Armah, 'Going back to my Roots', BBC News, 23 Mar 2007 (http://news.bbc.co.uk/1/hi/magazine/6480995.stm).

'became more important than church': Dr Robert Beckford, quoted in Kwei-Armah, 'Going back to my Roots'.

'you looked at people': Doreen Lawrence, quoted in Kwei-Armah, 'Going back to my Roots'.

'called all the black', 'I remember going': Lenny Henry, quoted in Kwei-Armah, 'Going back to my Roots'.

'To see the spirit': Clifton Jones, quoted in 'Why "Roots" Hit Home', *Time* magazine, 14 Feb 1977 (http://content.time.com/time/subscriber/article/0,33009,914824-3,00.html).

'Nobody ever told him': quoted in Erica L. Ball and Kellie Carter Jackson (eds), *Reconsidering Roots*, University of Georgia Press, 2017, p. 90.

Mercator Projection: see *Encyclopaedia Britannica*, https://www.britannica.com/science/Mercator-projection

Peters Projection: see http://www.petersmap.com/index.html.

'You're telling me that Germany': *West Wing*, Season 2, Episode 16, Warner Bros Television, Oct 2000.

'We're racist, we're racist': Angelique Chrisafis, 'Chelsea football fans convicted of racist violence in Paris', *Guardian*, 3 Jan 2017 (https://www.theguardian.com/world/2017/jan/03/chelsea-football-fans-convicted-of-racist-violence-in-paris).

'It was very crowded', 'I was ashamed': Paul Nolan, 'Why I filmed Chelsea fans on the Paris metro', *Guardian*, 18 Feb 2015 (https://www.theguardian.com/world/2015/feb/18/why-filmed-chelsea-fans-paris-metro).

'Not only am I humiliated': Souleymane Sylla, quoted in Tracy McNicoll, 'Paris court hands Chelsea fans suspended terms', France 24, 1 Mar 2017 (http://www.france24.com/en/20170103-france-chelsea-fans-trial-paris-over-racist-metro-taunts).

'Oh Crombie Ron is colourful': Ron Shillingford, 'Chelsea still struggling to shed racism from the terraces – a black fan speaks out about the club he supports', http://www.goal.com/en/news/1717/editorial/2011/11/08/2748108/chelsea-still-struggling-to-shed-racism-from-the-terraces-a.

'**thrown it straight back**': Howard Gayle, quoted in Ian Herbert, 'Howard Gayle: If they had thrown that banana at me at Goodison Park, I'd have thrown it straight back', *Independent*, 5 Oct 2016. (https://www.independent.co.uk/sport/football/news-and-comment/howard-gayle-liverpool-john-barnes-1980s-racism-anfield-first-black-liverpool-player-a7346961.html).

'**My first experiences of football**', '**Back then**': Sadiq Khan, quoted in Kevin Maguire, 'MP says it's time to call out the racist thugs who "spat on me and used the P-word"', *Mirror*, 5/6 Nov 2015 (http://www.mirror.co.uk/news/uk-news/mp-says-its-time-call-6775580).

'**As soon as I came here**': Mrs Jagger, Rowntree Trust Study, 1965, quoted in Chamion Caballero and Rosalind Edwards, 'Lone Mothers of Mixed Racial and Ethnic Children: Then and Now', Runnymede Trust, 2010 (http://www.runnymedetrust.org/uploads/publications/pdfs/LoneMothers-2010.pdf).

'**Dennis Marsden, the son of the Methodist mill worker**': obituary, *Times Higher Educational Supplement*, 15 Oct 2009 (https://www.timeshighereducation.com/news/people/obituaries/dennis-marsden-1933-2009/408646.article#survey-answer).

'**If you've got coloured children**': Mrs Jagger, Rowntree Trust Study, 1965, quoted in Caballero and Edwards, 'Lone Mothers'.

'**She said: "Don't come here with your coloured children"**': Mrs Whiteman, Rowntree Trust Study, 1965, quoted in Caballero and Edwards, 'Lone Mothers'.

'**I think there's a stereotype**', '**Society does portray**', '**Being white**': 'Chloe', 'Lucy', 'Zoe', Rowntree Trust Study, 1965, quoted in 'Lone Mothers'.

'**painlessly and in no way interfering**': Marie Stopes, *Australian Women's Weekly*, 4, 1934.

Pauline Black: Pauline Black, *Black by Design: A 2-Tone Memoir*, Serpent's Tail, 2011, p. 6.

'**Keep a generation GAP, try wearing a CAP**': from 'Too Much Too Young' by The Specials. All rights reserved. Used by permission.

'**Stop your messin' around**', '**Better think of your future**', '**Time you straightened right out**': from 'A Message to you, Rudy' by The Specials. Words and music by Robert Thompson. © 1967 Sparta Florida Music Group. All rights controlled by Round Hill Carlin,

LLC. Exclusive worldwide print rights administered by Alfred Music. All rights reserved. Used by permission.

'I got one art O level, it did nothing for me': from 'Rat Race' by The Specials. All rights reserved. Used by permission.

'The devil's chord': Jerry Dammers interview in *Mojo*: http://www. mojo4music.com/19782/jerry-dammers-devils-chord- split-specials/.

Two Tone and Walt Jabsco: see http://2-tone.info/articles/label.html.

'show them the error', 'Rather naïve': Michael Friedman, 'Pauline Black and the Art of Confrontation', *Psychology Today*, posted 10 Nov 2015, https://www.psychologytoday.com/blog/brick-brick/201511/ pauline-black-and-the-art-confrontation.

'There were very few black': Red Saunders, quoted in Dorian Lynskey, *33 Revolutions Per Minute: A History of Protest Songs*, Faber and Faber, London, 2011, kindle edition.

'Enoch was right', 'I think we should send them back': Eric Clapton, quoted in Sarfraz Manzoor, 'The year rock found the power to unite', *Observer*, 20 Apr 2008 (https://www.theguardian.com/music/ 2008/apr/20/popandrock.race).

'Come on Eric. Own up...': Sarfraz Manzoor, 'The year rock found the power to unite'.

'Britain is ready for a fascist leader', 'Adolf Hitler', 'You've got to have an extreme right': David Bowie interview for *Playboy*, quoted in 'The Musicians' Union: A History: 1893–2013': https:// www.muhistory.com/from-the-archive-2-mu-response-to-david- bowies-nazi-salute/.

'Later putting his statements': Amanda Borschel-Dan, 'From "Heil Hitler" to "Shalom, Tel Aviv", the many incarnations of David Bowie', *Times of Israel*, 11 Jan 2016: http://www.timesofisrael.com/from-heil- hitler-to-shalom-tel-aviv-the-many-incarnations-of-david-bowie/.

'exhausting', 'how to manoeuvre': Friedman, 'Pauline Black and the Art of Confrontation'.

CHAPTER 5 HAPPY FACE

'perfectly balanced, he's got a chip on both shoulders': Derek Redmond, quoted in 'Christie: Legend under fire', BBC News, 4 Aug 1999: http://news.bbc.co.uk/1/hi/sport/412020.stm.

'**deliberately unintelligible**': Sebastian Coe, *Daily Telegraph*, quoted in 'Christie fury at Coe's "racial" jibe', BBC, 15 Feb 2001: http://news. bbc.co.uk/sport1/hi/athletics/1171320.stm.

'**People say 100m is not that far**': 'The Linford Christie Story: Tunnel vision with gold in sight', *Independent*, 21 Oct 1995 (http://www. independent.co.uk/sport/the-linford-christie-story-tunnel-vision-with-gold-in-sight-1578885.html).

'**a nigger like you was doing in a tracksuit**': Linford Christie, interviewed by Michael Parkinson, 'Respect the Reputation', *Telegraph*, 10 Jun 2000 (https://www.telegraph.co.uk/sport/othersports/athletics/4747 240/Respect-the-reputation.html).

'**moment when they played God Save the Queen**': 'The Linford Christie Story', *Independent*, 21 Oct 1995.

'**I felt the Queen knew who I was**': Linford Christie.

'**I sit in my house minding my own business**': Linford Christie, quoted in John Davison, 'And what, inquired M'lud, is Linford's lunchbox?' *Independent*, 19 Jun 1998 (https://www.independent. co.uk/news/and-what-inquired-mlud-is-linfords-lunch-box-1165856.html).

'**Keep on movin'. Don't stop, like the hands of time. Click clock, find your own way to stay.**': from 'Keep on Movin'' by Soul II Soul. All rights reserved. Used by permission.

'**the mission was not wanting**': Alan McGee, quoted in Tim Jonze, 'If there's one thing Creation Records wasn't, it was boring', *Guardian*, 21 Sep 2010 (https://www.theguardian.com/music/2010/sep/21/alan-mcgee-creation-records).

'**what really saved me**': Alan Davies, quoted in Patrick Sawer, 'Alan Davies reveals Margaret Thatcher "saved" him, despite his Left-wing leanings', *Telegraph*, 25 Aug 2013.

'**It's our time, time today. The right time is here to stay. Stay in my life, my life always. Yellow is the colour of sun rays**': from 'Keep on Movin'' by Soul II Soul. All rights reserved. Used by permission.

'**Technically speaking**', '**We set up**': Trevor Beresford Romeo, 'Jazzie B's 1980s: from Dole to Soul', BBC2, 21 Nov 2016 (http://www.bbc. co.uk/programmes/po4h7fx4).

'Well it's like dreaming of your goals, ambitions and feeling free.
I'm on this mission to achieve. Achieve what? What's in your
mind's eye': from 'Get a Life' by The Specials. All rights reserved.
Used by permission.

Fashion: 'Jazzie B: "Fashion was integral to what Soul II Soul did"',
Guardian, 11 Apr 2013 (https://www.theguardian.com/fashion/
fashion-blog/2013/apr/11/jazzie-b-fashion-soul-ii-soul).

'aliens with passports': Beresford Romeo, 'Jazzie B's 1980s'.

'the shiny arena of the infotainment telesector': Paul Gilroy, *There
Ain't No Black in the Union Jack*, Routledge Classics, 2002 (first
published 1987), p. xxvii.

'Stephen Lawrence's murder': Sir William Macpherson, 'The Stephen
Lawrence Inquiry', Feb 1999 (https://www.gov.uk/government/
uploads/system/uploads/attachment_data/file/277111/4262.pdf).

'Each had a little rising blue and red arrow': Kamal Ahmed, 'Society
allowed my son's killers to make a mockery of the law', *Guardian*, 25
Feb 1999 (https://www.theguardian.com/uk/1999/feb/25/lawrence.
ukcrime5).

'What I see is that black people': Doreen Lawrence, quoted in Ahmed,
'Society allowed my son's killers'.

'I think I can speak for the whole House': Jack Straw, quoted in Ahmed,
'Society allowed my son's killers'.

'We feel a sense of shame': Sir Paul Condon's statement, published in
Guardian, 24 Feb 1999.

'This society has stood by': Doreen Lawrence, quoted in Ahmed,
'Society allowed my son's killers'.

'Stephen Lawrence deserved to die', 'a fucking pair', 'had the right
idea', 'will regret the day': *The Secret Policeman* documentary, BBC
Panorama, Oct 2003 (see http://news.bbc.co.uk/1/hi/programmes/
panorama/7650207.stm).

'In an experiment in the 1960s': George L. Kelling and James Q. Wilson,
'Broken Windows', *The Atlantic*, Mar 1982: https://www.theatlantic.
com/magazine/archive/1982/03/broken-windows/304465/.

police initiatives: 'Police and Racism', Equality and Human Rights
Commission, pp. 2–36 (https://www.equalityhumanrights.com/en/
race-britain/ten-years-macpherson-research-reports).

'**The sculpture was unveiled in 2005**': 'Manchester B of the Bang sculpture core sold for scrap', BBC News, 4 Jul 2012: http://www.bbc.co.uk/news/uk-england-manchester-18703854.

CHAPTER 6 DEAR SUDAN

'**the non-Arab and non-Muslim**': Jok Madut Jok, *Sudan: Race Religion and Violence*, Oneworld Publications, 2007, pp. 2–3.

'**When you visited the north**': Makwec Kuol Makwec, quoted in Jok, *Sudan*, p. 1.

'**mowed down the mass tribes of the Mahdiya**': Cockett, *Sudan*, p. 14.

'**mercury uncontrolled**': James Muller (ed.), *Churchill as Peacemaker*, Cambridge University Press, 1997, p. 92.

'**discontented class of semi-literate**': Cockett, *Sudan*, p. 32.

'**Imperialism was in effect**': Walter Rodney, *How Europe Underdeveloped Africa*, Bogle-L'Ouverture, 1973, preface and Chapter 1: http://abahlali.org/files/3295358-walter-rodney.pdf.

'**Armed conflicts continue**': Sudan, Human Rights Watch: https://www.hrw.org/africa/sudan.

'**Arab slave-takers**', '**The capture and sale of**': Madut Jok, *War and Slavery in Sudan*, University of Pennsylvania Press, 2001: http://www.antropologias.org/files/downloads/2011/10/War_and_Slavery_in_Sudan.pdf.

'**Human Rights Watch**': Human Rights Watch report on Sudan, 2002: https://www.hrw.org/legacy/backgrounder/africa/sudanupdate.htm.

Ahfad University for Women: http://www.ahfad.org/history.html.

'**fashion girls**', '**small tops**': Cockett, *Sudan*, pp. 120–23.

Psychology experiment, 1974: Rupert Brown, *Prejudice, Its Social Psychology*, Wiley-Blackwell, 2010, p. 94.

CHAPTER 8 PREJUDICED, ME?

'**vast majority**': Eddo-Lodge, *Why I'm No Longer Talking*, p. ix.

'**uplift suasion**': Ibram X. Kendi, *Stamped from the Beginning*, Bodley Head, 2016, p. 505.

'**showed a group of people a video of a woman**': Neil Macrae, Charles Stangor and Miles Hewstone, quoted in Brown, *Prejudice*, p. 91.

'**parallel universe Britain**': Lynskey, *33 Revolutions*: https://33revolution sperminute.wordpress.com/2012/01/05/racism-vs-racism-why-diane-abbott-was-right/.

Mel Sealy case: 'Man Compensated for "Cordless Gun" Arrest', BBC News, 31 Jan 2001: http://news.bbc.co.uk/1/hi/wales/1142312.stm.

'**No one can be taught**': Allport, *Nature of Prejudice*, pp. 488–99.

'**counter-productive**', '**strategically dumb**', '**The commercials**': quoted in Vikram Dodd, 'Anti-racist ad fuels debate on strategy', 15 Feb 1996: http://www.campaignlive.co.uk/article/advertising-anti-racist-ad-fuels-debate-strategy/58154.

'**To be maximally effective**': Allport, *Nature of Prejudice*, p. 489.

'**Catharsis alone**': Allport, *Nature of Prejudice*, p. 498.

'**Research by the data-scientist**': Seth Stephens-Davidowitz, *Everybody Lies: what the internet can tell us about who we really are*, Bloomsbury, 2017, pp. 128–31, 162–63.

'**our friends, our co-workers, our neighbours**': President Barack Obama's St Bernardino speech, 6 Dec 2015: https://obamawhitehouse. archives.gov/the-press-office/2015/12/06/address-nation-president.

'**We'd walk in late**': Shabina Aslam, Bradford Local Oral History Project: http://www.bussingout.co.uk/Images/Bussing_Out.pdf.

bussing policy: 'The child immigrants "bussed" out to school to aid integration', BBC News, 30 Jan 2017: http://www.bbc.co.uk/news/ uk-england-leeds-38689839.

CHAPTER 9 RECONCILIATION

Police telephone calls and contact with Bijan Ebrahimi: 'Investigation into police contact and response to calls for assistance by Mr Bijan Ebrahimi between Thursday 11 July 2013 and Sunday 14 July 2013', Independent Police Complaints Commission: https:// www.ipcc.gov.uk/sites/default/files/Documents/investigation_ commissioner_reports/Bijan%20Ebrahimi%20-%20Part%20A%20 report%20-%20for%20publication.pdf.

'**We failed Mr Ebrahimi in his hour of need**': Steven Morris, 'Police failed to protect Bijan Ebrahimi prior to his murder, IPCC',

Guardian, 5 Jul 2017 (https://www.theguardian.com/uk-news/2017/jul/05/police-failure-protect-bijan-ebrahimi-murder-ipcc).

Zahid Mubarek: The Hon. Mr Justice Keith, *Report of the Zahid Mubarek Inquiry*, TSO, 2006 (https://www.gov.uk/government/uploads/system/uploads/attachment_data/file/231789/1082.pdf).

'**They thoughts these two sisters … we read every report**': Gary Younge, ' "It was pure racism": the family of Bijan Ebrahimi on their fight for answers', *Guardian*, 5 Jul 2017 (https://www.theguardian.com/world/2017/jul/05/it-was-pure-racism-the-family-of-bijan-ebrahimi-on-their-fight-for-answers)

Educational performance by ethnic group: 'Social Mobility Commission, Ethnicity, Gender and Social Mobility', 28 Dec 2016, p. 3 (https://www.gov.uk/government/uploads/system/uploads/attachment_data/file/579988/Ethnicity_gender_and_social_mobility.pdf)

Pay of different ethnic groups: Equality and Human Rights Commission, *The Ethnicity Pay Gap*, London, 2017 (https://www.equalityhumanrights.com/sites/default/files/research-report-108-the-ethnicity-pay-gap.pdf).

Attitudes towards immigration: Eric Kaufmann, 'Why Culture is More Important than Skills: Understanding British Public Opinion': http://blogs.lse.ac.uk/politicsandpolicy/why-culture-is-more-important-than-skills-understanding-british-public-opinion-on-immigration/.

Casey on 'British values': Dame Louise Casey, The Casey Review: a review into opportunity and integration', HMSO, 2016, pp. 66–7 (https://www.gov.uk/government/publications/the-casey-review-a-review-into-opportunity-and-integration).

'**takes people on a journey**': 'Amanda Spielman's speech at the Birmingham Education Partnership conference', Ofsted and Amanda Spielman, 22 Sep 2017 (https://www.gov.uk/government/speeches/amanda-spielmans-speech-at-the-birmingham-school-partnership-conference).

Attitudes to prejudice: NatCen Social Research, 'Racial Prejudice in Britain Today', Sep 2017: http://natcen.ac.uk/media/1484235/racial-prejudice-report-final.pdf.

On the 'brand analysis' of capitalism: Legatum Institute, 'Public Opinion in the post-Brexit Era', Oct 2017: https://lif.blob.core.windows.net/lif/docs/default-source/default-library/1710-public-opinion-in-the-post-brexit-era-final.pdf?sfvrsn=0.

'Rule Britannia mindset': 'The Commission on the Future of Multi-Ethnic Britain', Profile Books, 2000.

'they shared a playground', 'On one side': Oona King quoted in Professor Ted Cantle, 'Segregation of schools – the impact on young people and their families and communities', Interculturalism Community Cohesion Foundation, Feb/Mar 2013 (http://tedcantle.co.uk/wp-content/uploads/2013/03/075-Segregated-schools-divided-communities-Ted-Cantle-2013a.pdf).

VeryBritishProblems: see https://twitter.com/SoVeryBritish @SoVeryBritish. Used by permission.

AFTERWORD

MR POWELL AND MR TRUMP

'Important speeches are ones that endure': Cody Keenan on 'Rivers of Blood', piece written for this book, Aug 2017.

INDEX

Abbott, Diane 237
al Abdin, Tayib Zein 53
Africa Centre 166
African National Congress 124
Ahfad University for Women 213–14
Ahmed, Abubaker Ismail (Seddig)
    45–50, 52–8, 105–6, 288
    childhood friend Kamal 217–18
    death 223–7
    medical career 195–7
    and Sudan 204, 212–13
Ahmed, Maud 178–9, 199–201,
    212–14, 217, 225–7, 288–9
Ahmed, Noah 178–9, 199–201,
    212–14, 217, 225–7, 285–9
Ali, Muhammad 114
All London Teachers Against Racism
    and Fascism (ALTARF) 122–3
Allport, Gordon 245, 247, 253, 279
Amin, Idi 44, 83
Arabic 21, 54, 203
Armstrong, Neil 165
Aslam, Shabina 255
Attlee, Clement 38
Austen, Jane 85
authoritarian personalities 239–40
Avon and Somerset Police 264–5, 267

B of the Bang 166–7, 192
Bacon, Francis 251
Badri, Babiker 213
Baldwin, James 8, 85, 212
Barnes, John 149, 151
al-Bashir, Omar 210

BBC 59, 123, 142, 171, 286
Beard, Mary 100
Beat, the 158
Beatles, the 3, 45, 176
Beckford, Dr Robert 143
Bedruthan Steps 84
Beresford Romeo, Trevor 172–4,
    192
Bessemer, Henry 33
Betjeman, John 103
Beveridge, William 155
Bickley, John 51
Biko, Stephen Bantu 202
Bilaszewski, Marcin 268
bilharzia 45, 54, 225
Billo, Nills 200
bin Laden, Osama 204
Black, Pauline 156–7, 159
Black and White Minstrel Show 57
Black is Beautiful movement 143
Blair, Tony 30, 178
Blondin, Charles 103
Boat People 120
Bourne, Jenny 90
Bowie, David 159
Boyle, Sir Edward 254
Brand New Heavies 174
Breakfast Club, The 109
Brexit 20, 40, 272–3, 288, 297
British Airways 276
British Crime Survey 191
British Election Study 78
British Movement 123
British Museum 276

British National Party (BNP) 62–5, 67, 276, 279
British Social Attitudes Survey 272
'British values' 4, 241, 278–9
Britten, Benjamin 277
'broken windows' theory 190
Brooks, Duwayne 181–2
Brown, Gordon 278–9
Brunel, Isambard Kingdom 104
Burke, Edmund 97–8

Caballero, Chamion 154
Callaghan, James 84
Campaign for Racial Equality 246
Camus, Albert 117
Carlos, John 175
cartography 144–6
Casey, Louise 278–9
catharsis 252–3
Centre for Policy Studies 172
Centre for Urban Education Studies (CUES) 122–3
Chagger, Jaswinder 93
Chelsea FC 147–51
Christie, Linford 163–71, 189, 192
Church of England 29
Churchill, Winston 41, 146, 208
Clapton, Eric 159
Clash, the 177
Clemence, Ray 147
Coard, Bernard 134
Cockett, Richard 214
Coe, Jonathan 85
Coe, Sebastian 167
Coleman, David 164
colonialism 46, 68, 209
Commission for Racial Equality 180, 185
Condon, Paul 182–3
Connolly, James 276
Conservative Party 29–30, 40, 87–8

Smethwick election victory 50–1
Conservative Political Centre 73
Constable, John 277
contact theory 247, 252–7
Cooksey, David 172
Corbyn, Jeremy 51
Correll, Josh 244
Cotterill, Druscilla 95
Cranmer, Archbishop 103
Creation Records 173
Crown Agents 44, 57
Cry Freedom 202

Dad's Army 207
Dalglish, Kenny 151
Dammers, Jerry 158, 160
Darfur 204, 206, 210
Davies, Alan 174
Davis, Miles 85
de Botton, Alain 17
Diana, Princess of Wales 165
diversity 257
Diwali celebrations 249
Domingo, Plácido 154
Donald, Kriss 267
Duffy, Kevin 265
Duncan, Dr 39
Dunkerton, Julian 174
Dylan, Bob 176

Eagleton, Terry 276
Ebrahimi, Bijan 14, 261–7
economic stagnation 19, 269, 287
Eddo-Lodge, Reni 77, 232
Eden, Anthony 43
education
    attainment levels 133–6, 179–80, 231, 274
    bussing policy 254–6
    comprehensive schools 130
Edward I, King 7

Edwards, Rosalind 154
El Keiry, Ismael Sajer 46
Elsony, Asma 199–200
Emin, Tracey 174
Empire Windrush 37, 40, 84
employment opportunities 179–80,
    195–6, 231, 251–2, 274–5
Ennals, David 84
Enterprise Allowance Scheme (EAS)
    172–4
Equality and Human Rights
    Commission (EHRC) 12, 63, 65–
    6, 185–8, 191
eugenics 155
European Union 182, 271, 273, 288
Everitt, Richard 268

fairness 248–9, 252
Farah, Mo 85
fascism, post-war 36
Fawcett, Millicent 16
Fielding, Henry 103
fighting 109–15, 263
financial crisis 251, 271–2
Fitzgerald, F. Scott 85
football 146–52
Forsyth, Bruce 278
Foucault, Michel 19
Franklin, Rosalind 277
French Revolution 98
Front National 63
Funki Dreds 175, 177

Gaddafi, Colonel Muammar 217
Gaitskell, Hugh 81
Gall–Peters Projection 145–6
Gallagher, Tony 270
Gandhi, Mahatma 16
Gayle, Howard 151
Gezira irrigation scheme 207
Gilbert and Sullivan 57

Gilmour, Lord 81
Gilroy, Paul 177, 179
Global Fund 200
Golding, William 85
Gordon, General Charles 207–8
graffiti 116, 118–19
Great Western Railway 104
Greenhoff, Jimmy 147
Griffin, Nick 62–3, 65, 68
Griffiths, Peter 50, 52

Hadid, Zaha 277
Hailsham, Lord 38
Hall, Terry 156–7
Hamed al-Nil Mosque 213
Hansen, Randall 39
Harari, Yuval Noah 5, 287
Harris, Helen 265
Healey, Denis 69
Heath, Ted 73, 78, 88
Heatherwick, Thomas 166–7
Heffer, Simon 69, 71–2, 77–8, 291
Heighway, Steve 151
Henry, Lenny 63, 143
Hewstone, Miles 236
History Boys, The 236
Hitler, Adolf 155, 159, 188, 268
Hola massacre 68–70, 72
Holmes, Sherlock 277
Homo sapiens 4–5, 186
Honeyford, Ray 124–5
Hope, Doug 67
Human Rights Watch 210–11
Hume, David 251
Hungary 65
Hussein, Saddam 204

immigration 13, 36–40, 272–3, 288
    Birmingham debate 65–8
    Enoch Powell and 66–81, 83–100,
        291–9

European 37, 234–6
fiscal contribution of immigrants
    252
Huguenot 39
post-war Polish 40–2
and race 80–100
In the Heat of the Night 62
Independent Police Complaints
    Commission (IPCC) 265–6
Index of Dissimilarity 280
Institute for Public Policy Research
    252
Institute of Ophthalmology 55
Institute of Race Relations 90
interviews 180, 196, 229
Iqbal, Karamat 67
Israel 43

Jagger, Mrs 152–4
James, Lee 265, 267
Janjaweed militia 206
Jazzie B 173–7
Jesus Christ 198
Jews 7, 36, 39, 52, 63, 184
Johnson, Michael 169
Jok, Jok Madut 205, 211
Jones, Arthur Creech 37
Jones, Charles 104
Jones, Claudia 155
Jones, Clement 77–8
Jones, Clifton 143
Joseph Rowntree Foundation 152

Kapila, Mukesh 204
Kedong massacre 82
Keegan, Kevin 151
Keenan, Cody 291, 299
Kendi, Ibram X. 232
Kennedy, John F. 165
Kenyatta, Jomo 82
Keynes, John Maynard 155

Khan, Sadiq 151
Khartoum University 46, 204
Khayatian, Mojgan 261
King, Martin Luther 61, 92, 140, 186,
    202, 297–9
King, Oona 280
King's Cross 136–9
Kitchener, Lord 207
Knott, Czeslaw 40–1
Ku Klux Klan 188
Kwei-Armah (Ian Roberts) 142–3
Kynaston, David 36

Lane, Elizabeth 45
Lawrence, Doreen and Neville 143,
    181–4, 187–8, 192, 266
Lawrence, Stephen 14, 180–5, 187–9,
    191–2, 237, 266
Lego 107
Liverpool FC 85, 146–7, 149–52, 285
London Olympics 167
Lumumba, Patrice 43
Lynskey, Dorian 237

MacBride, Maud Gonne 178
McGee, Alan 173
Macpherson Report 181–4, 187–8
McQueen, Steve 134–5
Macrae, Neil 236
Madness 158
Madonna 135
Magic Roundabout 45
Mahdi, the 208
Makwec, Makwec Kuol 205
Mandela, Nelson 16
Mandelson, Peter 272
marissa 216
Marsden, Dennis 152
Marx, Karl 85
Match of the Day 150–1
Mau Mau 68–70

Mercator Projection 144–5
Mexico Olympics 175
Mill, John Stuart 85, 251
Ministry of Labour 37
Mona Lisa 137
Moore, Brian 150
Moores, Manizhah 261, 266
Moorfields Eye Hospital 55
Morris, Desmond 156
Morrison, Toni 227
Mosley, Oswald 39
Mossman, James 91, 93
Mrs Brown's Boys 278
Mubarek, Zahid 266
Mullins, Peter 67
multiculturalism 123, 125,
    176, 271
Muslim Brotherhood 48
Muslims 16, 52, 59, 65, 184, 196, 231,
    253–4, 270, 272, 280–1

names 120–1, 160, 180, 196, 205–6
Nasser, Gamal Abdel 43
national anthem 277
National Assistance Board 153
National Citizen Service 256
National Front 62, 108, 141,
    151, 286
National Health Service (NHS) 85, 89,
    195, 225
National Trust 84
Nationality Act 124
Nazi salute 286–7
Nelson, Trevor 177
Newton, Isaac 251, 277
Nkrumah, Kwame 43
Nolan, Paul 148
Norley, Stephen 265
Northern Ireland 68
Notting Hill Carnival 155
Nour, Mohamed 216

Obama, Barack 6–11, 254, 291, 298–9
Ofili, Chris 166
Omdurman 1, 47–8, 57, 140, 204, 213
Orton, Joe 277
Osborne, Sir Cyril 83–4
Owen, David 44

'Paki-bashing' 90
Palestine 43
Parekh, Lord Bhikhu 279
Parker, Ross 267
Passmore, Andrew 265
Patel, Nikesh 85
patriotism 77, 168, 271, 292
Payne, Keith 243–4
Peters, Arno 145–6
Philip, Prince, Duke of Edinburgh 57
Phillips, Trevor 65–8, 75, 78
Pickett, Kate, and Richard Wilkinson
    251
pillar boxes, red 276–7
police 180–4, 187–92
    see also Avon and Somerset Police
Policy Studies Institute 8
Polish Resettlement Act 41
Popplewell, Mr Justice 170
Powell, Enoch (and 'Rivers of Blood'
    speech) 13, 40, 61–2, 66–81, 83–
    100, 124, 159, 185, 291–9
Prince 165
prisons 256, 266
'Protect and Survive' leaflet 245
Proust, Marcel 17
Public Enemy 77
pyramids 46–7, 218

Quant, Mary 45

Race Relations Act 45, 89, 94, 98
Racism – the Fourth R 123
Rampton, Anthony 134

Redmond, Derek 167
Reed, Lou 176
Richard, Cliff 72
Rock Against Racism 159
Rodney, Walter 209
Rolling Stones 45, 176
Roots 141–2
Rousseau, Jean-Jacques 85
Rowntree, Joseph 152
Royden, Maude 29
Runnymede Trust 154
Rushdie, Salman 124

St George's flag 151, 276, 279–80
St Pancras Hotel 138
St Paul's Cathedral 218
Salacrou, Armand 42
Salih, Tayeb 53
Salisbury Review 124
Sampson, Andy 133–6, 138–44, 146, 151, 154
Sánchez, Ilich Ramírez (Carlos the Jackal) 204
Sandhu, Tarsem Singh 98
Saunders, Red 159
Scarman Report 183, 266
Sealy, Mel 242–3, 245
Secret Policeman, The 187
Selecter, the 156–7
Sellers, Peter 125
sense of self 249–51
Shakespeare, William 85, 100, 277
sharia law 216
Shaw, George Bernard 155
Shepherd, Cybill 172
Shillingford, Ron 149–50
Sikhs 97–8
single mothers 152–4
Sivanandan, Ambalavaner 90
Skinner, Mike 175
slavery 89, 139–41, 143, 238

in Sudan 211–12, 215–16
Smith, Adam 85
Smith, Gill 123
Smith, Tommie 175
social dominance theory 240–1
Soul II Soul 18, 85, 166, 172–6, 180
South Sudan 204
Specials, the 84, 157–60, 175, 177
Spice Girls 277
Spielman, Amanda 278
Stangor, Charles 236
Staple, Neville 156–7
steel industry 32–3, 212, 273
Stephens-Davidowitz, Seth 254, 272
stereotyping 236–7, 256
Stewart, Robert 266–7
Stonehouse, John 97–8
Stopes, Marie 155–6
Straw, Jack 183
Streets, the 175
Sturman, Anthony 29, 34–5, 71
Sturman, Elaine Mary 29–36, 41–5, 49–50, 53–4, 106–9, 289
    and anti-racism 117–18, 121–5
    marriage and divorce 56–8
    and single motherhood 152–4
Sturman, Philip 29, 35
Sturman, Roland and Norah 29, 32, 34–6, 56
Sudan National Museum 207
Sudan People's Liberation Army 211
Suez Crisis 44
Sufi Muslims 213
Swift, Jonathan 250
Sylla, Souleymane 147–9

taqiyah 55, 218
Tebbit, Norman 40, 172
Thames Valley Harriers 168
Thatcher, Margaret 30, 133, 165, 172–4
Thomson, George 81

Thorpe, Jeremy 78
tolerance 278–80
Tomblin, Mark 247
Tricky 166
Trump, Donald 296–8
12 Years a Slave 135
Two Tone 156–60, 165, 174, 212, 278
Tyson, Cathy 137–8, 156

Uber 20
Uganda Railway 82
UKIP 51, 67
Uncle Tom's Cabin 96
Union flag 62, 117, 151, 169, 177, 246, 279
United Nations 43, 210

Verwoerd, Henrik 117
Virgil 99
Voltaire 250

Walker, Anthony 187, 189, 192
Walker, Patrick 52
Wells, H. G., 80, 169
Welton, Dr 39
West Wing, The 146

Wheeler, Caron 176
'white British' population 166
White City Estate 122
white working class 269–70, 274–5
Whiteman, Mrs 153–4
Wiles, Sir Harold 37
Wilhelm of Cleve, Duke 144
Wilkinson, Ellen 103
Williams, Jan 267
Williams, Shirley 133
Willis, Bruce 172
Wilson, Harold 3, 50, 74
Wilson, Jane and Louise 174
Winter, Leanne 265
Wollstonecraft, Mary 251
women, in Sudan 213–14
World Health Organisation 200

X Factor, The 277

Yates, Derek 175
Young Disciples 166, 174

Zephaniah, Benjamin 100
Zimbardo, Philip 191
Zoo Time 156

A NOTE ON THE AUTHOR

Kamal Ahmed is Economics Editor of the BBC and one of Britain's most respected journalists. He joined the BBC in April 2014 as Business Editor after a twenty-year career in newspapers. He has worked for the Guardian, the Observer and the Sunday and Daily Telegraph. He started his career in local newspapers in Scotland and subsequently worked for Scotland on Sunday. He has also served as Group Director of Communications for the Equality and Human Rights Commission and is a board member of the Media Trust. He lives in London.

A NOTE ON THE TYPE

The text of this book is set in Minion, a digital typeface designed by Robert Slimbach in 1990 for Adobe Systems. The name comes from the traditional naming system for type sizes, in which minion is between nonpareil and brevier. It is inspired by late Renaissance-era type.